YOUR FIRST YEARS TEACHING SECONDARY MATHEMATICS

SUCCESS from the START

Rob Wieman
Rowan University
Glassboro, New Jersey

Fran Arbaugh
The Pennsylvania State University
University Park, Pennsylvania

NCTM® | NATIONAL COUNCIL OF
TEACHERS OF MATHEMATICS

Copyright © 2013 by
The National Council of Teachers of Mathematics Inc.
1906 Association Drive, Reston, VA 20191-1502
(703) 620-9840; (800) 235-7566; www.nctm.org
All rights reserved

Library of Congress Cataloging-in-Publication Data

Wieman, Robert.
 Success from the start : your first years teaching secondary mathematics / Robert Wieman, Rowan
University, Glassboro, New Jersey, Fran Arbaugh, Pennsylvania State University, University Park,
Pennsylvania.
      pages cm.
 Includes bibliographical references.
 ISBN 978-0-87353-673-8
 1. Mathematics—Study and teaching (Secondary)—Standards—United States. 2. Mathematics—Study
and teaching (Middle school)—Standards—United States. I. Arbaugh, Fran. II. Title.
 QA13.W554 2013
 510.71′273—dc23
                                  2012045335

The National Council of Teachers of Mathematics is the public voice of mathematics
education, supporting teachers to ensure equitable mathematics learning of the highest
quality for all students through vision, leadership, professional development, and research.

Printed in the United States of America

Dedication

To the students and teachers of Urban Academy, New Design Academy, and the Institute for Collaborative Education, and to Wally Warshawsky.

R.M.W.

To Sandi, who taught me much and left us far too soon.

F.A.

CONTENTS

ACKNOWLEDGMENTS

As mathematics teachers, mathematics teacher educators, writers, and researchers, we are lucky to have been supported by, and have learned from, a wide range of people and experiences. We thank Lucy West and the Educational Materials Committee of the National Council of Teachers of Mathematics (NCTM) for envisioning this book and entrusting us with writing it. Myrna Jacobs at NCTM has been invaluable in navigating the publication process. The authors of the elementary version of this book, Kathy Ernst and Sarah Ryan, shared ideas throughout this project. Their thinking about how to organize the book was pivotal in helping us decide what to focus on in our writing.

We hope that this book, instead of introducing a host of new innovations, organizes and presents the collective wisdom of the field at large—of countless mathematics educators. We ascribe much of the content of this book to others; many ideas that we do not specifically ascribe came to us through colleagues, mentors, students, and our own experiences as mathematics teachers. Our colleagues, teachers, and mentors at Penn State University, the University of Delaware, the University of Missouri, Bank Street College of Education, and other institutions have contributed tremendously to our own understanding of what it means to know and teach mathematics as well as what it means to teach mathematics teachers. We also acknowledge the countless other mathematics educators whose work we drew on. Finally, our own work as teacher educators and researchers has given us the opportunity to learn both a great deal about the practices of educating teachers and effective ways to communicate those practices.

Our most heartfelt thanks go to the teachers, professional developers, and students we have worked with over the past quarter century. At a time when the popular discourse tends so much to the negative—when teachers and adolescents are portrayed as parodies of the worst that schools have to offer—we have found teachers and students to be a constant source of insight, knowledge, humor, and inspiration. From them we have learned about mathematics, instruction, persistence, honesty, and above all, humility.

Finally, we acknowledge the support from our closest friends and family, who endured long periods of authorial obsession and doubt and encouraged us to carry on.

INTRODUCTION

If you are like most beginning teachers, you are excited to embark on your career. You may envision your classroom as a place where students engage with mathematics, where they learn important content and are inspired to do their best. But you may also worry about how your teaching will actually play out—how you and your students will interact and what they will learn. We wrote this book for beginning middle and high school teachers who want to grow and improve throughout their first years in the profession.

You have chosen a profession that is both familiar and unfamiliar. With your years spent as a math student, along with your experiences in teacher education, teaching math is familiar to you. As a student, you spent hours in math classrooms, observing what teachers did and said and how that affected students. Perhaps you completed a teacher preparation program, succeeded in student teaching, and got certified to teach mathematics at the middle or high school level. You probably know what kind of math teacher you want to be—and do not want to be. You feel well prepared.

During your first years of teaching, though, you will probably find unfamiliar aspects of teaching math that you had never thought about. What do math teachers do when students do not "get" the lesson? What about students who struggle with math they supposedly learned in elementary school? Or absent students who need to make up work? How do teachers decide where students should sit? How do math teachers figure out whether their teaching is effective? Some students will have different ideas about what they should be doing in mathematics class, what is important about school, and how they should engage with the content and one another. Like most new teachers, you may find that what seemed familiar is full of the unknown.

HOW THIS BOOK HELPS BEGINNING TEACHERS

We wrote this book to help you navigate this recognizable yet unfamiliar terrain. This book will be especially helpful to new teachers of middle and high school mathematics.

Demystifying teaching

Many in the United States believe that teaching is simply a matter of talent and intuition, that great teachers come by it naturally—that they were "born to teach." Akin to this belief is that bad teachers are simply not dedicated, talented, or smart enough. We hope to debunk this belief so that it does not block your effectiveness and improvement.

Teaching is incredibly complex: what appears simple is extremely difficult. Furthermore, many aspects of teaching are quite unnatural and run counter to "normal" interaction in the adult world (Ball 2007). For instance, mathematics teachers often pretend not to understand what a student is saying in order to force the student to more clearly explain his or her thinking. Such interaction does not happen in normal adult conversations. Similarly, when people outside a classroom ask for our help, we would not direct them to ask their neighbor first, yet that is a common tactic in student group work. Outside the classroom, we would never do many of the things we do to support our students; it would be unnatural.

Moreover, much of what a teacher does is invisible to outsiders. Students see teachers handing out worksheets, checking homework, showing how to do a mathematical procedure, asking and answering questions. Students do not see the planning, the bureaucratic work (such as organizing papers and grading), or the thinking that goes into decisions teachers make in the classroom and in creating assignments. This book makes some of those invisible aspects of teaching more visible and then offers strategies to make this work more manageable.

Focus on mathematics

This book focuses on the teaching and learning of middle and high school mathematics. Dozens of self-help and how-to books are available for beginning teachers. These books exist mainly to help beginning teachers with general issues, such as creating a safe and challenging academic culture, organizing the classroom, engaging students, and setting high expectations. Although helpful, these books lack a focus on any particular content area—they do not address specific challenges and needs of middle and high school mathematics teachers.

We wrote this book to address important issues of mathematical teaching and learning, while offering information and advice about diverse issues that new teachers need to master quickly. Especially for secondary school teachers, who teach mainly just one subject, situating concerns of new teachers within mathematics is important and useful—and mostly absent from teacher how-to books.

Linking theory and practice

This book helps beginning mathematics teachers by linking theory and practice in a new way. First we describe what it means to know mathematics, how students come to know mathematics in powerful ways, and how teachers can orchestrate such learning. We then connect these (theoretical) ideas about content, learning, and teaching to advice about teaching moves and classroom routines that support learning.

In a well-known mathematics education article, Skemp (1976) argued that the ability to perform mathematical procedures, devoid of any greater set of ideas or connections, is like being able to follow directions from point A to point B. As long as you do not make a wrong turn, or no one closes a street for construction, you can find your way. However, if you make a wrong turn, or something blocks your way, you are completely lost. In contrast, understanding mathematical concepts and connections between representations, ideas, and strategies is like having a map. A map enables you to chart various routes from point A to point B and to deal with unexpected obstructions. Truly understanding mathematics offers a similarly powerful tool to solve mathematical problems.

We feel the same way about teaching. A list of suggestions is akin to a set of directions, but if your students do not respond as expected, or if your school has a culture that does not support those suggestions, then you may get lost. If you have a larger set of understandings about teaching and learning mathematics, you can use them to chart your own course and make informed decisions about what you and your students do in your mathematics classroom. We offer directions, though in the context of a larger map, so that you can adjust them to your context while staying true to larger goals and understandings about teaching and learning.

EQUITY IN MATHEMATICS LEARNING AND TEACHING

"Excellence in mathematics education requires equity—high expectations and strong support for all students" (National Council of Teachers of Mathematics [NCTM] 2000, p. 11). This statement of the Equity Principle in *Principles and Standards for School Mathematics* captures an overarching theme for this book: that effective mathematics teaching supports all students—regardless of personal characteristics or background—to develop a deep understanding of mathematics.

Issues of equity in learning and teaching mathematics are complex and lie at the intersection of complicated histories, group and individual identities, personal beliefs, and political ideologies. Although we acknowledge this complexity, untangling these issues is beyond the scope of this book. But this book does highlight the influence that teachers wield in ensuring that all middle and high school students have access to learning interesting and important mathematics.

Teaching practices that account for equity support students in developing connected mathematical knowledge. Students must engage in the mathematical processes of reasoning, representing, solving problems, communicating, and making connections (chapter 2), and you must hold high expectations as your students do so. Equitable teaching practices are supported by viewing teaching through the triangle of instruction (chapter 3) and include cultivating a positive learning community (chapter 4), choosing accessible and rich tasks (chapter 5), planning for and enacting inclusive instruction (chapters 6 and 7), creating clear expectations for positive behaviors (chapter 10), and working with struggling students (chapter 11, especially the section on redefining mathematical success).

Your teaching decisions greatly influence your students' experiences in learning mathematics, their access to interesting and important mathematics, and ultimately how they come to know mathematics. This book presents both a vision of mathematics teaching and strategies for realizing that vision that promote equitable learning environments for all middle and high school students.

STRUCTURE OF THIS BOOK

The structure of the book flows from a link between ideas (theory) and suggestions (practice). First, we offer beginning secondary mathematics teachers a set of ideas about learning and teaching that can guide instructional decisions. Later chapters deal with aspects of teaching. Each chapter offers guiding principles that connect the content to the larger framework. We then offer habits of practice—practical suggestions that align with the guiding principles and with the overarching framework of teaching and learning mathematics. These habits of practice are based on our own experiences as mathematics teachers as well as our experiences working with mathematics teachers over the past twenty years. As appropriate, we also draw on work done by other mathematics educators. In drawing on a variety of sources, we give you advice grounded in solid research and practical experience.

The book is organized in four sections. Section I (The Big Picture) begins with a visit to a prealgebra classroom. The vignette in chapter 1, interspersed with reflective questions, establishes the kinds of mathematics learning and teaching that you will encounter through this book. Chapters 2 and 3 describe connected knowledge of mathematics, the fundamental role of the NCTM (2000) Process Standards in learning mathematics, and the kind of teaching that lets students develop connected mathematical knowledge.

Section II (Laying the Groundwork) focuses on how you can create a successful mathematics classroom. Chapters 4 and 5 present strategies to forge collaborative relationships with more experienced colleagues; learn about students, curriculum, and context before the students arrive; and envision and create a classroom community to support student learning during the first weeks of school.

Section III (The Lesson Cycle) focuses on the core activities of teaching: planning, enacting, and reflecting on instruction. Chapters 6–9 cover mathematical problems/tasks/activities, effective planning for instruction, enacting instruction that supports students in building connected knowledge of mathematics, and reflection as a tool for improvement.

Section IV (More Elements of Effective Teaching) focuses on elements of effective teaching not contained in sections II and III. Chapters 10–15 address group work, assessment, classroom management, and teaching struggling students, as well as technology, interacting with parents/guardians, and standardized testing and test prep.

TEACHING AND THE COMMON CORE STATE STANDARDS FOR MATHEMATICS

Over the past twenty-five years, the mathematics education community has created standards for learning and teaching mathematics in U.S. schools (NCTM 1989, 1991, 2000, 2006). Through these standards, the community has attempted to define broadly what content students should learn at what times, the kinds of thinking at the core of what it means to know and be able to do mathematics, and practices teachers can use to support such learning.

More recently, the National Governors Association Center for Best Practices (NGA Center) and the Council of Chief State School Officers (CCSSO) published the *Common Core State Standards for Mathematics* (CCSSM; NGA Center and CCSSO 2010). CCSSM addresses two different topics. First, CCSSM describes what mathematical topics students should master at specific times during their schooling. For instance, by the end of fourth grade, students should be able to "add and subtract mixed numbers with like denominators" (p. 30), and some time in high school they should "understand that the graph of an equation in two variables is the set of all its solutions plotted in the coordinate plane, often forming a curve (which could be a line)" (p. 66). Second, CCSSM contains Standards for Mathematical Practice, which describe what it means to know and understand math-

atics deeply, as well as the kinds of thinking and behaviors that should
he larger goals of mathematics instruction in all grades:

1 Make sense of problems and persevere in solving them.

2 Reason abstractly and quantitatively.

3 Construct viable arguments and critique the reasoning of others.

4 Model with mathematics.

5 Use appropriate tools strategically.

6 Attend to precision.

7 Look for and make use of structure.

8 Look for and express regularity in repeated reasoning. (NGA Center and CCSSO 2010, pp. 6-8)

The writers of CCSSM stress that students should engage in these practices while learning the mathematics contained in the Standards for Mathematical Content.

Although this book addresses teaching middle and high school mathematics, it is not about mathematical content. Yet this book does connect to CCSSM. We see the Standards for Mathematical Practice as powerful descriptions of what both learning and understanding mathematical content looks like. The theory about learning and teaching in section I of this book aligns well with these practices, is inspired by much of the same research and foundational documents, and addresses many of the same core issues in mathematics teaching and learning. If you reflect on the ideas about learning and teaching mathematics, as well as use this book's suggestions in your teaching, your classroom will be a place where students engage in CCSSM's mathematical practices.

WHO SHOULD READ THIS BOOK

We wrote this book explicitly for beginning teachers of middle and high school mathematics, whom this book can help in several contexts. Newly certified mathematics teachers could read it during the summer before starting a first teaching job and find valuable information to help with those first days and weeks of school. Groups of beginning mathematics teachers could read it as part of a formal induction program. Beginning mathematics teachers struggling in their first few months could find advice to address areas of immediate concern. The book can help preservice teachers looking to prepare and learn from student teaching or who are about to move from their own training to full-time teaching. Finally, the book will help beginning teachers continue to reflect on and improve instructional practices over the first few years of their career.

OUR FIRST PIECE OF ADVICE

This book is full of suggestions to improve your teaching and thus your students' opportunities to learn mathematics. You will not be able to enact all our suggestions right from the beginning of your career, nor would we want you to. Although effective mathematics teaching is complex, improvement can come from working on one aspect of practice at a time. Many chapters present strategies to improve your practice. Choose one or two strategies to work on first and see how it goes. We hope that, in working to achieve small changes in your practice, you can create gradual, sustained growth and positive change.

This is an exciting time to be a math teacher. As a field we have learned much about how students learn and how we can support them in learning mathematics in a deep and connected way. Across the nation, mathematics teachers are working together to improve their teaching, enabling more and more students to experience mathematics as a living, powerful, creative, and elegant discipline. You are entering a profession that lets you demonstrate caring as well as engage in challenging and stimulating intellectual work of great importance: improving instruction so that all students can learn mathematics with understanding and power. Welcome aboard.

The Big Picture

Different students can learn at such different levels. Some students understand math so well; others have much more difficulty learning the same content. Similarly, some teachers can teach difficult math to a wide range of students, whereas other teachers, working just as hard, find that students continue to struggle. Why? Do successful students and teachers do something specific?

Certainly, successful teachers and students often have strategies. Whatever these strategies may be, they are based on a core set of ideas about what it means to understand mathematics, how students gain that understanding, and how teachers can support them. These core ideas also can inform effective teaching. As mathematics teacher educators, we have worked with beginning middle and high school teachers for many years. An overarching framework of ideas about mathematics learning and teaching helps beginning teachers make sense of why a lesson succeeded (or not) and helps them decide what to do when planning and teaching.

Section I presents ideas for learning and teaching mathematics that frame the rest of the book. Chapter 1 includes vignettes from a mathematics classroom that help describe how we believe middle and high school math classes should look and sound. Chapter 2 describes what we mean by "knowing and understanding" mathematics and how students acquire that knowledge and understanding. Chapter 3 explores what it means to teach mathematics, given what we know about how students learn mathematics with understanding. Together, these chapters offer a theoretical grounding for our advice and for many practical decisions you will make as a mathematics teacher.

Being a new math teacher is exciting, but it can also overwhelm: you have so many aspects of teaching to master and details to remember. Sometimes, identifying the most important things to know and think about may be difficult. This section's framework will help you feel less overwhelmed. It will help you make sense of the tremendous variety in your students' understanding and your colleagues' effectiveness, and it will help you figure out what to focus on while planning, teaching, assessing, and doing the countless other tasks that constitute the work of teaching.

SUCCESS
from
the START
Your first years
teaching SECONDARY
MATHEMATICS

chapter one

How Should Middle and High School Math Class Look and Sound?

Ms. Barker is a second-year mathematics teacher at a rural Missouri grades 6–12 combined middle and high school. As one of three math teachers, Ms. Barker will teach many of the same students as they progress through the grades and graduate. Her grade 8 prealgebra class has many students that she taught the year before. Ms. Barker likes the continuity of teaching students for multiple years, and she establishes classroom norms that support mathematical learning. She also designs and enacts instruction focused on her students' making sense of the mathematics they are learning. After each vignette, stop and reflect about particular aspects of Ms. Barker's instruction and her students' learning.

A VISIT TO MS. BARKER'S PREALGEBRA CLASS

Ms. Barker planned an introductory lesson on solving linear equations. Her goals were for her students to understand that solving an equation means finding a value for the variable(s) that—

- makes the equation "true";

- creates the same value on both sides of the equation; and

- "balances" the equation across the equals sign.

First she would have students figure out values for the variable in several different equations that make those equations true. Then she would engage her students in several writing tasks to help them articulate what it means to solve an equation, followed by a whole-class discussion around their writing. In ensuing lessons, students would develop and practice strategies to solve linear equations.

When the bell rang, Ms. Barker said, quietly, "I am ready to begin. Are you?" As the students settled into their seats and got out their notebooks, Ms. Barker directed their focus to instructions she had written on the board:

> For each equation, figure out what value(s) for x makes both sides of the equation equal.
> $$2x + 6 = 20$$
> $$5x - 4 = 21$$
> $$-3x - 4 = -13$$
> Explain how you figured out each answer.

Ms. Barker continued, "To start today, I have written three equations on the board. Your job is to figure out what value for x makes each equation true. Stephan, what do you think I mean by 'makes each equation true'?"

Stephan replied, "I think it means that you are looking for the number that makes the equation work."

Ms. Barker said to the class, "What do you think Stephan means by 'work'?" She paused to let the students think and then said, "Who will share?"

A few hands shot up, and Ms. Barker called on Jasmine, who said, "Makes both sides of the equation equal the same value."

Ms. Barker wrote both Stephan and Jasmine's phrases on the board. "I think those are very good explanations of what you are looking for. Who has a question before we start?"

Sandi raised her hand. "Will x be the same or different?"

Ms. Barker said, "Do you mean from equation to equation?"

"Yes," Sandi replied.

"Well," Ms. Barker said, "for these equations, it will be different, but you ask a very good question. We'll talk about times when x can have the same value for lots of different equations. OK, let's get started."

STOP+ REFLECT

» Why did Ms. Barker want her students to understand the meaning of a solution to an equation before she wanted them to master methods to find solutions?

» What beginning-of-class routines has Ms. Barker established with her students?

» What did Ms. Barker do at the beginning of class to focus the students on the math?

» Ms. Barker asked a question and then paused for her students to think before asking for a response. How did this practice benefit her students?

As students began working, Ms. Barker quickly scanned the room, noting empty seats. She stepped to her computer, at the back of the room, to record absences (because of assigned seating, she could readily tell who was absent). As she was doing so, Maggie came into class and took her seat. Ms. Barker finished recording absences. On the way back to the front of the room, she stopped at Maggie's desk, stooped down so that her face and Maggie's were on the same level, and asked quietly, "Maggie, do you have a late pass?" Maggie shook her head. Before standing, Ms. Barker said, "Let's talk after class. For now, talk quietly with Shari to catch up on what we're doing."

Ms. Barker went around the room, peeking over students' shoulders as they wrote in their notebooks. Mike had little written on his paper beyond the original equations and his answers. Bending down to speak to Mike, Ms. Barker said, "If you are satisfied that these answers are correct, and that there aren't other correct answers, then I want you to think about how you're going to explain how you found your answers. I'm going to ask you to explain your reasoning when we come back together." As she walked off, Ms. Barker noted that Mike was not doing what she had asked but was instead turned around, talking to Edie. Ms. Barker reversed direction, as if walking back to her desk to get something she forgot. As she passed Mike's desk, she put her hand on his shoulder and then walked on. She was gratified to see, once she reached her desk and looked back, that Mike was again working.

Once back at the front of the room, Ms. Barker asked Mike to join her at the board. "Let's start by focusing on the first equation," Ms. Barker said while writing $2x + 6 = 20$ on another part of the board with room for more writing. She said to Mike, "Tell us what value you got for x that makes the equation true, and then help us understand how you were thinking about it."

Ms. Barker moved to the side of the room as Mike said, "Well, I just thought, I have to have a number that, when you multiply it by 2 and add 6, you get 20. I just figured out that it would be 7."

Ms. Barker said, "Is this the only value of x that makes the equation the same on both sides?" She paused for a few seconds. "Mike, what do you think?"

Mike replied, "I'm pretty sure it is, because I can't think of any more numbers that would work."

"Well, let's see what others think, too. Maybe that will help us decide whether 7 is the only value for x that works. Did anyone think about it differently?" As hands went up, Ms. Barker said, "Mike, can you run this conversation?"

Mike nodded and then chose Jill, who said, "I looked at it a little bit differently. I thought, 'I have to have a number that, when you multiply it by 2, you get 14.'"

Several students looked puzzled about what Jill had said. Before Mike could pose a follow-up question, James asked, "Wait a minute. Where'd you get 14?"

Jill asked to go to the board, and Ms. Barker said, "Of course." Jill wrote the following:

$$2x + 6 = 20 \rightarrow 2x = 20 - 6 \rightarrow 2x = 14$$

"So," Jill continued, "then I just thought to myself, 'What times 2 equals 14?'" Jill and Mike returned to their seats.

STOP+ REFLECT

>> Ms. Barker tracked absences by using assigned-seating charts. How does this system compare with yours?

>> Note how Ms. Barker handled Maggie's tardy and Mike's off-task behavior. How did she help keep the focus on the math they were learning rather than on their behavior?

STOP+ REFLECT

>> Ms. Barker involved Mike in leading the discussion. How might that strategy have affected Mike's behavior and engagement with the mathematics?

>> Consider Jill's equations. If Jill had no experience solving equations, how might she have explained her thinking? How did she make sense of what it means to solve a linear equation?

"That's very interesting, Jill," Ms. Barker said. "Who can explain why Jill can rewrite this equation [pointing to $2x + 6 = 20$] as this equation [pointing to $2x = 20 - 6$]?" No one answered. "OK, working with a couple of people around you, discuss what Jill did and why it makes sense." After a few minutes, Ms. Barker brought the students back together and said, "OK, who will share an idea from their group?"

Adam raised his hand and said, "Well, we just kinda thought that it just made sense, but we couldn't really explain it." Other students nodded in agreement.

Jill raised her hand and said, "Can I explain why it makes sense to me?" She continued, "I was just thinking about it like I used to in elementary school. Like, $8 + 3 = 11$, so $11 - 3$ has to equal 8. It's like a fact family thing. It's just that here, we have $2x + 6 = 20$ to start out, so one of the family members is $2x = 20 - 6$."

Ms. Barker paused to let the other students think about what Jill had said. "So, what if we started with the second equation [pointing to $5x - 4 = 21$]? Look at what Jill wrote on the board, and in your notebooks, write a 'family member' that will help us find the value for x that works." After a minute or so, Ms. Barker said, "Now, turn to your neighbor and talk about what you wrote. When you are done talking about number 2, work on the third equation."

Students began to write in their notebooks and then talk to their neighbors. "Raise your hand if you need a little more time," Ms. Barker said after a few minutes. Several hands went up. "We'll take a few more minutes, then. If you are finished, be sure you can explain your thinking." A bit later, Ms. Barker called the students back together and said, "Let's focus on equation 3. Who will volunteer to show us the 'family member' you wrote?"

Jasper said, "I will," and moved to the front of the classroom, where he wrote $-3x = -13 + 4$ on the board.

"Jasper," Ms. Barker said, "I'm a little confused. When Jill wrote her family member, she used subtraction, but you used addition. Can you explain what you were thinking?"

Jasper paused and then wrote $-5 - 6 = -11$ on the board. "See, this example is the same pattern as the original equation—something minus a positive number equals a negative number—and I know that -5 minus 6 is -11. Then I figured out a family member for this one, $-5 = -11 + 6$, which I know works. Then I just did the same thing to this equation [pointing to $-3x - 4 = -13$] and ended up with this [pointing to $-3x = -13 + 4$]. Can I finish it?" Ms. Barker nodded and Jasper said, "Then I just added and got $-3x = -9$, so x has to equal 3."

"Thanks, Jasper." Ms. Barker glanced at the clock and noticed that class had about twenty minutes left. She liked this idea that Jill had introduced to the class and thought that it would prove useful as she taught students different steps for solving equations. She wanted to look in her book to find problems for students to work on for the rest of the period, so Ms. Barker said, "While I am looking for something in the book, write an equation similar to these we've been working on and give it to your neighbor to solve by using Jill's strategy." Ms. Barker then spent a minute looking in the textbook and then wrote on the board:

> Page 87, #1–18. For each equation, write a "family member" that would help you find a value for x that makes each equation true.

"Let's spend the rest of class working on these problems." As her students reached for their textbooks, Ms. Barker said, "I'll be walking around to check on your progress. Get to work, please."

CONCLUSION

Ms. Barker's classroom, though fictionalized, is based on our many observations of and conversations with beginning teachers. You may now be thinking, "There's no way that Ms. Barker is a beginning teacher," or "How did she learn to run class like that?" You may also be focused on the students in this classroom and thinking, "Can eighth-grade kids really think like that?" or "My kids could never figure out how to do something in math class like Jill did."

All teachers can develop practices similar to Ms. Barker's, and students of all ages and abilities can and should learn mathematics the way Ms. Barker's students are learning. Chapters 2 and 3 present ideas about learning and teaching mathematics that will help explain the decisions Ms. Barker made in planning and enacting this lesson. These ideas will underlie the suggestions in the rest of the book. We hope that these ideas will support you as you think about, plan, enact, and reflect on instruction.

STOP+ REFLECT

>> What might you notice if you entered Ms. Barker's room during class? You might see Ms. Barker standing to the side of the class and students at the board talking to the whole class. Or you might see Ms. Barker at her desk, looking at her computer or textbook while students worked in their notebooks. Or you might see students talking with each other in small groups. What would visitors see in your room during class? What would you be doing and where would you be standing? What would students be doing?

>> Ms. Barker has established several norms and routines in her class that facilitate her students' engagement with the mathematics they are learning. Think about the norms and routines you have established. Are some beneficial to you and your students? Have some norms not been particularly useful?

>> What do Ms. Barker's students understand about linear equations, and how do you know? Could observers in your class tell what your students understood?

>> Describe how students interacted with mathematics in Ms. Barker's class. How do your students interact with mathematics?

chapter **two**

The Learning of Mathematics

>> Think of an area of math
that you understand deeply.
How did you gain that
understanding? What was
your experience of math
class like while you were
learning that material? What
were you doing and thinking
about while learning?

>> Think of an area of math for
which you do not understand
the material deeply, even
though you may have
studied it. What was your
experience of math class like
while you were "learning"
that material? What were
you doing and thinking about
while learning?

>> Think back to Jill in Ms.
Barker's class. How well
did Jill understand linear
equations? Does Jill see
math as a set of arbitrary,
disconnected rules?

All students can learn math with deep understanding, and every teacher's goal should be for all students to gain this high level of understanding and knowledge.

Picture a typical middle or high school mathematics class you took as a student. Envision the classroom, the teacher, and your fellow students. If this class is typical, a few students should stand out—who appear to have understood the mathematics more deeply than their peers. Problems that may have mystified many in your class seemed, somehow, simple and clear for these students; for them it just all made sense. Perhaps you were one of those students, for whom the math all fit together and new topics grew naturally from math you already knew.

In this same class, you can probably also identify students who struggled. For these students, math was probably a set of arbitrary formulas, unconnected to what they already knew. Perhaps you were one of those students, for whom math class seemed like a difficult exercise in remembering some obscure code whose meaning was beyond your grasp.

The rest of this chapter presents a way of thinking about what it means to know and understand mathematics, and how students gain that understanding and knowledge.

UNDERSTANDING = HAVING CONNECTED KNOWLEDGE

As teachers, we want our students to know many things about the mathematics they study:

- How to perform procedures efficiently, and how and when to apply those procedures

- Different representations for important mathematical ideas and how those representations are related

- Diverse problem-solving strategies and how to see the same mathematics in several contexts

- The mathematical concepts underlying the methods and representations that they use

Knowing each of these things by itself, however, does not constitute deep understanding. Understanding mathematics means having knowledge rich in connections. Students who understand linear relationships, for instance, can solve linear equations. But they can also connect solution methods to the idea of equivalence—that removing or adding the same thing to equal quantities maintains the equivalent relationship—and that equivalence is central to why "doing the same thing to both sides" helps to solve any equation. Students who understand linear relationships deeply can connect algebraic solutions to graphical solutions and come up with a variety of situations and stories that involve linear relationships. They can recognize slope in many forms and see slope as a rate of change, which can surface from a situation about hourly wages or monthly fees for a cell phone. They can identify slope in a linear equation, on a graph, and in a table. They understand how repeated addition in a story of a plant growing a set amount each week can be represented by multiplication in an equation, or a difference in a table, and how each approach relates to the rise and the run of the line in a graph. They know that subjecting a shape on the coordinate plane to a linear transformation (say, $2s + 3$) will combine a dilation and a translation, and that the "slope" of the linear transformation is the same as the scale factor of the dilation.

Students who understand math in this way are more likely to remember and apply what they learn. For them, techniques and procedures to solve mathematical problems are not isolated sets of rules, but embody important mathematical ideas and take advantage of powerful relationships. When facing new problems, students with connected knowledge can look for what they already know and then apply this knowledge in new and powerful ways.

STOP+REFLECT

Think back to the math you said you understood well in the previous reflection questions. Do you think you have connected knowledge of this topic? What connections can you think of?

DEVELOPING CONNECTED KNOWLEDGE

In some ways, the idea of connected knowledge is wonderfully simple: we want students to make and understand connections between all the things we have them do and think about. But let's think more deeply about what we mean by connected knowledge. What kinds of mathematical thinking constitute knowing mathematics with understanding, and how do students develop mathematical understanding? The National Council of Teachers of Mathematics (NCTM) describes five processes that clarify different aspects of connected knowledge and point toward concrete ways that students can develop it:

1. Problem solving

> Instructional programs from prekindergarten through grade 12 should enable all students to—
>
> - build new mathematical knowledge through problem solving;
>
> - solve problems that arise in mathematics and in other contexts;
>
> - apply and adapt a variety of appropriate strategies to solve problems;
>
> - monitor and reflect on the process of mathematical problem solving. (NCTM 2000, p. 52)

Students who can engage in problem solving demonstrate one aspect of connected knowledge. To solve new problems, students need to think about the mathematics they know and how it might apply to a new situation. They need to see how different operations or models might connect to this situation. They need to monitor and reflect on their problem-solving process to ensure that the techniques and models they use are consistent and make sense. In solving problems, students show that they understand how different strategies, situations, and representations are connected.

By "problems" in mathematics, we refer to mathematical tasks that are problematic. If the person doing the task already knows how to arrive at an answer, then nothing is problematic about the task. Many tasks that students complete in mathematics classes are called "problems" but can be better described as "exercises." Students know, or are told, how to solve the exercise, and their job is to apply a known rule or algorithm. Real problems, however, are much different. Students encounter a situation and a question, and they must use what they know to figure out appropriate solution paths, choose a solution path that they think will work, and then use that path to solve the problem. Through this process, students make sense of the mathematical content they are learning and thus build new understandings or strengthen their mathematical knowledge. (For more about mathematical problems and tasks, see chapter 6.)

STOP+REFLECT

Think back to Ms. Barker's class. Asked to figure out what values for *x* make an equation true, the students did not know immediately what to do. They had to engage and apply their prior mathematical knowledge. Jill's "fact families" approach illustrates using previously learned mathematics to solve a "new" problem, thus engaging in problem solving. How often do your students engage in problematic mathematical tasks?

2. Representation

> Instructional programs from prekindergarten through grade 12 should enable all students to—
>
> - create and use representations to organize, record, and communicate mathematical ideas;
>
> - select, apply, and translate among mathematical representations to solve problems;
>
> - use representations to model and interpret physical, social, and mathematical phenomena. (NCTM 2000, p. 67)

Mathematical representations take many forms, such as symbols, numbers, graphs, tables of values, pictures, story problems, and physical manipulatives. A student with connected knowledge has access to several representations for the same mathematical content and can easily translate between them. These different representations are connected to each other, to underlying ideas, and to different contexts. Having to create representations for new situations forces students to attend to underlying mathematical structure. Students must either identify a representation already known and apply it to new situations or create a representation using previously known symbols or models.

3. Communication

> Instructional programs from prekindergarten through grade 12 should enable all students to—
>
> - organize and consolidate their mathematical thinking through communication;
>
> - communicate their mathematical thinking coherently and clearly to peers, teachers, and others;
>
> - analyze and evaluate the mathematical thinking and strategies of others;
>
> - use the language of mathematics to express mathematical ideas precisely. (NCTM 2000, p. 60)

Communication in the mathematics classroom can also take many forms and occur in various contexts. Perhaps the most familiar examples of communication are explanations. Teachers continually explain to their students (as oral communication), and students often explain on tests and quizzes (as written communication). Have you ever said something like, "I really understood it only after I had to explain it"? Explaining mathemati-

STOP+REFLECT

Ms. Barker's students mainly used one type of representation, symbolic equations. Ms. Barker could have also focused students on other representations of linear equations. For example, you could solve linear equations graphically in one of two ways:

1. Graph each side of the equation as its own function. The point where the lines intersect is the solution.

2. Set the equation equal to zero and then graph the nonzero side of the equation. The x-intercept of the line is the solution.

You could also use physical manipulatives such as algebra tiles and balance scales when solving linear equations. What representations do your students use?

cal ideas requires people to identify and clarify important features of those ideas and structure their explanations in ways that mirror the mathematical structure. In working to clarify their mathematical ideas, students often must use precise mathematical language or create analogies or examples that capture important elements of mathematical structure.

Communication can also take the form of questions, pictures, diagrams, acting out ideas with physical objects, and various other forms. Students who can ask clear and direct questions show an ability to identify important mathematical features and monitor their understanding of those features. Other methods of communication also force students to call upon an understanding of mathematical structure and how it applies to specific situations.

4. Reasoning and proof

> Instructional programs from prekindergarten through grade 12 should enable all students to—
>
> - recognize reasoning and proof as fundamental aspects of mathematics;
>
> - make and investigate mathematical conjectures;
>
> - develop and evaluate mathematical arguments and proofs;
>
> - select and use various types of reasoning and methods of proof. (NCTM 2000, p. 56)

Mathematical reasoning is at the core of students making sense of the mathematics that they learn (NCTM 2009b). Conjecturing, seeking patterns, generalizing, justifying, and proving are all components of mathematical reasoning. A student with connected knowledge is a sense maker. That student can reason mathematically to construct proofs that show understanding of mathematical relationships. When students reason, they argue for particular solutions based on underlying structure and concepts of mathematics. Proving requires beginning with knowledge we know and making logical connections to new ideas, often recognizing common mathematical structures in new situations or extracting and attending to important mathematical structures when making arguments.

STOP+ REFLECT

Look back at chapter 1 and consider Ms. Barker's students' opportunities to communicate. The students wrote explanations in their notebooks; they talked to each other in small groups about Jill's solution strategy; and some communicated to the whole class during discussions. What else did you see? When did Ms. Barker's students struggle to communicate their ideas? How do your students communicate?

STOP+ REFLECT

Ms. Barker's practices of asking students to explain their thinking, as well as when she asked her students to analyze Jill's thinking, support their capacities to reason and justify their thinking. Ms. Barker has established a norm of sense making in her class; her students seem comfortable, even eager, to explore mathematical relationships and to work toward understanding the math they are learning. Also, despite not anticipating Jill's solution strategy, Ms. Barker recognized an underlying mathematical structure in Jill's argument and thought it worthwhile to explore with the class. What opportunities do you give your students to reason and make sense of the mathematics they are learning?

5. Connections

> Instructional programs from prekindergarten through grade 12 should enable all students to—
>
> • recognize and use connections among mathematical ideas;
>
> • understand how mathematical ideas interconnect and build on one another to produce a coherent whole;
>
> • recognize and apply mathematics in contexts outside of mathematics. (NCTM 2000, p. 64)

When we describe mathematical understanding as having connected knowledge, students' abilities to make connections as described in the NCTM Process Standards take on great importance. By definition, students who can see how different mathematical representations are connected, explain and justify those connections, communicate those connections, and use those connections (both within and outside mathematics) to solve problems have connected knowledge.

STOP + REFLECT

Ms. Barker consistently gives her students ample opportunities to make mathematical connections. Her initial posing of the problem to figure out requires students to connect a new situation to their prior understandings. Her decision to follow up on Jill's solution strategy supported her students to make connections between different representations (linear equations and fact families). Ms. Barker's continually asking for justification and explanation also supports her students to make connections. What connections do you want your students to make?

How do students develop this kind of mathematical understanding? First let's think of expertise in another realm, long-distance running. Being a good long-distance runner means, at its most basic, being able to run long distances. Long-distance runners use different techniques to improve their ability to run long distances. However, one aspect of getting better at long-distance running is inescapable: long-distance runners get better by running long distances. Their coach can demonstrate proper running technique, create effective workouts, and suggest a proper diet, but ultimately the runner must put in the miles.

The same is true in mathematics. Building connected knowledge depends on planned instruction in which students engage in the five processes described above. A teacher can support that learning in many ways, but eventually students themselves must reason, represent, communicate, solve problems, and make connections.

Tradition holds that people learn by listening. If we push a little harder, we may say that people learn by paying attention. Years of research in cognitive science tell us that although listening and paying attention are important, students really learn what we want them to learn by thinking. If we want students to learn with understanding, we need to give them tasks that require them to make sense of mathematics and support them in the difficult work of struggling with new ideas in the context of solving problems (Hiebert and Grouws 2007; Stein and Lane 1996; Stein et al. 2009).

However, thinking alone is not sufficient. Students who memorize formulas, or decide whether they are on the right track by looking at their teacher's facial expressions, are certainly thinking—but not in ways that produce connected mathematical knowledge. Students who use the quadratic formula to establish that a quadratic equation has imaginary roots, while noticing that the graph is a parabola that does not intersect the x-

axis—and then wonder why that is—are thinking in ways that lead to connected knowledge. The key to their learning is in how they were thinking
and what they were thinking about. Certain kinds of thinking require students to make connections and thus yield the connected knowledge implic-
it in knowing mathematics with understanding (Stein et al. 2009). Engaging
students in the five processes above supports them in thinking about and
learning mathematics to build connected knowledge.

Until now we have argued that we want students to gain connected
knowledge, defined as students' capacity to problem solve, represent and
communicate, reason mathematically, and make mathematical connections. Although we described these five mathematical processes as separate,
they overlap. When students solve problems, they often begin by creating
representations of the situation. Representations also serve as frequent aids
for communication. While students reason mathematically, they generally
communicate this reasoning. To solve problems effectively, students must
continually examine the reasoning behind the methods they use to check
whether they are appropriate. All the processes generally involve making
connections—between problems and representations, between representations and justifications, and between the words or pictures we use to communicate and the mathematical ideas that we seek to describe.

Seeing mathematical understanding as connected knowledge also
helps us to think of mathematical understanding on a continuum. Mathematical understanding is constantly developing; it is not something that we
either have or lack. Because understanding is on a continuum, we can meet
a wide range of students where they are. We can support students who have
few connections already in connecting what they do know to new content.
And we can push students who have advanced understanding to make even
more connections.

REDEFINING "SUCCESSFUL MATHEMATICS STUDENT"

Traditionally, in the United States, we have defined what it meant to be a
good mathematics student in two ways:

1 By what successful students can do—good students execute
mathematical procedures quickly and accurately.

2 By how successful students behave in class and interact with
mathematics—good students listen attentively and diligently
practice the algorithms their teachers demonstrate during instruction.

These two definitions of success in mathematics are problematic. First,
they do not align with our goal of connected knowledge for all students—or
with what we know about how people gain it. Knowing math consists of
more than procedural fluency, and learning math is more than listening
and practicing. Second, these definitions are limiting. Defining success only
as attaining procedural fluency has excluded most Americans (and people
in other countries) from mathematical success. The emphasis on quickness
and accuracy obscures the need to think deeply about mathematics. This

definition also discourages students who do not develop this procedural fluency quickly. Many students leave U.S. middle and high schools thinking that they simply cannot do well in math because they had difficulty quickly and accurately reproducing the procedures that made up their mathematical experiences. Mathematical success is not solely about becoming procedurally fluent. Procedural fluency, though certainly important in mathematical success, is not sufficient in itself.

Success in mathematics depends on a range of skills. Successful math students engage in solving problems, communicating, representing, reasoning, and making connections. This definition is powerful because it combines what students should know and be able to do with how they should behave and interact with mathematics and with each other. It also allows teachers and students to identify a wide range of skills and abilities that can contribute to success in math class without having to master techniques and ideas right away.

Figure 2.1 lists concrete, explicit examples of the skills that mark successful mathematics students. As you incorporate the ideas and strategies from this book into your own teaching practice, you will identify from your students other indicators of success, which you can add.

Successful mathematics students . . .

Communicate

- Ask clear questions

- Give clear explanations

- Summarize or restate others' knowledge

- Rephrase problems

- Push for explanation and justification

- Ask for help if they need it

- Help others if they can

- Use precise language

- Understand and use standard notation to communicate ideas and arguments

Represent

- Make good drawings, graphs, tables

- Create models of situations

- Use manipulatives and other tools

- Use symbols and notation to represent problem situations and mathematical reasoning

Reason

- Justify their work

- Find good examples and counterexamples

- Are logical

- Critique the arguments of others

Solve problems

- Identify important information in problems

- Predict the kinds of answers they can expect

- Consider different solution strategies

- Use appropriate mathematical procedures

- Remember what they are trying to find

- Check to see whether their solution makes sense

Make connections

- Create contexts

- Move from one representation to another (graphs to tables to equations)

- Recognize similarities and differences between problems

Fig. 2.1. *Qualities of successful math students (organized by Process Standards)*

If we want students to see mathematics as more than being competent at reproducing mathematical procedures that we have shown them how to do, and we want them to engage in thinking that leads to connected knowledge, then we need to be explicit about the skills and behaviors we value. Furthermore, we need to teach these behaviors and give students feedback about how they are engaging in them. In so doing, we will send a strong message that all students can succeed in mathematics.

CONCLUSION

To teach effectively, begin with a clear idea of what you want your students to learn and an understanding of how they learn it. We have described an ambitious goal for all students—the deep understanding that we call connected mathematical knowledge. We have also described how students gain connected mathematical knowledge: by engaging in the mathematical processes of reasoning, communicating, representing, making connections, and solving problems. Chapter 3 continues to discuss the ideas about learning and teaching that frame the rest of this book, by describing a view of mathematics teaching that supports middle and high school students in building connected mathematical knowledge.

chapter **three**

The Teaching of Mathematics

C hapter 2 argued that students develop connected knowledge by solving problems, representing, communicating, reasoning, and making connections. But what about the teacher? How does a teacher engage students in the processes that lead to connected knowledge?

We describe an approach to effective teaching that aligns with research about how students learn. This framework recurs throughout the book with our guidance on topics such as preparing for classes, planning and enacting lessons, and learning from your teaching. Consider the following goals of effective mathematics teachers:

MEANINGFUL STUDENT INTERACTION WITH MATHEMATICS

Because students develop connected knowledge of mathematics through problem solving, representing, communicating, reasoning, and making connections, effective teachers engage students in these processes. Students need tasks that require them to use these processes—not just for a short period at the end of class, but for most of the time they spend studying math. Teacher support of students while they engage in these processes is crucial (section III, The Lesson Cycle, focuses on this area). Underlying teaching that leads to students' developing connected mathematical knowledge, however, is the conviction that students must do the mathematical thinking. If the teacher does all the mathematical thinking and arguing, if the students spend most of their time mimicking the mathematical thinking of the teacher or practicing demonstrated procedures, students will not develop deep, connected knowledge. Students must work hard in math class to engage in all five mathematical processes.

It is tempting to think that we can make students understand mathematics by breaking down big mathematical ideas into small chunks—that they will then put those small chunks together to understand mathematics as a whole. However, such teaching most often leads to students knowing those small chunks as distinct pieces of mathematical knowledge. Few students can reassemble the pieces into a coherent whole. Students who learn math through engaging in the five mathematical processes described in chapter 2 are more likely to build connected mathematical knowledge (Senk and Thompson 2003).

CLASSROOMS SUPPORTING POSITIVE INTERACTIONS WITH MATHEMATICS

If the focus of mathematics instruction is to engage students in important mathematical work, teachers need to create a classroom culture that supports that work, select tasks that require such work, and monitor students as they do that work. To achieve this vision of classroom culture, think of teaching as managing interactions between teachers, students, and mathematics within the context of the classroom. The triangle of instruction (fig. 3.1) captures this view of teaching.

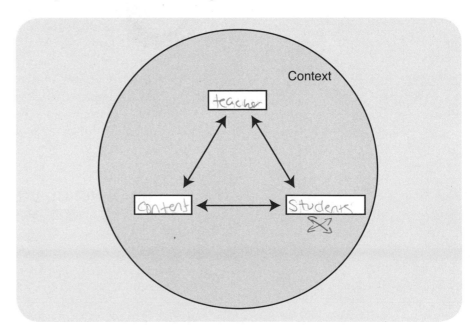

Fig. 3.1. *The triangle of instruction (adapted from Cohen and Ball 1999)*

The circle represents the classroom context, including how teachers and students normally interact and how they engage in discussions and schoolwork. The teacher, the students, and the mathematics are the key ingredients of any teaching situation. The arrows represent interactions—between teachers and content, teachers and students, and students and content. This framework is helpful in several ways. First, it aligns with research about student learning and allows us to situate this learning squarely in the student–mathematics interactions. Furthermore, we know what we want these interactions to look like. They should involve students' developing connected knowledge through problem solving, representing, communicating, reasoning, and making connections.

Second, this view lets us think of the other elements of teaching in relation to that primary focus. All the elements and interactions in this triangle should serve effective interactions between students and mathematics. The culture of the classroom should support students making sense of mathematics, working to build connected knowledge. For example, classroom routines, expectations, and normal modes of discussion should reinforce that mathematics is a sense-making activity, that solving math problems may require considerable perseverance, and that solutions should be reasonable and justifiable. Teacher–student interactions also should support students while they do mathematical work. For example, by maintaining a neutral facial expression after a student explains his or her thinking, and asking others whether they agree, a teacher supports students in attending to mathematical arguments when evaluating solutions. However, when a teacher always nods after a student makes a correct statement but looks quizzically after an incorrect statement, students learn to attend to nonmathematical cues when deciding whether mathematical thinking is correct or incorrect. Further, the mathematical problems or tasks teachers select are pivotal in creating opportunities for students to do meaningful mathematical work and requiring them to do so (see chapter 6). If the focus of your class is the teacher interacting with mathematics (that is, most tasks you choose require students to replicate something you just showed them how to do), you have moved the focus of learning away from students interacting with mathematics meaningfully. Figure 3.2 shows that learning occurs in student–mathematics interactions.

One problem with viewing teaching through this lens: if the focus is on how students interact with mathematics, much of what the teacher does is invisible and thus difficult to observe. As a beginning teacher, you have spent many hours observing in mathematics classrooms, both as a K–12 student and as a college student studying how to teach. Much of the work of teachers was hidden from view. We want to look "behind the curtain," to expose often-invisible teacher decision making that supports building a learning environment where students can build connected knowledge. To build learning environments that support students in building connected knowledge, teachers must strategically select—and plan how to introduce—tasks that promote productive work. During instruction, these teachers observe students as they work and analyze how they interact with the task, sometimes intervening to support that interaction. These teachers create a classroom culture that supports students in representing, reasoning, communicating, problem solving, and connection making (see sections II and III for specifics about enacting these ideas).

STOP+REFLECT

Think about your classroom through this lens. How would you describe the interactions among you, students, and mathematics? What interactions occur more often? Less often?

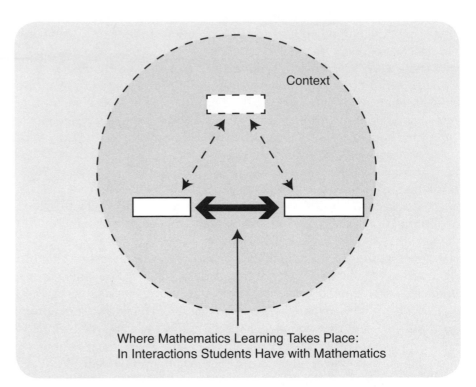

Where Mathematics Learning Takes Place:
In Interactions Students Have with Mathematics

Fig. 3.2. *Learning occurs when students, not the teacher, interact with mathematics.*

Adding a fourth arrow to the triangle of instruction is useful. To create learning environments that support students as they build connected knowledge, you must pay attention to how students interact with mathematics, as represented in figure 3.3 by the arrow connecting the teacher to the student–mathematics arrow. (Magdalene Lampert adds a similar arrow to this triangle in *Teaching Problems and the Problems of Teaching* [2001].) This arrow indicates that the teacher is paying attention to students' interactions with mathematics, how students engage with mathematical tasks, how they are (or are not) making sense of mathematical ideas, and how they are learning. Effective mathematics teachers notice whether and how the interactions in their classroom support students in building connected knowledge of mathematics.

In classrooms where students build connected knowledge, all the teacher's instructional decisions (before, during, and after the actual class) are well aligned. For example, a task may require students to solve a non-routine problem, justify their solution to classmates, and evaluate the solutions of others. When students press their teacher to say whether their solution is right, the teacher asks the students and their classmates to evaluate the solution. This teaching move focuses on students and mathematical reasoning. When a student group solved the problem incorrectly, the teacher does not correct them but instead asks how they know they are correct, points out that another group has a different answer, and asks both groups to work together to rectify the difference. This teaching move requires that students in both groups examine their own reasoning and evaluate the claims of others. Both teacher moves align with the task that students are working on as well as the goal for students to reason mathematically and then justify their reasoning.

When instructional decisions are not aligned, elements and interactions work against each other. If a teacher wants all students to think deeply

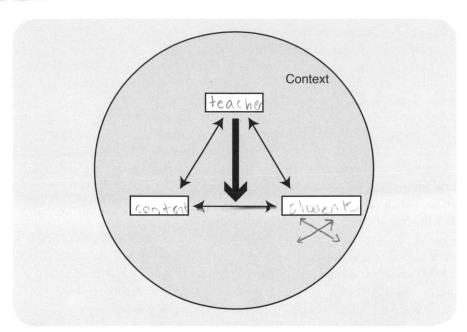

Fig. 3.3. *Effective teachers' focus during mathematics instruction*

about a question, but after a relatively short wait time he calls on the first student who raises a hand, his methods of calling on students do not align with his desire for all students to think about the mathematics. In this example, many students may not have had enough time to think in the way that the teacher wants, and his decision to call on the first person who raised a hand may inadvertently tell students that what he really wants is correct answers, arrived at quickly—not deep thinking.

This idea of alignment recurs throughout the book as a useful way to think about many aspects of teaching mathematics. Indeed, if we had to condense the whole book to one sentence, it might be this: When facing a problem in your teaching, look to see to what extent your actions, plans, and classroom environment are aligned with what you want for your students. In our experiences, many teaching problems stem from misalignment: tasks misaligned with learning goals, teachers' spoken words that do not align with actions, patterns of interaction that do not align with fundamental desires for engagement, and teaching practices that do not align with how students develop deep, connected knowledge. The triangle of instruction lets us isolate the interactions inherent in the classroom and examine how well these interactions align with student learning.

You can align your teaching by becoming more aware of your assumptions about students, mathematics, and teaching and learning. Assumptions are things we take for granted or suppositions that we unconsciously subscribe to. By themselves, assumptions are valueless, neither good nor bad. How teachers allow their assumptions to influence instructional decisions, however, can have positive or negative consequences for students' opportunities to build connected mathematical knowledge.

Becoming conscious of, testing, and examining your assumptions in light of your actions and conclusions will help you align your teaching. It will help you align your goals with your practices, and it will help you align

STOP+ REFLECT

Think back to Ms. Barker's classroom in chapter 1. How are her instructional decisions aligned? How does she keep the focus of her instruction on the interactions that her students have with the mathematics they are studying?

your perceptions of students' understanding and behaviors with what they actually understand and how they actually behave.

Many stories in this book about teachers improving their practice exemplify teachers identifying their assumptions and then either testing them to see whether they are true (for assumptions about what students do or think) or clarifying them so that students have a clearer idea of expectations (for assumptions about what students should do or think). In some stories, teachers' assumptions prove to be powerful ways of thinking that support students in sense making. By identifying and clarifying these assumptions and identifying the accompanying moves, the teachers moved from intuition to conscious use of effective teaching techniques. Sometimes, though, teachers' assumptions bar productive interactions. These teachers examined evidence and made decisions based on clearer and more realistic appraisals of student thinking and behavior, yielding more effective instruction. Other times, students and teachers did not necessarily share the same assumptions—then it was helpful for teachers to clarify their assumptions so that students had a much better sense of teachers' expectations.

As you read the stories in this book, think about the role of assumptions. Identifying, testing, and examining assumptions led teachers to adjust their instruction to better support students in reasoning and proving, representing, communicating, solving problems, and making connections.

CONCLUSION

We described teaching as planning for, observing, and supporting student interactions with mathematics so that students build connected mathematical knowledge. The triangle of instruction lets us think about teaching that aligns with our knowledge of developing connected knowledge of mathematics and that helps us think about how to approach problems of teaching. Alignment is a key aspect of effective instruction.

The rest of this book offers more specific guidance for beginning teachers, built on the ideas in the first three chapters. Section II, Laying the Groundwork, suggests how you can prepare for teaching before students arrive in the fall (chapter 4). Then we address the first few weeks of school and creating a classroom culture and routines that will place mathematics learning—through representing, communicating, problem solving, reasoning, and making connections—at the forefront of your students' experience (chapter 5).

II Laying the Groundwork

It was the beginning of August and Kim Washington was excited. The year before, the large suburban high school where she had completed her student teaching hired her to teach math. During her first year she learned more than she thought possible. To prepare for the coming year, she planned to—

- review and take better advantage of her curriculum materials;

- learn more about both the mathematics she would teach and how students think about the math;

- spend time before school planning lessons with other teachers; and

- think about how to create the precise tone she wanted in her class.

Kim looked forward to her meetings with other teachers. Some meetings were with colleagues who had taught the courses that her students took last year. She wanted to learn what her students had the opportunity to learn and what kind of mathematical thinking they were used to doing. She would also meet with a more experienced mentor teacher. Together they would plan routines to engage their students with mathematics.

Kim smiled when she thought of where she had been a year ago. Before her first year of teaching, the principal had told Kim that the school would be open during August for teacher preparation. Kim liked this idea. She went in for three days during the week before the first day of school. She chatted with her new colleagues, read the student handbook, and wrote a few lesson plans for the first week. She got paperwork ready to hand out to her students on the first day, made sure she had enough textbooks, and decorated her room. After the three days, she felt ready. She was not sure what else she could do to prepare. A year later, Kim thought to herself, "What a difference a year makes. If only I had known then what I know now, I would have spent much more time preparing." After a year of teaching, she now worried that she would not have enough time to prepare before the kids arrived for a new year.

* * *

One of the most vivid memories we have from our own beginnings as teachers is this sense that we should be working hard to prepare, yet not really knowing what to do. Equally vivid are memories of wishing we had prepared once the year got started, how studying the curriculum, setting up the classroom in a particular way, and introducing important routines and expectations would have made the whole year so much easier.

This section will help you prepare for teaching before the students arrive and get your class started off right. To help you teach more effectively from day one, we will give you things to think about and do as well as advice about what to plan for in your first few lessons. Although this section is especially important for new teachers, teachers with some experience will also find our suggestions useful.

This section also introduces a structure for the rest of this book. Each chapter opens with a story or example embodying some aspect of teaching that typically challenges beginning teachers. Each chapter outlines a set of guiding principles that (1) justify the chapter's suggestions and (2) serve as a tool for reflection on your current teaching practices. (Do your current practices align with these guiding principles? If so, how? If not, how does your current practice diverge from these ideas about learning and teaching mathematics?) The guiding principles, in turn, suggest specific habits of practice: concrete strategies and teaching moves to improve instruction and student mathematical learning. Finally, a summary connects the chapter content with the book's larger themes, described in section I.

SUCCESS
from
the START
Your first years
teaching SECONDARY
MATHEMATICS

chapter **four**

Gaining Important Background Knowledge for Teaching

Your primary job as a teacher is to support students as they work to gain connected mathematical knowledge. Expert mathematics teachers make this look easy: they often know what will happen before it does; they have the perfect strategy to help students who are stuck; they appear to be good at thinking on their feet. If you dig beneath the surface, you will find that expert mathematics teachers are usually responding in practiced ways to familiar situations that they expect. Their knowledge of students, curriculum, and pedagogy supports their teaching. Kim Washington (the teacher in the section II introduction) learned this when reflecting on the differences between starting her first and second years of teaching mathematics. This realization can also happen when reflecting on a shorter time—many days during her first year of teaching, Kim thought to herself, "If I had known at the beginning of the day what I know now, I would have done things differently."

Like experts in any field, expert teachers develop knowledge over time. Kim is often impressed by her more experienced colleagues' knowledge about students, curriculum, and teaching. However, you can take the initiative to develop much of this knowledge before students arrive. Because you will support students in making sense of mathematics, learn all you can before the school year about the students and mathematics that you are responsible for teaching.

Guiding Principles

>> Learn as much as possible about the mathematics you will teach, your students, and the culture of your school and the community—before students arrive.

>> Use knowledge about students, mathematics, teaching, and context to support your teaching.

>> Forge collaborative relationships with mentors.

Furthermore, more experienced colleagues will become valuable sources of information and professional support during your first year and beyond.

LEARN AS MUCH AS POSSIBLE BEFORE STUDENTS ARRIVE

Experience plays an important role in improving teacher instruction. But if you simply wait for improvement to happen, it may take longer than you want and improve less than you like. Conscious effort can accelerate natural growth that stems from experience. Before you begin teaching, put yourself ahead by learning as much as you can about the mathematics you will teach, the students who will take your classes, and the school and community contexts.

Think back to Ms. Barker's classroom in chapter 1 (set during her second year of teaching). Ms. Barker did not learn to enact this kind of teaching only through experience and time. In fact, in the middle of her first year, she thought the second semester would go much more smoothly. And yet many problems from the first semester persisted. Even with experience she had not learned how to get students to settle down to work more quickly, for example, or why some students struggled to understand slope. Some areas of her teaching had improved, but on reflection she noticed that her improvements came from specific things she had learned about and tried, or specific insights gained from looking at the teacher notes in her textbook or from conversations with colleagues. "Experience" proved to be specific information that she had actively sought and applied. She spent much of the summer between her first and second years of teaching studying her curriculum materials and going to a summer institute where she explored, with other teachers, methods to engage her students in problem solving and discourse. Consequently, the first semester of her second year was a vast improvement over her first year. Having learned early in her career that with knowledge comes power, she has consciously worked to learn all she can about her students, the math she is teaching, and new teaching methods before school starts each year.

USE KNOWLEDGE TO SUPPORT YOUR TEACHING

Effective teaching is something you can learn. It is not a matter of innate talent. What looks like talent to outsiders actually arises from knowledge about students, content, and context, which expert teachers use to plan and enact effective mathematics instruction.

So a visitor to Ms. Barker's class might notice that Mike spends five minutes at the front of the class sharing his thinking and then leading a discussion. The observer may even notice that Ms. Barker spoke with Mike during work time before the discussion. It may look like Ms. Barker has a great "way with students," that she can really inspire confidence. What the observer may not know is that Ms. Barker has learned that Mike is shy and lacks confidence in his academic ability, but that he is generally quick to use a systematic way of guessing and checking to solve problems involving finding unknown quantities. She also knows that cuing students before it is time to share, and asking them to share specific aspects of their solutions, makes overcoming fears of public speaking easier. Finally, she knows that several students will probably use a guess-and-check method that is less systematic than Mike's and that his method can serve as a bridge between haphazard guessing and the more efficient method of creating and solving equations.

The outside observer is right; Ms. Barker does have a "way with students." But her way is founded on knowledge that she gained and learned to apply. Her effective teaching is the enactment of this knowledge and technique.

FORGE COLLABORATIVE RELATIONSHIPS WITH MENTORS

As beginning teachers, and even as experienced teachers in new schools, we remember how overwhelming it could feel. We could not anticipate all the information we would need, and figuring out where to find it was hard. Experienced colleagues were invaluable sources of information that helped us navigate all aspects of teaching, including how to plan for lessons, what to expect from students, how to cope with bureaucratic and logistical demands, and other unexpected issues. However, relationships with helpful and experienced colleagues did not just happen. We had to seek out these relationships and then work to sustain them. We had to figure out which colleagues would be the most helpful and available, and overcome our own anxieties about asking for help or asking to collaborate. Our efforts were worthwhile because we became more knowledgeable through collaborating with mentors than we would have alone.

STOP+REFLECT

>> What aspect of your teaching do you think is going well? What knowledge do you use, perhaps even unconsciously, to support that aspect?

>> What aspect of your teaching is not going as well as you would like? How would knowledge of students, curriculum, or pedagogy help you improve this aspect?

>> What aspect of teaching, content, or your specific school context do you want to learn about? How might you learn more?

>> Who seems like a helpful experienced colleague you could learn from? How will that happen? How can you make that happen?

Habits of Practice

>> Find teachers and administrators to support you.

>> Learn about your students, school, and community.

>> Study your mathematics curriculum materials.

FIND TEACHERS AND ADMINISTRATORS TO SUPPORT YOU

All teachers deserve support throughout their career—especially beginning teachers. Regardless of whether your school or district offers a formal mentoring program for beginning teachers, you must take the initiative to ask for specific support.

Identify good mentors

As soon as possible after being hired, let your principal or department head know that you want to learn more about teaching mathematics and to work with a mentor or math coach, if one is available. Also ask for the names and contact information of teachers who are especially good at teaching math who could support you.

You will probably also need to seek out helpful, more experienced colleagues on your own. Look for people who talk about mathematics and seem excited about the kinds of solutions that students come up with. If possible, find another teacher teaching the same course as you, so that you can plan together, or share experiences about specific student solutions and misconceptions. Avoid teachers who spend a lot of time complaining about students or talking about what students cannot do.

Start the conversation

When you find a teacher or group of teachers who seem excited about their work and interested in talking about teaching and student thinking, ask whether they would talk with you about teaching. Approaching them will probably feel uncomfortable, but do so anyway. Teachers tend to be helpful and knowledgeable, but they also may be reluctant to offer unsolicited advice. If you want their help, you probably have to ask for it. If you are unsure what to ask, try these suggested topics to start the conversation:

- Setting up and maintaining a classroom environment that supports students to work productively and make sense of mathematics

- Anticipating and making sense of student thinking

- Planning and analyzing lessons

- Developing routines to support student learning

- Identifying and understanding the math you will be teaching

- Specific logistical demands that may be unfamiliar to you (such as classroom organization)

Once you identify mentor(s) willing to talk with you, talk to them as often as you can. If possible, set up a regular time to meet. Meeting with them before school begins to help plan for the beginning of school would be especially helpful.

LEARN ABOUT YOUR STUDENTS, SCHOOL, AND COMMUNITY

To enact instruction that will support your students to build connected mathematical knowledge, you must know all you can about your students, their school experiences (including experiences in previous math classes), and their community. You want to be able to plan for instruction with some knowledge about what your students have had the opportunity to learn in previous math classes as well as some idea of their mathematics learning environments. You want to be able to build on their previous experiences to create interactions that will support them in gaining connected mathematical knowledge.

Seek out specific information

As you begin teaching, learn about the following:

- What is a typical math class like in this school? Do students work in groups or individually? Do they work on nonroutine problems for long periods, or do they practice what teachers have demonstrated?

- What activities are students involved in? What are the big school events? Who takes part in them?

- How are parents involved in the school? Do substantial groups of parents not speak English? What language do they speak?

- Do distinct groups exist within the school? Who is in those groups? How do the different groups get along?

- What are the demographics of the school, particularly as they affect teaching and learning? Do many students have learning disabilities and individualized education plans? How many students speak English as a second language? Do many students have jobs outside school?

- What is the school's neighborhood like? Do the neighborhood and the school have cordial relationships?

- What strengths do typical students have in math class; what can you build on?

- What difficulties do students typically have? What part of your course will be especially difficult for them? Why?

- How do teachers typically deal with behavior issues?

- Do students generally do their homework? Do they participate in class?

- What are the most important bureaucratic requirements that a new teacher should know about (such as attendance routines and grading)?

Use different resources to find information

You can begin to gather this information in several ways. The most accessible is through local media and the Internet, both of which can help you answer basic, factual questions about the school, such as the size of the student body, graduation rates, and test scores. School websites will often describe the math courses offered, and what is required, as well as whether courses are tracked and the basis of those tracking decisions.

You can also find some of this information by spending time in the school while students are there. Doing so may not be possible if you are hired over the summer, but if you are hired before the school year is out, spend some time observing in math classes, in the lunchroom, and during passing time in the halls. Focus on how students talk to each other and to teachers, and what kind of work they do and appear to be used to in math class.

Finally, you can gain important information about the school and the students from your colleagues. If you can observe math classes, see whether you can talk to the teacher after or before the class. Ask what information would be important for new teachers to know, in addition to asking questions about the above information.

Some things to remember

When gathering information about your new school, be sure to keep an open mind and do not let first impressions shut you off from further information. Also remember to look hard for positive aspects of the school that you will be able to build on as a new teacher: routines that you observe, rules that everyone follows, interests and enthusiasms that students have. You cannot possibly learn everything about the students, the school, or the community. But get as much of a sense as you can to avoid surprises in the first weeks of teaching and to create a classroom that draws on the best the school has to offer.

STUDY YOUR MATHEMATICS CURRICULUM MATERIALS

Most U.S. schools and districts adopt a particular set of curriculum materials, textbooks, or a math program for their teachers to use in teaching mathematics. To maintain consistency across course offerings, schools may require mathematics teachers to use these materials as their primary resource for planning, teaching, and assessment.

Before 1990, mathematics textbooks generally contained content organized for one type of instruction: the teacher explains and shows how to correctly "do" the procedures from one part of the textbook, and then students practice by completing a set of related exercises. The supplementary materials for the student textbooks were often little more than a teacher's edition (a replication of the student text with answers) and a set of chapter tests. Students generally used these materials only when they did exercises assigned for homework, and perhaps to look at worked examples or explanations when they had difficulty with homework. Teachers used these textbooks as guides for what content to teach in what order and as a source of homework exercises.

During the 1990s, the National Science Foundation funded several new mathematics curriculum (or textbook) series designed to create opportunities for students to learn mathematics through engaging in the five processes in chapter 2 (problem solving, connecting, communicating, reasoning and proving, and representing). These curricula were also designed to help teachers learn more about the mathematics they were teaching, how students think and learn about mathematics (that is, what misconceptions they will probably have in learning particular mathematics), and how to assess student learning.

Currently, mathematics textbooks and curriculum series differ tremendously in how they structure students' learning opportunities and in how they present information useful for teachers to plan, enact, and reflect on their teaching. Some curriculum materials continue to stress explanation and practice, whereas others give students the opportunity to build their understanding of mathematics by working on problems that can be solved in a variety of ways. Some curricula have extensive guides for how to set up your classroom, how to lead discussions and what questions you might ask during lessons to support student learning, and how to assess students' understanding at various times through the unit. Other textbook series may contain less useful information. However, to various extents, mathematics textbook series typically include the following information.

- Things for students to do and think about:

  - Activities and problems for students to do in class and for homework

  - Assessments for students to take

  - Extra or alternative activities for struggling students or students who may need an extra challenge

- Suggestions for teachers:

  - How to present the work to students and how to lead discussions

  - How to set up your classroom and how to create norms that support the student work and discourse required for students to learn from this particular textbook series

  - How to adjust instruction for students with special needs

  - How to communicate with families, including letters home (often in English and Spanish) describing what students will learn, and how parents or caregivers can support their children in learning mathematics

- Things teachers should consider:

  - Mathematical goals for lessons and units

  - How the student activities support students achieving the goals

- How students might make sense of the mathematics, including examples of typical student work, or typical student comments, and how a teacher might respond

Textbook materials can be a tremendous resource for learning important knowledge for teaching, yet they can also overwhelm. To learn from them effectively, look at the materials in several different ways with several different questions in mind as you prepare to teach.

Six steps to knowing your textbook materials

Step 1: Familiarize yourself with the materials generally
Mathematics textbook materials can be confusing, and your first job is to learn what information is available and where. What resources does your curriculum offer and where can you find them? (Ideally, you got a complete set of textbook materials from your principal before you began teaching. If not, many textbook series have resources for teachers on the Internet that mirror those in print.) Many curricula have a student textbook and a teacher's edition. They also may have separate teacher's guides that give an overview of the multiyear program, supplemental lessons, answer keys, assessment guides and resources, Internet supplements with teacher tips, blackline masters for use with overhead projectors, blackline masters for worksheets, and many other resources for information and assistance.

Look through your materials with these questions in mind:

- What does a full set of curriculum materials contain?

    - What different kinds of materials are available?

    - What do students receive?

    - What do teachers get?

- Where can you find information about the mathematics you will be teaching and how students might think about that mathematics? Where can you get information about how to support students during lessons?

    - Does this information appear at the beginning of each unit, at the end of each unit, in a separate section at the end of the teacher's edition?

    - Does the information appear at the beginning of each lesson? Is it interspersed throughout the lesson in the teacher's edition?

    - Are supplementary materials available that offer information about these topics, such as separate teacher's guides or teacher sites on the Internet?

- Where are suggested assessments? Do the assessments include examples of student work and ways to score them?

Step 2: Familiarize yourself with the math you will teach

What is the mathematics that your students will need to know and understand? After skimming through the materials a first time, look more specifically to find out what mathematics you will teach. Begin by looking at the larger units. For each unit, find out the following:

- What overriding mathematics concepts are your students expected to understand by the end of the unit?

- What kinds of problems will they be expected to solve?

- What representations will they need to be able to use, generate, and interpret?

- What procedures will they be expected to be able to use?

- What connections should students be able to make between representations, procedures, concepts, and problems?

- How will students be asked to reason mathematically?

- How will students be required to communicate their mathematical thinking?

- How does the math of each unit build on the mathematics of earlier units, and how does it lead to the math of ensuing units?

Often mathematics textbooks contain unit introductions that address many of these questions, but not always. Even if the questions are addressed specifically, looking through the unit is still helpful to see how the mathematics comes out in the activities.

Step 3: Learn how the curriculum materials envision and support student learning

What kinds of activities does the curriculum supply, and what do teachers and students do during these activities? What support does it give teachers in helping students to reason, represent, solve problems, communicate, and make connections?

In the first unit you will teach, look more closely at the problems, activities, and any suggestions for teachers:

- Does this textbook give students open-ended problems? Where are these problems in each unit? What guidance do the teacher materials offer to support students in doing that work?

- Does the textbook present exercises that require students to practice procedures that the text explains? Where are these exercises in each unit?

- Do the curriculum materials describe full-class discussions or suggest questions to ask during class? If so, do the materials suggest how to lead those discussions? Where is that support? Do the materials describe typical student responses or what student misconceptions may come into play during the lesson? If so, where?

Chapter 6 contains an exercise in which you will more closely examine the different types of mathematical problems or tasks in the student edition of your textbook series. This would be a good exercise to undertake during the summer, before your students arrive.

Step 4: Become clear about specific mathematics in the first unit
One of the most important things to do as a teacher is to familiarize yourself with the mathematics that you will teach, and get used to anticipating and interpreting ways that students think mathematically. The best way to learn more about the mathematics you will teach is to actually do the work that students will do. As you work through the problems in the first unit, think about these prompts:

- How does each problem/exercise relate to the big mathematical ideas and concepts of the unit? How will working on these problems/exercises help students learn about this idea?

- How might students solve each problem/exercise? Try to solve problems/exercises in as many ways as you can imagine students doing, including ways that may result from students' mathematical misconceptions or that involve common mistakes. Completing this task will help get you into a mindset of attending to and anticipating student thinking.

As you work through the mathematics in the unit, take notes in the margins (or use sticky notes) to remind yourself of what you did.

Step 5: Begin planning lessons
As section III will describe, planning lessons is a core activity of teaching. At this point in getting to know your curriculum materials, practicing planning instruction using the materials is helpful. Planning a series of lessons without knowing your students well may seem inauthentic, but the more you can practice planning with a new set of teaching materials, the better off you will be when you plan instruction that responds to your students' mathematical needs. At this point, we suggest that you read chapters 6 and 7 and then choose a series of three to four lessons and practice planning. If possible, do so with a colleague—someone who teaches at your school or a friend you met in your teacher education program. Having someone else to talk with during this process is particularly helpful at the beginning.

Although you may have planned several lessons during your teacher education program (including student teaching), remember that this exercise will help you familiarize yourself with your own textbook series. Working through planning a lesson now will help you identify where the textbook has information to support you in thinking about how students might make sense of the mathematics and what questions you might ask them as they work to support their understanding. Doing so will also help you gain a sense of how useful and helpful your materials are during planning.

Step 6: Continue this process
Learning about and from textbook materials is not simply something teachers do over the summer before their first year; they do so throughout their careers. Working through the mathematics and reading the teacher notes offers tremendous opportunities for teacher learning, regardless of experience level. And what you may need from the curriculum materials may change. As a beginning teacher, you may want to pay special attention to suggestions in the material about setting up your room or creating a supportive environment for learning mathematics (some mathematics textbooks series have this kind of advice). As you gain experience and create routines for the beginning of the school year, you may want to look at the materials anew for suggestions in other areas.

Specialized vocabulary

Teaching embodies a great deal of specialized vocabulary concerning what teachers are supposed to teach and how and when they should teach it. Making sense of all the different terms and knowing the differences between them can be hard for beginning teachers. Here are some of the more common terms, what they mean, and how they overlap.

- *Curriculum:* In broad terms, the mathematics that you are responsible for teaching and that students are responsible for learning.

- *Curriculum materials:* A set of materials, usually produced by a publisher and purchased by a school or district, that supports teachers in teaching the curriculum. The materials may consist of textbooks, teacher's editions, assessments, alternative lessons and assessments for struggling or accelerated students, and a variety of other materials.

- *Pacing guides:* Documents that offer guidance for how to pace lessons (how much time particular lessons will typically take) or give directions about what mathematics should be "covered" by a certain calendar date. Districts or schools often produce pacing guides, which can vary both in their specificity and in how strictly teachers must follow them. Curriculum materials may include more general pacing guides as well.

- *Standards:* Lists of broad content goals, usually organized by grade, put out by states and national organizations. Curriculum

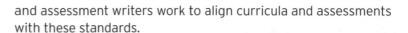
and assessment writers work to align curricula and assessments with these standards.

CONCLUSION

As you prepare for the beginning of school, remember that you want your students to spend their time in class engaging in reasoning, representing, communicating, problem solving, and making connections—with a goal to build connected mathematical knowledge. Recall the triangle of instruction, which helps you visualize teaching mathematics as orchestrating interactions between students, teacher, and content within the larger context schooling. Student learning takes place in the interactions between students and mathematics, and your primary job as a teacher is to plan and attend to those interactions. To do that effectively, you need to know as much as possible about the various aspects of the instructional triangle. Learn as much as you can about your students, the mathematics they will learn, and the context within which they live and go to school—all before school starts for the first semester.

SUCCESS
from the START
Your first years
teaching SECONDARY
MATHEMATICS

chapter **five**

Creating a Learning Community during the First Weeks of School

During the year we spent writing this book, Rob's daughter started at a new school. When he picked her up at the end of the first day, he asked how it had gone. She enthusiastically replied, "We learned stuff on the first day, which is a bit out of the ordinary." Her math teacher had asked all the students to draw a rectangle on graph paper, figure out the area, draw a new rectangle with each side twice as long as the original rectangle, and then find out the area for that new rectangle. They then shared the rectangles they had made and talked about what they had noticed. Rob's daughter was excited to show her dad the patterns she had found and looked forward to talking about it with the other kids in class the next day.

Although this was just the first day in a new school, Rob's daughter had already learned that in her math class she would be looking for patterns, describing those patterns so that others could understand them, and working to understand her classmates' ideas. From day one, her math teacher established what students would do in class and how they would engage with each other and the teacher, all while having students address important ideas from her curriculum. This math teacher knew that setting the tone and teaching her students how to work and interact with others in math was essential during the first days of class. She did not set this tone by telling her students how to act. Instead, she planned for and enacted instruc-

Guiding Principles

>> A mathematics learning community supports students in solving problems, reasoning, representing, communicating, and making connections.

>> Establish a supportive mathematics learning community during the first weeks of school.

>> You create community by aligning what you say, do, pay attention to, and require students to do.

tion that gave her students an interesting mathematical task that would result in students working in ways consistent with the culture she wanted to establish.

* * *

Your primary job as a teacher is to support your students to build connected mathematical knowledge, particularly in communicating, reasoning, representing, solving problems, and making connections. During class, your students' focus should be on making sense of the mathematical tasks you assign them, and your focus should be on their sense making (recall the triangle of instruction). Strive to create a learning community in your classroom, in which members have shared understandings about learning goals, intellectual and social values, and about how to interact with each other in ways that align with those goals and values. Establishing and nurturing a learning community in a math classroom requires conscious effort from the teacher and the students.

Establishing a learning community is some of the most important work that any math teacher does at the beginning of each school year. Beginning teachers especially must pay explicit attention to planning for and enacting instruction in the first weeks of school that supports building a learning community; many of the challenges beginning teachers face stem from not paying enough attention from the start to creating a classroom environment conducive to mathematical learning. To help you start off the school year in the best possible way, this chapter offers advice and strategies to establish and maintain a learning community in your classroom.

A MATHEMATICS LEARNING COMMUNITY SUPPORTS STUDENTS

We have all belonged to organizations or groups where we felt included and supported, where everyone seemed to know how to interact and support each other and work toward a common goal. Perhaps it was an athletic team, a book club, a scout troop, or just a group of friends. Think about a group you have been involved with that had this kind of environment. Within your group, people knew how to act and what to expect, and the members shared a common goal and worked together to achieve it in ways that were clear to everyone. When we think about creating a learning community in a math classroom, we can draw on our experiences outside the classroom in supportive communities. We can create an environment where members feel included, share a common purpose and expectations, and nurture supportive interaction.

A learning community in math class supports students in solving problems, reasoning, representing, communicating, and making connections. An environment that does not can make learning difficult for students. For example, if students expect the teacher to show how to do a problem before asking them to solve it, those students may resist if a teacher asks them to do problems that require mathematical reasoning—where they are not told exactly what to do. Here the students and the teacher do not have a shared expectation of what each should be doing in math class.

As you work to establish and maintain a learning community in your classroom, you will need to continually check what you are doing against this fundamental criterion: do the patterns of interaction that you model and encourage support students to engage in these processes, or do they serve some other purpose? For example, if you informally chat with students at the beginning of class, you are creating an element of your classroom community. Does this chat help create a feeling of inclusion and safety that will support students in taking the risks involved in reasoning, communicating, and solving problems, or does it allow students to avoid difficult mathematics? These are difficult questions without clear answers, but keeping your focus on creating a community that supports students to learn mathematics will help you avoid creating a community that distracts students, and you, from your main goal.

ESTABLISH A SUPPORTIVE MATHEMATICS LEARNING COMMUNITY

When we see math classrooms that run smoothly—where students solve problems, reason, represent, communicate, and make connections, where the focus is clearly on learning the mathematics at hand—we might attribute the positive learning environment to students' personal qualities. The students seem so engaged and motivated, so bright and kind and patient with each other, so independent and mature. Experienced teachers, however, understand that this behavior comes from a tremendous amount of teacher work. To a large extent, the teacher determines the community of the classroom.

Because your classroom's patterns of interaction will determine how your students learn mathematics, a primary task of teaching is to create a community to support interactions to help students reason, represent, communicate, solve problems, and make connections. If we think back to the triangle of instruction, a strong community creates a context in which both teachers and students can focus on the interactions between students and mathematics. Many problems of first-year teachers, especially in classroom management and student engagement, are actually the result of failing to create a strong supportive community in their classroom during the first weeks of school.

ALIGN WHAT YOU SAY, DO, PAY ATTENTION TO, AND REQUIRE STUDENTS TO DO

Chapter 3 argued that effective instruction is internally aligned. Issues of alignment also apply to establishing and maintaining a productive mathematics learning community. As teachers, we communicate our expectations to students in many ways: our actions, our words, the tasks we give them, our reactions to their behavior and ideas, and how we set up the physical space of our classrooms. One powerful way to create a positive mathematics learning community is to align these different ways of communicating and interacting with our values and expectations. Conversely, misaligning our words and actions sends mixed messages, undermining our effectiveness.

Imagine the first day of school in an algebra class. The desks are arranged in paired rows. As students enter, the teacher says hello at the door and directs their attention to the board, where she has written the following:

> Li went to buy presents for her cousins, who like hats and t-shirts. Hats cost $12 each. T-shirts cost $15 each. Li has $180. How many hats and how many t-shirts can she buy?
>
> Come up with as many different answers as you can. Write them down. Be prepared to share with a partner how you thought about this problem.

For the first five minutes of class, the teacher walks from desk to desk, asking some students what they have done so far and quietly commenting that she finds their solutions interesting. She then stops and says, "Now turn to the person next to you. I want the person sitting closest to the windows to share first. Tell your partner one of your answers and how you got it. The partner needs to listen and make sure that he or she understands both the solution and how the speaker got that solution. You have three minutes. Go."

Now imagine a first algebra class in which the following occurs: Students walk into the classroom, which is set up in rows. The teacher asks the students to quiet down and introduces herself. She takes several minutes to explain that this class will be about thinking deeply about mathematics, that she expects students to work hard on math and talk with others in the class about math, and that she values their ideas. She then spends fifteen minutes explaining the homework policies and handing out textbooks.

In the first example, the teacher gave a task that elicited student thinking and then structured a conversation that supported students in sharing their thinking. Her actions and words during student work reinforced her interest in their thinking. Everything she did and said was aligned with the type of work that she expected students to do in her class: she expected students to work on math problems and to share their mathematical thinking with her and with each other. The way she set up her room, the task she gave, and how she interacted with students all sent a powerful message to her students about how they would work and interact in math class. She has established expectations and patterns of interaction that will create and support a learning community.

In the second example, the teacher's statements, actions, and the tasks she gave to her students are not aligned and, indeed, send contradictory messages. This class does not convey nearly as powerful a sense of community. Students leave the class still not knowing exactly what they will be doing in math, but suspecting that despite the teacher's professed commitment to student thinking, she will do most of the talking, and their job is to sit still, listen, and follow the rules.

STOP+REFLECT

>> Think of your own mathematics classroom or a class that you were a student in. What values did the community of that classroom embody? How did the community support you in making sense of mathematics? How did it create barriers to your understanding?

>> What behaviors do you want your students to routinely exhibit by the end of the first few weeks of class? How will those behaviors support their learning?

>> Have you found ways that your actions and words do not align? How might you align them more closely?

ENVISION POSITIVE NORMS FOR CLASSROOM INTERACTIONS

Imagine yourself as a student on the first day of high school geometry. Your teacher has arranged the desks in groups of four and has handed out

Habits of Practice

>> Envision positive norms for classroom interactions.

>> Plan and use teacher moves that establish community.

>> Create initial routines for what to do.

>> Set up the physical space of the classroom.

>> Plan the first lessons with building community in mind.

>> Reflect on the first few lessons.

a problem. Before you begin work, the teacher says, "In this class we will work in groups because people learn better when they work together. I expect that you will all be responsible for your own learning and the learning of others in your group. Now as a group, see whether you can solve the problem I have given you."

STOP+ REFLECT

As a student, what do these directions tell you to do? What should you think about as you do the problem? How should you interact with others in your group?

Now imagine, instead, that your teacher has said, "I want each of you to read, quietly to yourself, the problem on the piece of paper in the middle of your group. Then I want you to think about the problem on your own for two minutes. What is going on in the problem, and what is the question you are supposed to be answering? Be ready to explain what the problem is asking or to ask a specific question about the problem that will help you understand the situation."

At the end of two minutes your teacher then says, "Now explain to your partner the situation described in the problem, or ask a specific question about the situation that you do not understand. Then I want you to say, in your own words, the question that the problem asks you to answer. I should hear things like, 'I don't understand what this word means,' or 'We need to figure out this part' or 'We know this, but we don't know this.' I'll be walking around listening to your conversations to see how you're doing and what questions you have."

STOP+ REFLECT

As a student, what do these directions tell you to do? What should you think about as you do the problem? How should you interact with others in your group?

The students in both examples are working in groups on a mathematical problem that will require them to reason, problem solve, and communicate. The major difference between these two sets of directions is the extent to which the teacher in the second example gives explicit instructions for how she expects students to interact with the mathematics and with peers.

Chapter 2 described teaching and learning as planned interactions designed to support students to achieve specific mathematical learning goals. Effective teachers begin creating community by envisioning, in specific detail, the interactions they want so that they can give explicit directions to their students and then look for specific behaviors. In imagining norms, they create explicit descriptions of what ideal interactions should look like and sound like in their classrooms. Specifically, teachers can describe how students interact with content, each other, and the teacher.

Student-mathematics interactions

The most important expectation to establish in your classroom is that students will spend their time working to build connected mathematical knowledge through solving problems, reasoning, representing, communicating, and making connections. Most of the time they will be figuring things out rather than simply following rules and directions.

What does that look like? Students look at a math problem and write down ideas or think about it when they walk into class. Students create representations of the problem, draw pictures, or create equations or expressions that represent the problem in some way. Students reread problems and look back and forth between the problem and their work. Students look back in their notes or textbook for information that might help them solve the problem, or at the work of their partners or group members to find out what they are thinking. Sometimes students gaze off into space, thinking about the problem, but then come back to their paper or the problem to check whether their understanding makes sense. Students get up to find tools that they need to solve the problems, be it graph paper, calculators, protractors or rulers, or other tools. During class discussions, students track the speaker with their eyes, looking at representations that the speaker describes or refers to.

What does student–mathematics interaction sound like? Students interacting with mathematics is sometimes quiet, with students thinking on their own and writing down thoughts and ideas or questions. Sometimes students ask questions of each other or communicate their thinking. It sounds like, "I understand this part, but I have a question about this part," or "I don't get what you did here? Could you explain this to me?" or "What is this number [picture, expression, etc.]? Where does it come from?" or "Why are you allowed to do that?" It also sounds like, "This is like what we did yesterday," or "My method is kind of like Leon's, but I started with a different picture," or "At the beginning I made an equation, but that was not helping, so I decided to make a few guesses," or "I realized that I needed to find out this piece first, so I started by figuring out _____."

Take a few minutes and envision your future classroom, where students are building connected mathematical knowledge. Now, on a piece of paper that you can refer to during class, write down five specific indicators to look for while your students work that will tell you that they are positively interacting with the mathematics they are learning. Make items from the lists you create in this chapter central in directions you give your students in the first days of a new school year so that they can come to know your expectations.

Student-student interactions

Because mathematics class is fundamentally about learning mathematics, students should interact with each other about mathematics. Indeed, some overlap exists between students interacting with mathematics and with each other. So students should communicate and reason with each other about mathematics problems, create and refer to representations as tools to solve problems and facilitate conversation, and make connections between what various students say and think. Student–student interactions should also foster a sense of safety and emotional support and respect so that students can risk being wrong or admit to being confused. Partial understandings, mistakes, and misperceptions are opportunities to learn (Yackel and Cobb 1996).

What does positive student–student interaction look like? Students converse. They look at each other; at the problem statement or other visual representations connected to the problem in the room; and at each other's writing, drawings, equations, and calculations. Students point at these representations and then look at each other as they ask questions or make statements. Students nod their heads in agreement, shake heads in disagreement, or look puzzled. Students are on the edge of their seat to see the paper of a partner explaining a solution. Students write or draw as they speak, write on each other's papers, take a partner's pen to add to a picture or set of calculations. Students look at each other to see whether their expression shows understanding or confusion.

What does positive student–student interaction sound like? Students talk with each other and say specific things about the mathematics they are learning. Students explain, saying things like, "I started by doing this . . .," or I knew we had to figure out _____ . . .," or "This is just like the ones we did yesterday. You just have to make an equation." Students ask questions like, "I just don't know what we are supposed to be figuring out here; is it the speed or some other thing?" or "What does this mean?" or "Why did you do that?" Students question each other's reasoning by saying something like, "I don't agree with this step," or "This answer seems wrong; you can't have a negative area," or "Why did you multiply here? The problem is talking about adding over and over again; shouldn't it be plus?" Finally, students check that they understand and are being understood. Students could say something like, "So tell me what I said so far," or "So what you are saying is . . .?" or "Which part do you not understand?" or "But why does it work?"

Take a few minutes and envision your future classroom, where students are building connected mathematical knowledge. Now, on a piece of paper that you can refer to during class, write down five specific indicators to look for while your students work that will tell you that they are positively interacting with each other around the mathematics they are learning.

Teacher-student interactions

Finally, the way that you interact with students models for them how you want them to interact with each other and with the mathematics. What's more, you are in complete control of what you say and do in any situation, so you have the power to create your half of any student–teacher interaction. Use this power to focus these interactions on students' mathematical thinking and model appropriate and supportive talk for students to emulate.

What does positive teacher–student interaction look like? You move around the class, observing and listening intently to students' discussions.

An Essential Element of Positive Norms: No Personal Attacks

To gain connected mathematical knowledge, students need to be in a classroom where students regularly share their thinking in public. Students must share not only complete, mathematically correct answers and strategies but also thinking that is not complete or that contains mathematical misconceptions. Partially formed solutions or misconceptions often offer the greatest opportunities to engage in the processes that lead to connected knowledge.

Unfortunately, sharing their thinking is often difficult for students. They need to feel safe and comfortable, secure that their mistakes or confusion will not bring ridicule or embarrassment. You must send a clear message that making fun of or ridiculing peers for any reason whatsoever is unacceptable in your classroom.

Thus far, we have emphasized that you create positive norms by envisioning and reinforcing specific behaviors that you want, rather than concentrating on negative behaviors that you do not want. You can certainly use this idea to make it safe for students to share their thinking. You can highlight mistakes you make yourself and not show embarrassment when you do so. You can praise students for sharing incomplete ideas and point out how it helped the class as a whole make sense of important ideas.

However, quashing personal attacks is so important that you need to be ready to recognize and address them from the beginning of your class. Establish a clear rule of "no personal attacks" in the first few days of school: define what that means for students, and talk with students as soon as you feel that they are attacking other students (as opposed to critiquing ideas). Talk with students individually when personal attacks occur (calling out students in front of their classmates is never a good idea). Speak quietly to an individual student or ask the student to stay after class. Other students do not have to witness your reprimand to get the message; they will know that their classmate did something unacceptable and that you are speaking to the student about the offending behavior.

New teachers often feel uncomfortable intervening when students engage in banter that is "on the border" between normal teenage kidding and personal attack. Although this discomfort is real, it cannot get in the way of your sending clear messages that students are not to engage in personal attacks. If their behavior makes you uncomfortable, it is more than likely affecting your students' ability to share their thinking. Do not let the offending behavior slide.

You kneel to get at their level and look at them and at their paper, as well as at others in the group to see whether they show signs of understanding or not understanding. You write down things while observing.

What does positive teacher–student interaction sound like? You ask questions probing student thinking, like, "What have you done so far?" or "What are you trying to find out?" or "Which part don't you understand?"

or "How is this like stuff you have done before?" You push for meaning or justification, asking questions like, "Why are you doing this?" or "How is this helping you solve the problem?" or "But why are you allowed to do this?" You check for understanding and ensure that students are involved: "Could somebody else explain Johnny's idea to me?" or "I see that Suzy has a different method on her paper. Can you explain your thinking, Suzy?"

Envisioning is generally about what students and teachers should be doing, rather than what they should not be doing. Effective teachers do not dwell on or attend to things they do not want from students; rather, they create the classrooms they want by naming and modeling specific behaviors, explicitly requiring those behaviors of students, and reinforcing those behaviors by attending to them. No one learns how to act solely by learning what not to do.

Envisioning what behavior should look like and sound like is not as easy as it would seem. We will spend much more time discussing specific talk moves you and students can make in chapter 8 and about classroom management in chapter 10. Furthermore, the specifics of how students interact with each other and the mathematics on any given day are related to the mathematical goal and the context, so much of your planning is anticipating and envisioning specific interactions in the context of the lesson. Even though it may be difficult, spending time before the semester begins thinking about what positive interactions in your class can look like and sound like, and getting in the habit of specifically describing ideal interactions, is a fundamental element of creating classroom community.

STOP+ REFLECT

>> Take a few minutes and envision your future classroom, where students are building connected mathematical knowledge. Now, on a piece of paper that you can refer to during class, write down five specific indicators to look for while your students work that will tell you that your interactions with them are positive.

PLAN AND USE TEACHER MOVES THAT ESTABLISH COMMUNITY

Some teacher moves and practices are especially helpful to establish a community that supports mathematical learning and are relatively simple to use. Using these moves at the beginning of the year will help students feel comfortable and safe engaging in the intellectual risks necessary in problem solving, communicating, connecting, reasoning and proving, and representing mathematics. Many of these practices will appear in chapters 8 and 10. But you can use these practices in the first weeks of school to establish a culture in your classroom that will support students in productive interactions with mathematics.

Greet students at the classroom door

Greeting your students at the door as they walk into your classroom on the first day of school sends a powerful message about you as a teacher. On the first day when you greet your students, you can introduce yourself, hear their names, and let them know what to do when they get in the classroom (for example, where to find the mathematics they should work on when they sit down) and where to sit. This practice communicates that you see your students as individuals and know who they are, that you expect them to work on math in this class, and that you are in control of the classroom. When students feel noticed, and sense that their teacher has clear expectations for academic engagement, they generally respond positively and work productively.

Be conscious of your stance and voice

How you address your students on the first day sets the tone for rest of the year. Your students must learn, through your actions, what you expect from them when you give oral instructions—mostly that they are silent and focused on what you say. Communicating those expectations the first time you speak to your students as a group will send a powerful message. Five teacher moves will help to communicate those expectations:

1 Stand still and tall (stay in one spot; try not to shift from foot to foot).

2 Look at your students (scan the room, looking directly into students' eyes).

3 Do not talk over student talk (wait until no students are talking; quietly say something like, "I am ready to begin, are you?").

4 Use a loud, clear voice (loud enough for students to hear, but not so loud that you are shouting).

5 Do not do anything else while you are giving instructions (students need to know that what you are saying is the focus).

Learn students' names early

Learning students' names, and then consistently using them, is a relatively simple and extremely powerful teacher practice. Addressing students by name from the first day tells them that you know who they are and are interested in their thinking and noticing them. This is especially important at the beginning of the semester, when you are working to set the tone of your class.

Not only should you get to know their names as early as possible, you should also use their names whenever possible (and appropriate). For example, you can name specific mathematical techniques, methods, and ideas after the students from whom they originate and continue to acknowledge them by name after they have shared a specific method with the class (such as Ms. Barker's use of "Jill's method for solving linear equations" in chapter 1). You can also use students' names in mathematical problems. Using students' names in new ways shows that you listen to their ideas and that the community values their mathematical ideas.

Recognize and reinforce positive behaviors

As often as possible, and particularly during the first weeks of school, identify students who engage in the specific behaviors that you want and then name the behaviors and the students displaying them. This teacher move helps students have a much more concrete and specific picture of positive behaviors and communicates that you believe that students can perform them. So, instead of spending time telling students what not to do, point out particular instances of students doing what you want and praise those students. For example, during the whole-group debriefing of a mathematical problem, you could say something like, "I like how Jason stopped his partner when he did not understand and asked him to explain his drawing," or "I appreciate how Shani turned her notebook so that the other members of her group could see what she was talking about."

Redirect

When students are off task, or engaged in behaviors that do not support learning, you can redirect them by telling them what they should be doing or by asking them a question about the math they are working on. Doing so is especially important at the beginning of a school year when students are still learning how you want them to behave. So, if students are off task, you can redirect them by asking something like, "How are you thinking about the problem?" or "What have you done so far?" Such questions focus on the student–mathematics interaction (recall the triangle of instruction) and limit time spent focused on nonmathematical topics.

Break the plane

As much as possible, from the beginning of the first day, walk around the classroom, observing and listening to as many students as you can. Far too many mathematics teachers position themselves behind an invisible vertical plane that exists between the front of the classroom (where the blackboard, teacher desk, and/or overhead projector are located) and the students' seats. Break this invisible plane whenever possible. This teacher move sends a strong message about how you value their mathematical work and thinking. Doing so will also help with managing student behaviors and increase the likelihood that your students remain on task. Moving around the room also allows you to reinforce positive behaviors on an individual basis (for example, "nice work, Paola") and redirect negative behaviors without making them the center of the class's attention.

Use "wait time" and "write first"

When asking mathematical questions, wait and give all students time to think about your question. Calling on the first student who raises a hand says that you care only about fast answers and that speed is the most important quality of a mathematical response—at the expense of other important qualities. Another powerful approach: have all students write down a response before asking for an answer. This technique will allow you, as you walk around, to assess what all students know, as well as give students a chance to rehearse and try out their thinking before putting it out to the whole group. Giving students time to think mathematically will help them begin to be comfortable with identifying what they know and do not know, and how they might begin to work on a problem.

Use "cold call"

Just like wait time/write first, cold call is a way to break students of the habit of simply not thinking about the questions that you ask and letting the "smart" kids do all the answering. In cold call, students refrain from raising hands, and you simply call on a student "cold." This teacher move signals that you expect all students to engage in the material; they cannot just sit quietly while their classmates do the thinking. With cold call, students never know when you might call on them, so they must think in response to every question. Establish early on that having the right answer is only one way to answer the question. Students could also respond to your question by asking another question to help clarify their thinking. Tell them that saying, "I need some help with answering your question" is an appropriate student response. Initiating cold call in conjunction with write first or with mathematical questions that pose little risk may be easier.

Use "turn and talk"

A powerful way to get students to talk to each other about math is to use "turn and talk" (sometimes called "think, pair, share"). Asking students to turn and talk with their partner about a specific question, or a statement that a fellow student made, is a great way to support student–student communication. You could use turn and talk to check whether students understand directions and to help them process new information or reason about problems and situations. Over time, you can expand turn and talk to include more complex mathematical reasoning and explanation.

CREATE INITIAL ROUTINES FOR WHAT TO DO

Our vision of a supportive classroom community emphasizes students interacting with mathematics and having mathematics-centered interactions with teachers and peers. For students and teachers to spend so much time and energy thinking about mathematics, they need to be able to not think about other things. They also need to develop habits that will support them in reasoning, representing, solving problems, communicating, and making connections.

Routines help students and teachers do exactly that. Establishing routines helps students and teachers deal with important logistical questions and helps students consistently behave in ways that support mathematical learning. Because the routines quickly become habits that students do not need to think about, they are free to think about mathematics. And because routines are so powerful, they will appear often in this book. Here we concentrate on the most important routines to establish during the first weeks of school.

Establish a routine for getting down to work

The most important routines support students engaging in mathematics from the beginning of class. From the first day, establish a routine that you and the students use to indicate that it's time to begin working. First, have a specific mathematical task(s) for students to work on as soon as they come into the room, and establish a consistent method to let the students know what that task is so that they can begin work without your telling them what to do. Here are some ways that you can do this:

- Have a task on a piece of paper that you hand to students as they come into the room, and tell them that they should start on that task right away.

- Have a specific space on the board where you write the task that they should work on. For the first few days of school, greet them at the door and tell them where to find the daily task.

- Have a task waiting for students on their desk or table. Again, greet them at the door by telling them that they have a problem waiting for them on their table.

- Have a task written on a piece of paper that students take from the same place every day as they come in.

No matter how students get the initial task, spend the first few moments of class walking around observing students as they work. Comment on their solutions and ask them about their thinking. If students are not working, first ask them what they have done on the problem so far. If their answer is "nothing," tell them you will be by in a few moments to hear what they are thinking, and then return. By giving them a task, and then attending to their thinking on that task, you show that you expect them to work. Another strategy is to create a specific time in which they need to finish the problem or at least have a solution in mind. By having a clear time limit on the initial task, you send the message that students cannot waste time.

Establish routines for basic logistical needs

When students first enter the room, they need to decide where to sit. Although this issue seems mundane, it is not at all a trivial question for adolescents and can involve, on their part, complex social calculations. We strongly suggest that you determine where students sit by assigning seats on the first day. Assigning seats serves several purposes. It takes away the students' deliberation about where to sit so that they can focus on mathematics rather than social calculations. It keeps you in control of seating arrangements, so that later you can create groups or alternative seating arrangements to serve various instructional purposes. Finally, it helps you learn student names and meet administrative needs, such as taking attendance, freeing up your energy to attend to students' mathematical thinking. You can let students know where to sit in several ways:

- Write their names on cards and tape them on the desks or tables. (Taping will prevent students from moving their card to a place next to their friends.)

- Display a seating chart near the door.

- Introduce yourself on the first day as students enter, and tell them where to sit by referring to a seating chart.

Several different ways exist to assign seats. As you get to know your students, you will get a sense of their relative strengths and weaknesses, which of their peers will distract them or help them focus, which students are outgoing or shy. You may want to account for all these factors as you modify seating arrangements throughout the year. (Chapter 10 discusses grouping students in more detail.) At the beginning of the year, assigning seats randomly or in alphabetical order is the best strategy. If students ask to change seats, ask them to stay in their seat for the first day and then have them write down their seating request and why they want to move. They can then hand you their request as they leave class on the first day. Immediately honor requests of students who may ask to change seats because of physical needs (such as needing to sit near the front because of sight or hearing issues).

Before the year begins, consider how you will deal with student requests to go to the restroom. This routine needs to—

- create a minimum of fuss;

- follow school procedures;

- give you a way to track who is out of the room, and how often;

- limit student trips to the bathroom to one at a time; and

- establish that you notice their absence.

Your students need to know that you expect them to use the restroom between classes rather than during class time. If your school does not have a predetermined routine (such as a written hall pass), consider one of these:

- Post a sign-out list on the wall near the door. After receiving your permission to leave the room, students should write their name, the date, the time they leave the room, and the time they return.

- Have some large, useless object serve as your bathroom pass (such as an empty detergent bottle or a large piece of wood with your room number on it). When students need to leave the room for any reason, they take the pass.

- Give each student three restroom passes (or vouchers) to use during the semester (have them write their name on the passes). Upon receiving your permission to leave the room, students give you their pass.

Finally, develop a routine to hand out and collect work and materials, such as the following:

- Assign every student a hanging file folder, which you store in a box. Place any work that you return, or assignment that they need to do, in their folder. Students check and empty their folder at the beginning of class every day. (This system is especially helpful to get homework to students who are absent. Place the assignment in their folder and they get it when they return to class.)

- Have students return papers by passing them up the row to the front. When all the work is in the front row, students can pass them to the left so that all papers are at one desk. You can pass papers and materials out by reversing this process.

- If students are seated in groups or at tables, they can place their work in the center of the table and then you or a designated student can gather the papers.

- If you need to hand out materials, designate a specific student to get the materials (such as the first student in the row or the student seated nearest the door in the group). At a specific time, they can go get the materials that you list.

- For expensive materials that you do not want to lose, such as calculators, have students give you their student ID or some other form of "deposit" to help you know who has what calculator and to help them remember to return it. Number all your calculators, and have a specific space for them to go that corresponds to their number. Often calculators come in boxes that allow you to have students put their ID in the slot where the calculator goes. Other teachers have used cloth shoe-storage pockets, with each "shoe" slot numbered, and students take a calculator and leave their ID in the shoe slot.

Establish routines for engaging in mathematical work

This section presents basic routines that you can establish in the first weeks of school for how students will work together and talk with each other and with you about mathematics. Chapters 8 and 10 will discuss mathematical discourse and group work, respectively.

First, although you will want to group students differently throughout the semester (partnered, in rows, in larger groups), keep the seating arrangement consistent for the first week of class and maintain a relatively consistent flow to lessons. Working within a consistent structure for the first week has several advantages. It will help students get used to talking with each other about math and give them the opportunity to get better at that particular structure before being expected to work successfully within a new lesson structure. It also allows you to practice giving directions for how students are to work together (and allows you to improve at giving those directions). For the first several days, give similar directions for mathematical tasks as well as similar directions for how students should engage with the math and with each other.

For the first week, structure the lesson so that students work in pairs. This arrangement allows for partner talk and individual work, as appropriate. It also allows you to move freely throughout the room. Here are some specific lesson structures that support students in working on math problems and discussing them with peers:

- Have students work on a problem individually for a short time. Then have them share what they understand about the problem with their partner. Ask them to describe the situation in their own words, as well as what the problem is asking, or to ask a question about something they do not understand.

- Have students work on a problem individually for a short time. Then ask students to share their initial thinking about how to solve the problem and then work with their partner to solve it.

- Have students work on a problem individually for a short time. Then ask students to explain their thinking to their partner after they are done. Ask that the partner listen to the solver's thinking and then explain back to the solver what he or she heard.

- Have students work with their partner to find different ways to solve the problem.

Second, establish and practice a routine for making transitions in your class. Specifically, create some consistent cue or signal for students to switch their focus between individual, partner or group work, and whole-class discussion. Here are some suggestions for effective transition routines:

- Give specific times for each part of the lesson (for instance, when you tell them to work on their own, tell them they have three minutes). Warn them before their time is up ("You have five minutes left to work on this problem . . . we will have a whole-group discussion in one minute").

- Use a visual or auditory signal to let students know that they should finish their conversations and pay attention to the larger group. Some teachers raise their hands, and if students see the teacher with a raised hand, they raise their hand and stop talking. Some teachers flick the lights. Some teachers ring a gong or bell. Whatever you do, practice so that students get better at finishing up their conversations. When you do practice, give positive feedback (for example, "12 groups of 16 got quiet quickly. That's three better than yesterday").

- Later in the year, you may want your students to reconfigure their desks (such as from groups to rows). Designate specific places where all students should move their desks, and practice doing it, keeping track of the time it takes them and praising them for specific improvement.

Some advice about how to establish routines

Although this section has suggested several routines, also talk with colleagues at your school about classroom routines that they have used successfully and adopt or adapt routines that the students may be familiar with from other classrooms. In the end, the specifics of these routines are not important. What is important is that students know how to do these things and that you create a system that enables you to hand out and collect materials and work with minimal fuss. Take time during the first week of class to practice these routines so that your students get good at it. It will save you hours of time over the year.

One common mistake that teachers make is trying to establish routines by describing them. Although clear description is important, students learn routines by consistently engaging in them and through feedback on how they are doing. So don't spend a lot of time at the beginning of the school year explaining what you and your students will do; instead, implement the routines from the beginning, explain them during implementation, and then praise students for doing them well or "tweak" what they are doing while they are doing it. For example: A student asks to go to the restroom during class on the second day of school and you have predetermined that you will use the sign-out sheet routine. You direct the student to fill out a row on the sheet, which he does as he leaves class. Upon return, he forgets to sign back in. You note that, and as you pass his desk, you bend down and remind him to complete the routine, which he then does. Other students in class will note that a routine exists and may ask about the routine. Then you can make a general announcement about the routine.

Introduce as few routines as necessary, and only when they are needed. Hold off describing many routines or policies until after the first few days, especially if introducing those routines takes valuable time away from doing mathematics on the first day of class. For example, defer doing things like handing out textbooks until after you have had at least a day or two of working on math for a whole period.

On the first day of class, plan to enact these routines:

- A routine for where students sit when they come into the room

- A routine of doing math right from the start of class (this involves having a consistent way of students finding out what task they should do, and of you attending to their mathematical thinking)

- A routine involving students sharing their thinking (by talking with a partner or writing something down)

- A routine for moving between individual work, small-group work, and whole-class discussion

SET UP THE PHYSICAL SPACE OF THE CLASSROOM

If you think back to the triangle of instruction in chapter 2, all the interactions between teachers, students, and mathematics took place within a circle that represented the larger context. Your classroom is one important aspect of this context. Your classroom's appearance and setup communicate important messages to your students and can facilitate student engagement and discourse in subtle, and sometimes not so subtle, ways. What's more, you control many aspects of the physical space of your classroom. Planning and arranging the physical space of the classroom before your students arrive will help establish a culture to support productive engagement and a smooth-running classroom.

Decide on a seating arrangement

How you arrange the desks or tables in your room will help structure your students' work and help direct their attention to the mathematics they are learning. Several seating arrangements can prove effective (fig. 5.1):

- Rows

- Paired rows

- Desks pulled together to make groups of three or four

- Desks arranged in a U shape, or concentric U shapes, facing a central board or discussion area

- Students seated at tables arranged in rows or a U-shape

Fig. 5.1. *Possible seating arrangements*

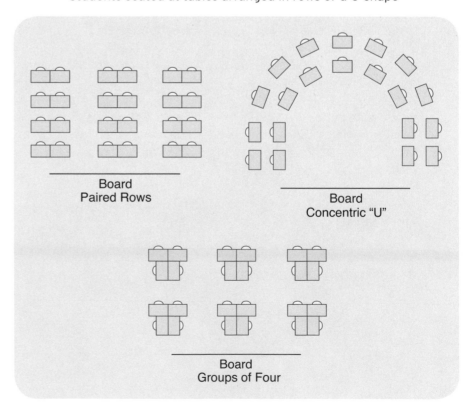

Board
Paired Rows

Board
Concentric "U"

Board
Groups of Four

The seating arrangement you choose should—

- allow students to look at each other while talking in small groups or partners, and provide a central focus for when you or a student leads a discussion or presents ideas or explanations;

- have room for you to walk around and observe all students from all angles; and

- stay the same for the first few days of school, at least.

As the semester proceeds, you may want to have more than one seating arrangement, and create routines for students to move the desks from one arrangement to another, but that should not be the focus of class during the first few days.

Establish a focal point for whole-group discussions

Part of the physical setup of your room should include a focal point for whole-group discussions. This space should be visible to all students and should include ways and spaces for sharing representations that students and you might use and refer to. For many classrooms this may be a black-board or whiteboard. For others it may be a screen for overhead projectors, LCD projectors, or document cameras. Students should be able to transition their attention from individual or group work to this focal point with minimal fuss. For example, arrange groups of desks so that no students have their back to the focal point (fig. 5.2).

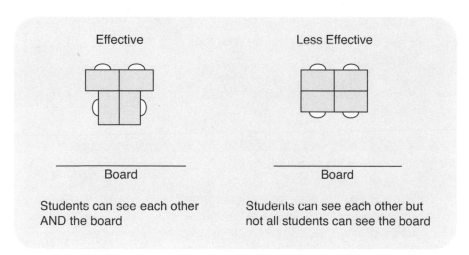

Fig. 5.2. *Effective and less effective seating arrangements*

Designate a specific area for available materials and tools

Students will need access to various materials and tools while solving problems. Some they may need consistently (rulers, protractors, graph paper, calculators), and others they will need to solve specific problems (such as weights and rubber bands for "Bungee Barbie"; motion detectors for "Walking the Graph"). Designate a place in your room that is accessible to students where you can store materials and tools. Depending on your classroom, you may have shelving, cabinets, or extra tables that you can use for this purpose. Before school starts, visit other teachers' classrooms to see how they store materials and tools—you may get some good ideas. Most important, your system for storing materials and tools should be one in which students know exactly what materials they can access, how to access them, and how to return them to their original storage spot.

Consider what to hang on the classroom walls

The walls of a classroom serve two main purposes: they are vehicles to communicate important information to students, and they send messages about what is important and valuable in math class. Many teachers use classroom walls to convey important information to students. You can use your classroom walls to support students' mathematical learning in several ways:

- Hang a whiteboard on which you routinely record homework assignments or present the mathematical problem for students to work on as they enter class.

- Hang a poster that details how you expect students to work on mathematical problems (fig. 5.3).

- Hang a poster with suggestions for what students can do when they are having trouble with their homework (see also chapter 13).

- Hang a poster with characteristics of productive group work (see also chapter 10).

- Hang a poster with suggestions for questions students can ask when they are confused.

- Hang a poster with indicators of what makes a good visual representation (that is, the presentation is legible; a reader can follow the thinking and solve the problem in the same way without further explanation).

- Many teachers designate wall space to display important mathematical representations (ideally created by students solving problems) that students can refer to when solving problems.

1 Make sense of the situation and clarify what the problem is asking you to figure out.

2 Think of what you know that can help you solve the problem, compare it with previous problems you have done, and identify a strategy to solve the problem.

3 Apply your strategy to solve the problem.

4 Evaluate your answer to see whether it makes sense.

5 Explain your answer and how you got it to a classmate.

Fig. 5.3. *Steps to work on math problems*

Many teachers also use the walls to create community and send specific messages about what they think mathematics is and what good work looks like. In addition to the suggestions above, you can do this by (1) posting pictures of your students working in ways that you envision and (2) posting exemplary student work, citing what they did well.

Whatever you hang on your wall, remember that the walls are a powerful way to show what you value, what your class is like, and what students in your class do.

PLAN THE FIRST FEW LESSONS WITH BUILDING COMMUNITY IN MIND

Effective teaching depends on effective planning; good lessons do not simply happen. Indeed, planning is so important that section III devotes considerable space to it. There we will help you think about choosing and adapting tasks, setting learning goals, anticipating student thinking, planning effective questions, and other aspects of preparing to teach each day. The planning process we describe applies to planning throughout the year and your career, including the first few weeks of school. Each lesson that you teach will require you to think about mathematical goals and social dynamics. At the beginning of any school year, however, social and behavioral goals loom large. The rest of this chapter will help you think about important decisions you will make during planning lessons for the first weeks of school that will foster a learning community in your classroom—focused on communicating, representing, reasoning, solving problems, and making connections.

Select problems/tasks for the first few lessons

The best way to let your students know what to expect in math class is to make sure that they work on mathematics as soon as the first class begins. The tasks should involve important mathematics. However, for the first few lessons, the specific mathematics of the problems is less important than the thinking and interacting the task will require from your students. The problems should be accessible to students; your students should all be able to start on the problems and make some progress. Problems should also be nonroutine, requiring students to figure out something mathematical. Consider using problems based on information gathered from the students (such as height and arm span) and then discussing patterns that emerge from the data. These guidelines will help you choose appropriately:

- Use mathematical problems/tasks/activities. Although some teachers use nonmathematical group-building exercises during the first week, doing so is antithetical to the "we do math in this class" message that we want you to send.

- Look for problems/tasks/activities that create opportunities to share multiple ideas and discussion among students. Give them something to talk about.

- Choose problems/tasks/activities that require students to engage in reasoning, representing, solving problems, and making connections.

For more about analyzing, choosing, and adapting problems/tasks, see chapter 6.

Plan to use a limited number of specific teacher moves

This chapter has presented many teacher moves and strategies to build a mathematical learning community. We do not expect that you will implement all these moves at the beginning of your first year of teaching. Our goal was to give you several options so that you can make informed decisions about how you want to start your school year. You will always be planning teacher moves; during the first few days of class, it is especially helpful to decide on just a few key and important moves you will use and practice, over and over again.

As you progress in your teaching, you will plan more content- and lesson-specific teacher moves. As the school year begins, however, stress more general teacher moves—those that you want students to get used to because you will be using them over and over again, such as asking, "What have you done on this problem so far?" (redirecting) or moving around the classroom during work time (breaking the plane). Pay particular attention to opportunities to use recognize and reinforce, because this move will show your students how you expect them to behave and help you refine your understanding of the behaviors you want.

Plan with an experienced colleague

Planning with an experienced colleague will be invaluable in creating effective beginning lessons and routines. Even if you cannot set up time to plan with such a colleague, asking questions and getting feedback about your plans will be helpful.

Example Plan for the First Day

This plan for beginning the first day of a math class illustrates attention to building community and a mathematical emphasis on reasoning and proof.

Before class begins

Set up desks in paired rows. Tape names onto each desk (blue for first period, red for second). Put a copy of the following task on each desk:

> Five students ran a race. A boy did not come in first, nor did a boy come in last. One person came between Susan and Diane. Joseph came in ahead of Diane, who did not come in last. Elizabeth wore a red t-shirt and did not lose to Susan. After the race, LeBron moved to Miami.

Directions: Figure out who won the race and what order the remaining students finished in. Be ready to explain how you figured it out.

At the beginning of class

- Stand at door, introduce self, greet students and ask their name, tell them to sit where their name is taped to the desk and begin on the problem on their desk.

- When the tardy bell rings, begin walking around the room.
  - Ask students what they have done so far.
  - Ask students how they know that they are right.
  - Look for students who do not have the same answer as their partner.

- After a few minutes, stand at front of the room, ask students to stop. For each pair, instruct the students who are closest to the window to turn to their partner, and for one minute describe—
  - the context of the problem and what they are supposed to figure out;
  - what they did first to try to solve the problem.

- Instruct the partners either to ask a clarifying question or to share how they started to find a solution (one minute).

- Have students continue to work on problem.

- Circulate for a few minutes. Identify different student solutions.

- Stop, gain the students' attention, and then recognize—
  - how students are working steadily;
  - how they are writing a variety of pictures or lists of names down;
  - how they are trying answers and then eliminating them, how they are working toward the right answer by trying incorrect answers.

This extremely detailed plan does not represent the documentation that you will need every day, but planning out questions and moves at the beginning of the year will help you as you begin teaching and help create patterns of interaction that will need less specific planning as the year goes on.

REFLECT ON THE FIRST FEW LESSONS

One of the most effective ways that teachers learn and improve their practice is through reflecting on their lessons after they have taught them. An entire chapter in section III is devoted to reflection; read chapter 9 before you begin teaching.

Reflecting on your teaching is an important activity throughout the year and your career. But it is especially important to reflect at the beginning of the school year on how students are behaving and interacting in your class, and where they appear to be experiencing difficulties. Reflecting on these difficulties will help you clarify what you want students to do and how you want them to behave and how you can support them in doing so. In reflecting on these first few lessons, ask yourself the questions on page 64 with regard to building a mathematics learning community.

- What did my students do when they first came into class? What did I want them to do? How have I let them know what I want them to do? How can I be more explicit?

- What did my students do when I asked them to share their mathematical thinking with another student? What did I want them to do? How can I be more explicit and support them in communicating?

This last question also can be focused on other aspects of the lesson that you are working to establish routines around (such as transitions, handing in materials, gathering materials, and working alone on tasks).

CONCLUSION

Many new teachers find the first weeks of school stressful and overwhelming. Creating a well-run classroom takes time, effort, and patience. However, if you can send consistent messages, institute sensible routines, and align your actions with your words and your goals, your students will learn how to behave and act in ways that will support their learning of mathematics.

The hard work that goes into creating a supportive and consistent classroom culture will pay large dividends throughout the year—most important, the freedom it gives you to concentrate on students' mathematical thinking and learning. Planning for students' mathematical learning, enacting that plan, and then reflecting on how to improve that plan and what students actually learned is the core activity of mathematics teaching—and the topic of the next section.

III

The Lesson Cycle

Ms. Garcia was looking forward to the Columbus Day weekend. She had recently begun teaching math in a large urban high school similar to the one she had attended just a few years earlier. She hoped to use the small break to think about her first few weeks and strategize about how to address some recurrent problems.

Writing in her journal about the first few weeks, Ms. Garcia first listed things that she thought were going well. She had just given a test on chapter 2 in her algebra class and was pleased with the students' grades overall. She noted that she would need to keep an eye on Megan and Thomas, who were still having difficulties solving multistep equations. Ms. Garcia was also pleased that she was getting to know her students and thought that showing interest in their activities outside her classroom (such as last week's soccer game) was a good idea.

Although she recorded several positives about her first few weeks of school, Ms. Garcia knew that some areas needed improvement. Beginning her list of things to work on, she thought that her biggest problem was unexpected student behaviors, which she sometimes did not know how to react to. Some students also made mathematical mistakes and had misunderstandings that she had not anticipated. Although her students did well on the test overall, their work on the last two problems—which required them to apply the mathematics they had learned in new ways—troubled her. Even students who did well on the rest of the test did poorly on these two problems. Ms. Garcia thought applying knowledge to problems students had not seen before was important and was puzzled why they could not do so on the test.

Ms. Garcia was disappointed that her list of positives had only a few items, whereas her "things to work on" list was longer. Although her more seasoned colleagues had told her that her experiences were normal and that being a new teacher was full of surprises, they also tried to assure her that she would develop a much better idea of what to expect. However, Ms. Garcia wondered whether something more than experience could help with the problems she identified. Closing her journal, she planned to talk with her mentor during their weekly meeting, both to get advice about problems and to explore resources that might help her as a beginning teacher.

* * *

During the first weeks of school, all new teachers have experiences like these. Although yours might differ slightly from Ms. Garcia's, you would probably be able to include multiple items on your "what's going well" and "things to work on" lists. Some of your items may involve your students' engagement with and understanding of the math content; other items might be more general (such as students' behavior problems or getting yourself organized).

Whatever items are on your list of things to work on, the most important aspect of teaching—and the best way to improve—is to concentrate on what many educators and researchers call the lesson cycle. The lesson cycle consists of defining goals; choosing or adapting tasks for students to work on; planning instruction; enacting instruction; and then reflecting on whether and how the task, your plan, and your enactment supported student learning. This cycle is the heart of teaching, and in learning to plan, enact, and reflect, you will make the most progress in learning how to teach well. Concentrating on choosing tasks, planning and enacting instruction, and reflecting on how it all went is the best way for Ms. Garcia to address the items in her list of things to work on.

This section focuses on aspects of instruction that support students in building connected knowledge of mathematics and offers strategies to address items on your "what to work on" list. If you have not yet begun teaching, this section will give you advice about how to plan for and enact effective mathematics instruction as well as use targeted reflection to improve your practices.

Chapter 6 focuses on mathematical tasks (or problems), the impact that different tasks have on students' learning of mathematics, and advice for decisions about the tasks to help your students build connected knowledge. Chapters 7 and 8 present strategies to plan and enact instruction that will support you to interact with your students in ways described in chapter 3 (The Teaching of Mathematics) and illustrated in the triangle of instruction. Chapter 9 suggests strategies for purposeful reflection, a practice that offers powerful opportunities to explore your own instruction, how students think mathematically, and the connections between the two.

SUCCESS
from
the START
Your first years
teaching SECONDARY
MATHEMATICS

chapter **six**

Choosing Mathematical Tasks for Your Students

Have you ever thought about the different ways that students interact with different math problems? Think about your own math classes in high school. How did you and your fellow students react when your math teacher assigned the word problems at the end of a section or chapter? What did you think about being assigned thirty-five math problems for homework, knowing how to do them all (sometimes before you even started) and working through the problems just to get your homework done? How did you and your fellow students react when your math teacher gave you problems that couldn't be done in a minute each, and you had to put real effort (and brain power) into finding a solution? Did you do math projects in high school?

STOP+REFLECT

How did different kinds of math tasks (or problems or activities) affect how you had to think about mathematics to solve them?

For students to develop connected mathematical knowledge, they need opportunities to engage with a variety of mathematical tasks—particularly problem solving, communicating, connecting, representing, and reasoning/proving. This chapter offers strategies to assess the kinds of thinking that problems in your textbook require; to adapt them (if necessary) to better support building connected mathematical knowledge; and to choose supplementary mathematical problems, tasks, and activities. First revisit the discus-

Guiding Principles

>> Different tasks require different levels of thinking.

>> Students need to engage with tasks that support all levels of thinking.

>> Be deliberate in your choice of tasks for student learning.

sion in chapter 2 about the difference between problems and exercises (this chapter uses the words *problems* and *tasks* interchangeably).

DIFFERENT TASKS REQUIRE DIFFERENT LEVELS OF THINKING

Two truths about mathematical tasks: (1) much of what students have the opportunity to learn in math class depends on the types of tasks they are working on, and (2) different tasks require different types of thinking. Some math tasks require students to recall some memorized fact or practice some learned procedure. Other tasks may require students to look for and generalize about a pattern in a set of data. Still other tasks may require that students make connections between different representations (say, a graph of a function and that function's table of values). Figure 6.1 lists some of the mathematical actions that students are asked to perform when working on mathematical problems. Different verbs suggest different levels of thinking (for example, compare *list* and *critique*).

define	list	state	label	measure
use	match	illustrate	calculate	expand
factor	solve	graph	construct	compare
relate	distinguish	interpret	infer	summarize
estimate	show	develop an argument	assess	represent
investigate	critique	reason	draw conclusions	hypothesize
formulate	prove	create	analyze	connect

Fig. 6.1. *Verbs used in mathematical tasks (adapted from the Depth of Knowledge Levels framework created by the Wisconsin Center for Educational Research)*

Consider the two tasks in figure 6.2, both of which involve factoring polynomials.

Task A	Task B
Factor the following polynomials:	Solve this equation by factoring:
(*a*) $x(x + 1) - 3(x + 1)$ (*b*) $x^2 + 5x + 6$ (*c*) $4x^2 - 25$ (*d*) $27x^3 + 8$	$x^2 - 7x + 12 = 0$ Explain how the factors of the equation relate to the roots of the equation and how you could use that information to draw a sketch of the parabola. Then draw the sketch.

Fig. 6.2. *Two tasks about factoring polynomials*

Task A requires that students first recognize different kinds of polynomials, remember rules for factoring those polynomials, and then apply those rules. For example, students need to recognize that part (a) has two terms and that each term contains a factor of $x + 1$. They then need to remember how to factor out the common term, yielding $(x + 1)(x - 3)$.

Task B also requires that students recognize this polynomial as a trinomial with a leading coefficient of 1, remember the rule for factoring such a polynomial, and apply the rule. Doing those steps correctly will yield $(x - 3)(x - 4) = 0$, which returns the solutions $x = 3$ and $x = 4$. Thus far, the two tasks require basically the same type of thinking: recognition, remembering a mathematical procedure, and applying that procedure. Task B stands out from task A by requiring students to think in ways that make mathematical connections among different representations.

ENGAGE STUDENTS IN ALL LEVELS OF MATHEMATICAL THINKING

To build connected knowledge, students need to engage in tasks that require all levels of mathematical thinking. Examine the verbs in figure 6.1, considering the thinking students have to do for each. The list grows in complexity of thinking—*reason* often requires more complex thinking than *calculate*.

Consider the following tasks that students could complete as they learn about slope.

Task 1

Graph the following lines by using a graphing utility (such as a graphing calculator or computer graphing program):

$$y = x$$
$$y = 2x$$
$$y = 3x$$
$$y = -x$$
$$y = -2x$$
$$y = -3x$$

Describe how the graph of the line $y = x$ changes as the coefficient of x changes.

Make a conjecture about the graph of the line $y = 4x$. Graph $y = 4x$ to check your conjecture.

Task 2

The line $y = 3x$ appears "steeper" than the line of $y = x$ (when you graph the lines on the same coordinate plane). Discuss this with a partner and explain why this happens. You may want to look at a table of (x, y) values for each line to help with your explanation.

Task 3

Which line will produce a steeper graph, $y = 10x$ or $y = 5x$? Why?

Task 4

Write the equation of a line that, when graphed, is steeper than the graph of $y = -3x$.

As students complete these four tasks, they must look for patterns, make conjectures, determine mathematical explanations, use multiple representations (symbolic, numerical, and graphical), and make connections between those representations. Just by doing these four tasks, students can begin to build connected knowledge about slope. They begin to internalize that slope has something to do with steepness and that slope is identified as the coefficient of x in a linear equation. You can build on this foundational knowledge as students progress in their understandings of functional relationships.

Research on classroom factors that influence how students learn mathematics indicates that when learning a new mathematical topic (such as slope), students should first do problems that require them to figure out something mathematical—to understand what is going on mathematically—before engaging in tasks that require them to learn the formal conventions of the mathematical topic (Hiebert and Grouws 2007).

Think about this progression of work in the context of a student learning about slope. Traditional instruction on slope starts with formal conventions: the definition of slope as "rise over run," using that definition to evaluate slope given the graph of a line, learning to identify slope in an equation in the form of $y = mx + b$ (where b is defined as the y-intercept, or "where the line crosses the y-axis"), and then putting those skills together to graph the equation of a line such as $y = 2x + 6$. These tasks may result in students' being able to look at and graph an equation such as $y = 2x + 6$. But they do not require underlying mathematical connections about linear equations and their graphs, nor do they lead to understanding why $y = 2x + 6$ produces a particular line on a coordinate plane.

If students, however, begin learning about slope with exploratory tasks (such as tasks 1–4 above), then they have some conceptual foundation for connecting the more formalized conventions of slope—all leading to a more connected knowledge of slope.

BE DELIBERATE IN CHOICES OF TASKS

When teachers commit to teaching for connected mathematical knowledge, they must also commit to deliberate choices of tasks for students. Teachers must explicitly consider what kinds of thinking different tasks require. They have to be strategic about the sequence of tasks that their students engage in. They have to know what kinds of tasks are in their textbooks, what supplemental materials they may have access to, and where to find tasks to supplement those they already have. This chapter's habits of practice focus on helping you become more deliberate about choosing tasks so that students can engage in problem solving, connecting, communicating, reasoning and proving, and representing, which will support them as they build connected knowledge.

About This Chapter

The QUASAR (Quantitative Understanding: Amplifying Student Achievement and Reasoning) project has influenced our work with teachers about mathematical tasks. QUASAR was a five-year project that a group of university mathematics educators undertook to improve middle grades mathematics teaching and learning in five large urban districts. Through offering professional development and studying its impact on teacher knowledge, teaching practices, and students' mathematical understandings (Stein, Grover, and Henningsen 1996; Stein and Lane 1996), QUASAR ultimately produced the Mathematical Tasks Framework (Stein et al. 2009). Through this work, these researchers argue that the types of tasks that teachers choose for their students, as well as how those tasks are set up and implemented during instruction, have a major influence on the quality of student learning of mathematics.

Chapter 8 includes findings from the QUASAR project about effective (and ineffective) teaching practices to support students' engagement in tasks as they build connected mathematical knowledge. But because researchers have written much more about the Mathematical Tasks Framework than we can include here, you should explore these ideas further through the following resources:

- *Implementing Standards-Based Mathematics Instruction: A Casebook for Professional Development* (Stein et al. 2009)

- "Mathematical Tasks as a Framework for Reflection: From Research to Practice" (Stein and Smith 1998a)

- "Selecting and Creating Mathematical Tasks: From Research to Practice" (Stein and Smith 1998b)

Habits of Practice

>> Analyze tasks available in your textbook.

>> Adapt textbook tasks (if necessary).

>> Choose supplemental tasks (if necessary).

ANALYZE TASKS AVAILABLE IN YOUR TEXTBOOK

Once you have decided to become more deliberate in your choice of tasks for students, become as familiar as possible with what your textbook already has. The following exercise will help you to familiarize yourself with your textbook and accompanying materials by focusing you on the types of tasks contained in those materials.

Choose one of your mathematics textbooks and complete the following steps:

1 Choose a chapter to focus your analysis on.

2 Working through the problem set in each section of the chapter, identify and keep track of the verbs of mathematics (such as those in fig. 6.1) used in the tasks or in the directions for the tasks. Note whether the verbs appear in the beginning, middle, or end of the problem sets. Make a separate list for each section such that you can look across the lists in the next step (fig. 6.3).

Fig. 6.3. *Sample chart for textbook analysis exercise*

Section no.	Verbs used in tasks from:		
	Beginning of problem set	Middle of problem set	End of problem set
1			
2			
. . .			

3 Look across the lists of verbs and identify patterns that you see. Ask yourself questions such as the following:

- Do certain verbs appear multiple times? If so, what kinds of thinking are required by students who complete those tasks?

- Are any verbs from figure 6.1 missing from your lists? If so, what verbs are those and what kinds of thinking are "missing" from the problem sets in this chapter of your textbook?

4 Write a general statement about the types of thinking that the tasks available in your textbook require, such as the following:

- The tasks in my textbook mostly require that students _____.

- Tasks at the beginning of problem sets tend to require that students _____.

- Tasks in the middle of problem sets tend to require that students _____.

- Tasks at the end of sections tend to require that students _____.

5 Identify any supplemental materials that came with your textbook. Using steps 1-4, analyze the tasks available to you through these supplemental materials.

Now that you have analyzed the tasks readily available in your text book and supplemental materials, you should have a good idea of the thinking that your students engage in while doing those tasks. You should also be able to identify "holes" in the types of thinking that your textbook requires. Many tasks in your main textbook may require low-complexity thinking. Sections might typically start with tasks that require thinking that is low in complexity but also contain tasks near the end that require more complexity in thinking. Or your textbook may have a good mix of tasks. Whatever your analysis reveals, you now have more insight about the tasks readily available to you, which supports you to choose tasks that will best help your students build connected knowledge.

ADAPT TEXTBOOK TASKS

After your textbook analysis, you may decide that your students need access to different tasks to experience a range of mathematical thinking. Adapting the tasks in your textbook is one way to require different kinds of mathematical thinking. Below are three strategies to "tweak" existing textbook tasks.

Require that students explain "why"

Requiring your students to routinely explain why mathematics works the way it does is one of the most powerful things you can do. This is an easy strategy to incorporate into your students' daily work. Say that your eighth graders are in a chapter about integer operations (addition, subtraction, multiplication, and division of signed numbers). After the section on addition, you could pose a question such as, "When we add a positive number to a negative number, sometimes that answer is positive and other times the answer is negative. Why does that happen?" Students can write their answer to the question in their notebooks, share their answers with a partner or small group, and then you can orchestrate a whole-group discussion.

Students perform many procedures in mathematics and follow many rules that they have no explanation for other than "it just works that way." This paradigm starts early in students' mathematical learning ("ours is not to question why, just invert and multiply") and extends through high school (division by zero is undefined; you can't take the logarithm of a negative number). Tweaking tasks to require that students address the "why" question pays considerable returns for their building connected mathematical knowledge.

Extend students' thinking about related tasks

You do not always have to adapt exercises to increase the complexity of thinking required. Say that your algebra 2 students were graphing equations of ellipses on a coordinate plane. In the previous section, students had done similar exercises with circles. For an exit slip for class, you could ask them to respond to a prompt such as, "We know that every square is a rectangle, but not every rectangle is a square. Can we say the same for circles and ellipses? Write an explanation to support or refute the following statement: Every circle is an ellipse, but not every ellipse is a circle." This prompt requires that students connect mathematical concepts, communicate their thinking in writing, and create a mathematical justification, all of which increase the complexity of thinking required about the tasks they have just completed.

Ask students to create problems with particular solutions

Appearing in most geometry books, the exercise in figure 6.4 focuses students on applying area formulas for polygons. To complete this exercise, students need to correctly identify the type of polygon (recognize), identify (or remember) the associated area formula, substitute values for the corresponding parts of the polygon into the area formula, and correctly calculate.

Fig. 6.4. *A common task in geometry textbooks*

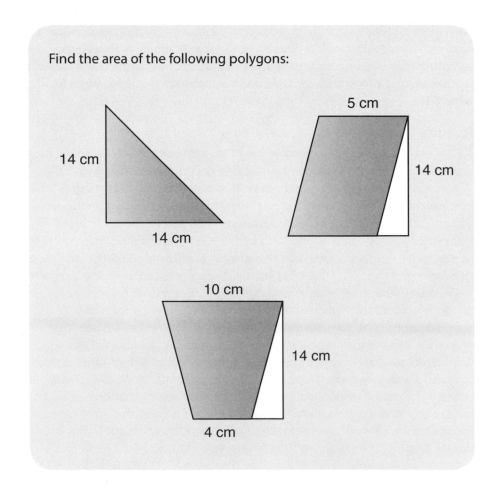

Find the area of the following polygons:

Increasing the complexity of mathematical thinking for this exercise is relatively easy. Using the answers in your teacher's edition, you could assign the task in figure 6.5.

Create a polygon for each of the following conditions:

1. A right isosceles triangle with an area of 98 cm^2

2. A parallelogram with an area of 70 cm^2

3. A trapezoid with an area of 98 cm^2

Fig. 6.5. *A tweaked problem about polygon area*

To complete this task, students must work backward with the area formulas of polygons. Students would need to draw on their knowledge of the properties of different polygons, identify (or remember) appropriate area formulas, identify and connect variables in the formula to corresponding parts of the polygon, estimate possible values for those parts (reasoning about factors of the value of the area), calculate, and reason to revise estimations if necessary. Engaging students in both "doing" and "undoing" (or working backward) can build connected knowledge (Driscoll 1999) and, again, is a relatively easy modification.

We cannot list every possible way to modify tasks to increase their complexity of thinking. But if you keep in mind the goal to engage your students in the five processes from chapter 1 (problem solving, representing, communicating, connecting, and reasoning/proving), then adapting textbook tasks on occasion will get easier, as will incorporating them into your instruction.

CHOOSE SUPPLEMENTAL TASKS

To engage your students in reasoning, communicating, representing, connecting, and problem solving, you will sometimes need to go outside your textbook. Consider the following advice about resources that you can tap into to find "good" supplemental tasks as well as questions to help you assess the usefulness of tasks you find.

Consult colleagues

Your colleagues are a good first source for supplemental tasks. Many experienced math teachers have amassed great collections of supplemental tasks over the years. Try asking a question like, "Next week I start a unit on parabolas. Do you have any good activities that you've used with your students that I could see?" Colleagues can also give you advice about what students learn from the activity, parts that students may have difficulty with, and how to organize students' work. Also check with your colleagues about what activity books are available at your school or in your district. Commercial companies such as Scholastic, Dale Seymour, and Delta Publishing, as well as organizations such as the National Council of Teachers of Mathematics, regularly publish books of good tasks/activities to use in various math courses.

Use the Web

Identify useful online resources for tasks/activities. We suggest three useful places to start your search:

1 The National Council of Teachers of Mathematics sponsors sites (such as Illuminations, http://illuminations.nctm.org) with tasks, activities, and lesson plans for diverse topics.

2 The Math Forum (http://mathforum.org) is a good source of supplemental tasks/activities.

3 The Texas Instruments website (http://education.ti.com /calculators/downloads/US/Activities/) emphasizes technology.

Many other useful sites offer supplemental activities; ask your colleagues what websites they have found particularly useful.

Caution about supplemental tasks/activities

Using supplemental tasks can be tricky. First, you must carefully choose supplemental tasks/activities to ensure that they match your mathematical learning goals for particular content. Second, remember that your goal is to build connected knowledge, so make sure that supplemental tasks/activities engage students in at least one mathematical process (problem solving, communicating, connecting, representing, and reasoning/proving).

CONCLUSION

This section is about the lesson cycle: planning, enacting, and reflecting on instruction. The tasks that you assign have a tremendous effect on what students learn. To learn how to reason, they need tasks that require them to reason. To communicate, students need tasks that explicitly require them to communicate. Furthermore, you control the work that your students engage in. You can choose tasks that ultimately may limit their mathematical thinking or tasks that allow students to think in multiple ways about mathematics. This chapter described ways to think about and adapt tasks to help you give your students tasks that will require them to reason, represent, communicate, solve problems, and make connections. In chapter 7 (Planning the Mathematics Lesson), you will learn to plan lessons so that the rich tasks you select will yield the effective learning that you want.

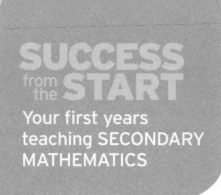

SUCCESS
from
the START
Your first years
teaching SECONDARY
MATHEMATICS

chapter **seven**

Planning the Mathematics Lesson

Linda Kelly is a first-year mathematics teacher at a large high school in Tucson. The district's beginning-teacher mentoring program requires Linda to spend two class periods per month observing other math teachers. The program also requires a monthly meeting of first- and second-year teachers, facilitated by an assistant principal, Pat Brown. In mid-November, Linda starts to observe notable points in her colleagues' classrooms. She wants to discuss these at the upcoming mentoring meeting. To prepare, Linda sends out the following e-mail:

Dear Colleagues,
At the next meeting, I hope that we can talk about two observations from my classroom visits:

> **1** Many of the math teachers I have observed seem to rarely get "stumped" by students' questions. I feel like I get stumped a lot.

> **2** During my visits, I've been writing down the questions that teachers have asked students during the lesson. Some teachers seem to really ask good questions that

"work" with the students. I'd like to be able to do this better in my classes. Are there ways to get better at questioning?

Thanks, and see you next week!

Linda

When the teachers and assistant principal gathered the next week for their meeting, Jamie Swift, a second-year history teacher, said, "I am so glad you wrote that e-mail. I felt that I got stumped a lot my first year also, and I still feel that way many days. Sometimes planning really helps, and my lesson goes great. Other times it feels like my plan is way off, and the lesson veers off course almost right from the start because a student has asked a question that I hadn't anticipated." Others around the table nodded. Linda asked, "So does planning really help?"

* * *

Our answer to Linda's question is an unqualified "yes." In our own teaching as well as when we have worked with beginning mathematics teachers, a focus on planning paid huge dividends in the classroom. Orchestrating a classroom full of twenty to thirty teenagers is a challenging and complex job, and trying to do so without a well-thought-out plan of action is just asking for trouble.

Not all planning, however, is equally effective. Sometimes our plans, and those of colleagues, have not yielded the productive lessons and increased knowledge that we wanted. How and what teachers plan is important. This chapter will give you ways to think about and execute plans that will help you avoid some common pitfalls of poor preparation.

First, let's confront a strongly held cultural belief that the best teachers are effective because they have good instincts or that they just naturally know what to do with students to support their learning. We don't deny that effective teachers often have good "teaching" instincts. However, expertise and effectiveness come from hours of preparation, practice, and learning from reflecting on lessons. Developing expertise in teaching requires explicit planning—for instruction, students' learning, and your own learning. This chapter examines what it means to plan effectively and offers strategies to help you become an effective planner.

CREATE LESSONS THAT SUPPORT STUDENT LEARNING WITH UNDERSTANDING

A successful mathematics lesson results in students gaining connected knowledge of new mathematics, one in which they learned with understanding. More than any other factor, good planning leads to student learning. Many factors help determine whether a lesson is successful, including the ability and motivation of your students, the nature of the activities, your own ability to manage discussions and classroom behavior, and countless others. Many of these factors seem beyond your immediate control. But you can control how much, and how well, you plan.

The goal of effective mathematics instruction is that students learn mathematics. A good lesson engages students in challenging, yet accessible,

Guiding Principles

Effective planning enables you to—

>> create lessons that support student learning with understanding;

>> plan for student learning;

>> reduce the complexity of teaching; and

>> learn from teaching.

mathematical work from which they learn something new. We have heard teachers describe a "good lesson" by using criteria that do not focus on student learning, such as "The lesson needs to be entertaining," or "I need to get through a certain amount of material," or "The students are well-behaved." Although those criteria may underpin a successful lesson, the most important goal for building connected mathematical knowledge is that the students learn mathematics during every lesson.

PLAN FOR STUDENT LEARNING

Students learn mathematics by solving problems, reasoning, representing, communicating, and making connections—by thinking mathematically. Your planning, therefore, should begin with your clarifying what you want your students to think about and how that thinking will lead to learning. Sometimes teachers can lose this emphasis on student learning and instead focus first on choosing the activities that students will do. Other times, as teachers, we focus on what we will do during instruction and put student learning in the background. By concentrating on what we will do, we forget to plan what we want students to think about as they complete the tasks we

> Cartoonist Bud Blake wrote the comic strip *Tiger*. In the first panel of one of his strips, we see two boys and a dog. The first boy says, "I taught my dog to whistle." In the second panel, the other boy bends close to the dog and says, "I don't hear him whistling." In the last panel, the first boy says, "I said I taught him to whistle. I didn't say he learned it."

have given them. We lose the focus on their learning.

Planning for learning means clarifying what you want students to think about and then planning teaching moves that support students in doing so. The questions that a teacher asks students while they work on an activity or task influence how students think mathematically. How students interact with each other during an activity influences how students think mathematically. How a teacher orchestrates whole-group sharing of small-group work affects how students think mathematically. Effective planning includes specific and explicit attention to what the teacher will do, what the students will do, and how those actions will support students' mathematical thinking. None of this is possible without a clear idea of what you want students to learn, what they need to think about to learn it, and how tasks and questions can support them in that thinking.

REDUCE THE COMPLEXITY OF TEACHING

Teaching is a complex job. During class, you are responsible for several concurrent dynamics and processes. You will have to make sense of a wide range of student statements and actions and decide how to respond. You must monitor students' understanding. You must decide whether to adjust the pace of the lesson according to your appraisal of student understanding.

You must monitor student behavior to make sure that it stays consistent with social norms and supports student learning.

Effective planning can reduce the complexity of teaching in three ways. First, it helps teachers know better what to expect so that they will be less surprised by events or the reactions of students and themselves. Being surprised by events in the classroom is often a source of major stress for teachers, especially if those surprises require some action or decision.

Second, effective planning enables teachers to consider how they will react to specific situations. For example, while planning a lesson on similarity, you may predict that some students will make a "similar" version of a 3×5 rectangle by adding 10 to each side. You can have some 3×5 and 13×15 cutouts ready, as well as a planned question: Is the bigger rectangle a larger version of the smaller rectangle? Or perhaps you have students work in groups to predict how much rain will fall this year on the basis of data from ten previous years. You may identify ahead of time the strategies that students are likely to use and which would be good to use during whole-group debriefing. Having already thought about possible strategies and their usefulness allows you to concentrate on what students are doing and thinking during class, giving you space to look for responses like those that you anticipated.

Third, effective planning helps teachers focus on specific aspects of their students' work and behavior. At any given moment, so many things are happening in a classroom that no teacher can focus on them all. Beginning teachers, in particular, often have a hard time figuring out what to pay attention to. Without a plan, they often pay attention to things not connected to the lesson's learning goals. For example, a teacher who has not been explicit with himself or herself about learning goals for a lesson may be led off focus by a student asking a question only tangentially related to the topic at hand.

Recall Ms. Barker's classroom in chapter 1. She had a learning goal in mind, and when Jill presented an unexpected solution strategy, Ms. Barker decided immediately to spend class time exploring Jill's strategy because Ms. Barker could see how it "fit" with the learning goal of the lesson. The thinking she had done before teaching the lesson affected even her improvisation. By planning ahead and identifying exactly what mathematics is connected to the goal of the lesson, a teacher can decide which student-generated ideas to explore further or work to clarify.

LEARN FROM TEACHING

Teachers learn from experience. This learning, however, does not simply happen. Just as you must plan for your students' learning, you must plan for your own. Just as you must identify what you want students to think about as they interact with mathematics, you need to identify what you will attend to and think about as you interact with teaching mathematics. By planning to gather evidence of student thinking, you learn about how students make sense of the mathematics you have to teach. By planning teaching moves and observing their effects, you learn how to enact different practices and under what circumstances those practices might be effective. By establishing the planning habits of practice we describe below, you will position yourself to have tools necessary to reflect on and learn from your teaching. Again, without thoughtful planning, you may find yourself simply reacting to situations in ways that leave no time or energy to systematically ask and answer questions about teaching and learning.

Habits of Practice

>> Plan for instruction before writing a lesson plan.

>> Create a lesson plan.

>> Plan differently for different purposes.

>> Find supports to help you plan.

PLAN FOR INSTRUCTION BEFORE WRITING A LESSON PLAN

Effective teachers do not write out a lesson plan from scratch. By following the tasks below, you will be prepared to write a lesson plan that will support your students to build connected mathematical knowledge about specific mathematical content.

Answer important questions

Before creating a useful plan, effective teachers answer important questions about mathematics, students, and tasks so that their eventual plan represents informed choices and predictions. Begin by reading through the section you chose in your textbook and thinking about the following questions:

- What is the mathematical goal for the lesson? What will students understand and be able to do at the end of the lesson? How does it connect to other math that you have taught and will teach?

- How do the tasks and activities in the curriculum materials access this mathematics?

- What are typical ways students solve such problems? What typical difficulties might students have with this content?

- How will students reason, represent, make connections, communicate, and solve problems during this lesson?

- How will you know what your students understand?

Without answers to these questions, you will not have meaningful criteria to make the decisions at the heart of planning. Without knowing what math you want them to think about, and what kind of problems students may run into, you will have difficulty writing down specific questions, or specific solutions to look for and highlight on your lesson plan. These questions are so important that we suggest the following activities to help you think about and respond to the above questions.

Although the words *lesson plan* seem so concrete and simple, the concept actually covers a wide range of documents, ideas, practices, and requirements. Lesson plans can be a set of vague ideas in your head about what you will do and say in class. They can be a form that you fill out for your supervisor that includes space for a specific goal and a list of questions that you will ask. In your teacher education program, lesson plans may have contained extended responses to lists of questions covering many aspects of teaching.

For many beginning teachers, lesson plans are documents they have prepared for others—professors, cooperating teachers, principals. For us, a lesson plan is much more immediate and useful, created solely to help you teach. The lesson plan should be a tool that you use during instruction that contains the "nuts and bolts" of the lesson. It includes important things for you to say at key times during the lesson. It includes questions to ask. It may include information about student responses you want to look for, or it may contain blank places to record evidence of student learning. It also includes important logistical information, such as student groupings or specifics of the homework assignment. This kind of lesson plan is informed by extensive thinking about the lesson, but it is not an exhaustive documentation of all that you have thought about. It is best thought of as a "cheat sheet," a piece of paper to guide you at times during the lesson so that you will remember aspects of the lesson that you identified as important during the planning process.

Engage with the mathematics

Begin your planning by working to understand the mathematics of the lesson as deeply as possible. First identify the mathematical goal of the lesson. Many curriculum materials have a written goal for each lesson, but understanding this goal means more than simply reading it and copying it down. What, exactly, should students understand and be able to do at the end of the lesson? How does it connect to mathematics they already know and understand, and how does it connect to mathematics that will come later?

Once you have become familiar with the mathematical goals of the lesson, do the mathematical activity yourself. Do the problems in as many ways as you can think of, paying particular attention to how you think students may do them. Anticipate mistakes and misconceptions that may come out as students do the problems. After completing the problems, revisit the goal and clarify how the mathematical goals are connected to the mathematics of the problems. Often, in doing the mathematics you will find that your understanding of the mathematical goal changes and deepens.

To reap the most benefit from your planning, you must both do the mathematics of the lesson and anticipate student responses to the mathematics. More than any other aspect of planning, this strategy helps you clarify the mathematical goal of the lesson, predict student responses, and create a basis for how you might adjust the problems or how you will support students in their thinking. Without this step, students will consistently react to mathematical problems in ways that you have not predicted and you will confront difficult decisions that need to be made in the moment of teaching.

You also need to identify, at this point, exactly what mathematics you want students to think about during the lesson. What aspects of the problems and the solutions do you want students to notice, struggle with, and make sense of? What misconceptions do you want them to wrestle with? What connections do you want them to make? How does the task, as it is written, explicitly draw their attention to those ideas, representations, techniques and connections?

Adapt the mathematical tasks (if needed)

Once you have done the math, clarified the goals, and anticipated student responses, decide whether you need to revise or adapt the task so that students will be more likely to think about the ideas and connections that will support their learning. You may need to revise the task to give students more explicit opportunities to represent, reason, communicate, solve problems, and make connections. (Chapter 6 gave strategies to adapt textbook tasks.)

Choose an appropriate lesson structure

Closely connected to choosing and adapting student tasks is deciding exactly what lesson structure would most support students to achieve the mathematical goals. Would students learn best by working with peers on one problem for a relatively long time and then discussing several solutions as a whole class? Would students learn better by following along as you presented a series of shorter problems, periodically asking them to think about the problems and discuss them with a partner? Would they learn better by working independently on a series of problems, choosing when to move on to more complex ones?

You can use many different possible lesson structures; we describe three of the most common below. The structure of your lesson will affect, and be affected by, both the tasks that you choose and the mathematical goals of the lesson. Regardless of the structure of the lesson, however, students must actively communicate, solve problems, represent, reason, and make connections for most of their time during math class.

The workshop lesson

In a workshop lesson, students work in groups for a long period on a few problems and then discuss different solutions to these problems as a whole group. The typical workshop lesson begins with a "launch," during which you present the problems to the entire class. Most of the lesson is dedicated to students working on the problems in groups and developing solutions. The lesson ends with a whole-group discussion during which students present and discuss different solutions that highlight the mathematical goals of the lesson. A workshop lesson should pose a rich problem that offers access to a range of students and has a variety of solution strategies. A workshop lesson can elicit various student strategies and give students opportunities to make sense of and connect different solutions and ideas. By working in small groups, students also can engage in communicating, reasoning, representing, connecting, and problem solving throughout much of the lesson.

Orchestrating a workshop lesson requires much of a teacher. You must plan a launch that will enable all students to understand what the problem is asking for, have a sense of what prior knowledge they can bring to bear on the problem, have an idea of how to start on the problem, and have a clear sense of how they are expected to work on the problem and what they are expected to produce. During group work, you will need to monitor groups to make sure that they are engaging in productive mathematical work and to assess their specific strategies and understanding. Finally, during the discussion you will have to choose which groups will present their solutions and in what order. You will also have to listen attentively and ask questions that help students connect different solutions.

The discussion is more than simply a show and tell, where all groups get to share their solutions. The point of the discussion is for students to make sense of different solutions and make connections between them that help them reach the learning goal. You must carefully plan which solutions to share, in what order, and what questions will bring out the important mathematics (for more on different kinds of questions, see chapter 8).

The interactive lecture

For most of us, our high school and college mathematics classes were lectures, where teachers explained how to solve problems and worked examples on the board. Students were expected to listen carefully and take notes; perhaps the teacher would occasionally stop the lecture and ask a question to check for understanding. After the lecture, students practiced the demonstrated technique. The traditional lecture lesson format is problematic if the goal is for students to build connected mathematical knowledge because it limits students' opportunities to reason, represent, communicate, solve problems, and make connections.

The interactive lecture lesson format, however, can give students opportunities to solve problems, communicate, represent, connect, and reason about the mathematics of the lesson. In an interactive lecture, the teacher requires students to do much of the mathematical thinking that the teacher does in a traditional lecture. For example, in an interactive lecture about the area formula of a triangle, rather than draw a parallelogram and then showing how it is made up of two triangles, the teacher may start by asking students to draw a parallelogram in their notebooks and then determine how many ways they can divide the parallelogram into two triangles (the students are doing the mathematical thinking). After a minute or two, the teacher calls for the students' attention, debriefs about what they found, and then gives them another small task. This pattern of "bouncing" back and forth—the teacher prompting work, the students doing work, and the teacher debriefing that work—repeats multiple times during the lesson, all building toward a mathematical goal. Planning for a traditional lecture entails developing clear explanations of mathematical concepts/procedures ahead of time. Planning for an interactive lecture entails developing related questions or problems, anticipating various student responses, and working to string those responses together into a cogent mathematical story. Ms. Barker's lesson in chapter 1 is a good example of an interactive lecture.

Independent work

In independent work, students work on problems by themselves. Teachers can use this lesson structure in several ways. They use it often when students are completing an activity worksheet that requires them to use software. Teachers also use this format when students work with problems that build on each other (such as the four problems about slope in chapter 6).

In the independent work lesson structure, the problems are designed to require that students make sense of the mathematics and monitor their own understanding. The teacher's role in such a lesson is to observe students, assess their progress (through observation or short conversations), and support them to make sense of the problems. To plan for such lessons, teachers choose (or create) tasks that lead to a particular mathematical understanding or find already developed activities that meet the mathematical goal of the lesson.

Choosing a lesson structure

Whatever structure you choose for a particular lesson, remember two things. First, for most of your math class, students should be communicating, reasoning, representing, solving problems, and making connections. Second, having clear titles for these structures and clear routines connected to each of them will help your students know what to expect and will make your class run much more smoothly.

Plan questions and anticipate student responses

Once you know what tasks your students will work on and have chosen an appropriate lesson format, you should now plan, in more detail, what questions you will ask them during instruction. These questions should be geared to the responses you anticipate students giving and should support them to gain connected knowledge of the mathematics. Chapter 8 describes asking different questions for different purposes.

Generally, plan to ask your students questions that—

- are specific to the mathematical content focus of the lesson ("Who can explain why we are allowed to divide each term in an equation by the same number and not change the solution?");

- are open-ended ("What determines when a negative number plus a positive number results in a positive number?" as opposed to "Does a negative number plus a positive number always result in a positive number?"); and

- require students to think mathematically.

Plan visual aids and representations

Boards have always occupied a prominent place in mathematics classrooms, for a good reason. Visual representations of mathematical relationships and arguments lie at the heart of mathematics. Many of the most successful math students often have a picture in their heads that helps them make sense of, remember, and connect important mathematical ideas. Mathematical symbols, expressions, and diagrams serve as important ways to efficiently and effectively communicate mathematical arguments and justifications.

Mathematics teachers in Japan generally spend a great deal of time planning exactly how they will use their board; they believe that the content that they display needs to be carefully organized to tell a coherent mathematical story, to draw attention to important mathematical connections, to compare student ideas, and to present a model of good organization (Takahashi 2006). Boards in American mathematics classrooms generally do not exhibit such coherence. They typically contain hand-drawn diagrams, pictures, and equations, often without a clear order or hierarchy.

Given the central importance of representations in learning mathematics, your planning should include carefully thinking about the representations you will present during the lesson and how you will organize those representations to create a coherent story line. Consider the following questions when thinking about this aspect of your teaching:

- How will you present the problems? Where will you display them? What pictures or diagrams will go with the task, and how will those require students to make sense of important mathematics?

- How might various student strategies be represented? How will those representations help students make sense of essential mathematical ideas?

- What representations (pictures, diagrams, charts, equations, graphs) do you want to share with the whole class? In what order?

- Which representations will stay visible (such as on a poster) and which ones will be erased or put away? Where will you put the representations that you want to keep visible?

- How will you position various representations as the class progresses? How will this help students see connections between important mathematical ideas?

- How will you label the visuals? What aspects of the representation might you need to clarify?

- Which visual will you or the students make in class versus beforehand?

In addition to these questions, having specific routines around visual representations helps:

- Have a clear visual focus for whole-group discussions, so that the representation that is the focus of any discussion is in the same place as much as possible.

- Early in the year, work with students to develop criteria for good visual presentations. These criteria are mostly about clarity; people looking at the poster should clearly follow the poster makers' thinking.

- Have a clear way to discern between "working" representations, ones that people can add to and edit, and final representations that should not be changed or written on.

- Have a space for calculations and other necessary mathematical work that does not need to be part of any kind of permanent record. This approach allows for calculations to be made publicly, but in a way that does not clutter up and obscure the mathematical ideas of important representations. It will also help you avoid filling the board with calculations and then having to desperately look for space for the next important idea, or asking your students which part of the board you can erase so that you can put up the next important thing.

Imagine that someone comes into your classroom, after you and all the students have gone, with the board still intact. In a well-planned and well-executed lesson, the board and other visual representations should give a clear picture of the mathematics of the lesson, how students thought about that mathematics, and how the mathematics was developed during the lesson. In a well-run classroom, the walls should give a clear picture of how students interact with mathematics and each other, and the kind of thinking that is expected and that they engage in. To create this impression, plan the images you will use in lessons and keep on your walls. Inspirational posters of cute kittens and Olympic athletes do not show what students actually do. Classrooms with clear examples of student work, and pictures of students working on mathematics, as well as clear directives for how to talk in groups or approach difficult problems, tell us much more about what to expect when we actually see students in the classroom.

Plan to gather evidence of student learning

The aim of teaching is student learning. Effective teachers continually work to find out whether students have actually learned the mathematics; waiting until an end-of-week quiz or an end-of-unit test is not good enough.

Planning to gather evidence of student learning is an essential part of any lesson. Though trusting your perceptions and gut feeling for evaluating student understanding may tempt you, those perceptions can often lead you astray. Find a systematic way to gauge what all students have understood about the mathematics. The evidence that you consider can be student work, a checklist where you mark what solution strategies students used, notes from group observations, a list of questions students ask, or any number of other data sources. Whatever it is, however, you need to plan what data you will gather as well as how you will gather and record them.

Though this idea may seem simple, it actually goes against deeply ingrained cultural definitions of teaching. Most of us grew up with the idea that effective math teachers monitored behavior, explained well, and helped struggling students. Noticeably absent from this list is assessing what students understand about the mathematics. Without a plan to assess students' understanding during class, we are all inclined to fall back to the familiar approach of monitoring behavior and helping students who ask for it. If we do not plan ways to assess students and record what we find, we end up not assessing at all.

As chapter 3 described, attending to how your students are making sense of, and interacting with, the mathematics of the lesson is your primary job as an instructor. The knowledge you gain from this information will inform your future predictions about how students will approach this content and how you structure subsequent lessons.

Plan for logistics

Lessons have many moving parts. They often involve distributing materials and tools or changing the focus from a small group to a large group and having students move around the room. When you plan for a lesson, determine the materials students will need and how they will get them. You may need to create some materials. Plan exactly what to tell them so that they do not waste time confused about logistics. Decide how to group students and how you will let them know where, and with whom, they will sit. (If you have implemented strategies from chapter 5 about establishing routines, then you simply need to plan for enacting an established routine(s) appropriate for the mathematical content of the lesson.)

CREATE A LESSON PLAN

Now you are ready to create a lesson plan, a "short plan" with the essential information that you need to remember. This plan takes up no more space than one side of one piece of regular paper. This paper should include the problems that you will give your students, as well as essential questions you will ask to support students as they work. It should include the logistical details of the lesson so that you will not forget to include them. It should include reminders of how you will collect evidence of student understanding, and essential ideas to ask about in discussion. It is your plan, for you, so it should include what you need to remember while teaching.

Once you have completed your lesson plan, make sure that you have everything else ready for the lesson, such as any problem sheets you need to develop or make copies of. You may also need to spend time before the school day rearranging desks or tables in your classroom to "fit" the lesson structure you chose. Do you need to borrow materials or tools from another teacher?

If you have to fill out a specific lesson-planning template for your supervisor, figure out how to integrate the activities we have described into that template. If you do not have to fill out a lesson plan for a supervisor, this does not mean that you do not have to write anything down and that you will be able to keep it all in your head. The teaching approach we advocate is different from how many of us were taught in our own schooling and from the widespread images of teaching in popular films and media. Changing patterns of interaction between teachers and students will require conscious planning and concrete reminders for yourself; otherwise, you will simply fall back into old learned ways of interacting.

PLAN DIFFERENTLY FOR DIFFERENT PURPOSES

Although planning should always entail thinking through mathematics and how students might approach that mathematics, not all planning looks the same. As you gain more experience, you will become able to concentrate on different aspects of your lessons. The planning we described is the kind we expect that you will do for most lessons throughout your career. However, at different times of the year and in your career, you will engage in specialized planning to address specific teaching and learning issues.

Unit planning

In addition to planning lessons, effective teachers plan units. Most curriculum materials are organized into units of study defined by a particular content focus, such as the geometry of circles, chords, secants, and tangents or solving linear equations. When planning a unit, first identify the mathematics of the unit. What are the major mathematical ideas, representations, relationships, and strategies that students should learn about? What tasks or problems should they be able to solve? What are the activities that students engage in, and in what order? How do these activities build on each other?

When planning a unit, try to clarify exactly how you will know that students have met the learning goals. Often this means getting clear on what tasks students should be able to do. Knowing what these tasks look like and the thinking necessary to succeed in them will help you design instruction to support students. While teaching a unit, make sure that the tasks and the thinking you require of students are similar to the thinking that you will assess at the end of the unit. Students often complain that the test was nothing like what they did in class; teachers get frustrated when students fail to solve problems that they could do in class with teacher support. Both complaints stem from teaching that did not require in class what was required on assessments. If your tasks on assessments look different from those they have done in class, you are not assessing fairly. If the tasks look the same, but they get considerable support from you in class but not during the test, you are asking them to do different things in class and on the test.

Planning at the beginning of the year and semester

Planning, like much of teaching, is supported by routines that structure regular activities for you and your students and by norms that structure how you and your students interact with mathematics and with each other. Once these routines and norms are firmly established, you do not need to spend as much time planning how to manage transitions, for example, or how to hand out materials. You can spend more planning time thinking about the mathematics, how students will approach the mathematics, and content-specific questions you can ask to support them.

At the beginning of the semester, you should spend much of your planning time thinking about the routines and norms you want to establish. Much of your planning will entail choosing tasks that will not only support mathematical goals but also support students in having the kinds of conversations with each other, and interacting with the mathematics, in ways that you envision. You will have to plan what you will say, and how you will model and reinforce the kinds of behaviors you are looking for. Certainly throughout the semester you will have to continue to reinforce these norms and routines, but during the first days and weeks of the semester, these aspects of your planning and teaching will be especially important.

For instance, if you plan to have your students work in groups for substantial amounts of class time, the first time you have them do so you will have to plan, in great detail, how you introduce and monitor this lesson format. Clarify what behaviors you want them to exhibit, how you will make those behaviors clear and explicit, what kinds of behaviors you will look for as they engage in group work, and how you will respond to those behaviors. Select a task that will require and support collaboration. Plan what visual aid you will have to remind them of positive group behaviors and how you will assess and give feedback for how they work in groups. Once you have established powerful norms to support positive collaboration, you can spend more time planning other aspects of your teaching. (See chapter 5 for an example plan for the beginning of the semester.)

Planning throughout your career

Many aspects of a lesson were simply not on your radar screen before you began teaching. Part of what makes being a new teacher so exciting (and exhausting) is learning just how much you must manage and be conscious of. Planning gives you as a new teacher a chance to think about many of those details before they take you by surprise: Plan how to react to students who ask to go to the bathroom or who do not want to sit in their assigned seats. Plan for how to move from a group discussion to seatwork with partners. Plan how to respond to wrong answers or requests for assistance. So much of the work of teaching that was invisible to you as a student will become visible because you had not anticipated it, and then you will have to plan how to deal with it. That is one reason that the lesson-planning templates for methods classes are often so extended. Professors want you to think about a wide range of issues, decisions, and actions.

With experience, many of these elements of teaching will become easier. You will have gained a set of techniques for dealing with many of them, and you will not need to plan for many situations that are no longer new. After twenty years on the job, you will not need to write a reminder to yourself to stand at the door on day one of class or write the homework in the same place every day. As you gain experience, you will have already established ways of interacting with students, using strategies that you have practiced and become comfortable with. Many of the questions that you had to consciously ask yourself as a new teacher should become part of what you simply do by habit.

Later in your career, you may have a different challenge. You may need to uncover some of the things that you learned to do intuitively, and examine them again, to see whether they align with your purposes and goals. You may be able to use your planning to systematically improve your teaching, planning and trying new techniques and tasks, for instance, and collecting data to see whether they work as you hoped.

FIND SUPPORTS TO HELP YOU PLAN

Although planning is essential, it can be overwhelming and complex. Supports are available to help make your planning more manageable and successful. First, use your curriculum materials to help you plan. Many published curriculum materials have extensive notes for teachers that give useful information about the mathematical goals of lessons and units, typical student responses to tasks and problems, and effective questions you can ask to support students. They also suggest ways to create routines and norms that support students in gaining connected knowledge of mathematics as well as ways to assess student learning and understanding. Study and make the most of these materials. Second, collaborating with colleagues will help you plan much more effectively, especially if you plan with a colleague who has experience with the curriculum materials and students similar to those you teach. Such planning takes time, but you will gain tremendous knowledge and find that working with others stimulates your thinking. Collaborating during planning will also give you access to a much wider range of ideas, techniques, and solutions to possible teaching conundrums than you might have developed alone.

CONCLUSION

Section I of this book described learning as resulting from students thinking about mathematics. We situated this thinking in the arrow between students and mathematics in the triangle of instruction. We also argued that teachers are most effective when they spend much of their time paying attention to what, and how, students are thinking about mathematics. This chapter describes how thoughtful and consistent planning will have tremendous effects on the quality of the thinking and learning your students do, as well as your ability to pay attention to their interactions with mathematics. This chapter's strategies will enable you to plan lessons in which you can, as illustrated in the triangle of instruction, focus your attention on supporting your students' interactions with the mathematics they are learning.

SUCCESS
from
the START
Your first years
teaching SECONDARY
MATHEMATICS

chapter **eight**

Enacting the Mathematics Lesson

Before you read this chapter, reread the vignette of Ms. Barker's classroom from chapter 1 and consider how her enactment of the lesson—

- focuses students on building connected knowledge of mathematics (see chapter 2);

- illustrates the relationships found in the triangle of instruction (see chapter 3); and

- reflects the ways that Ms. Barker knows her students (see chapter 4) and has established a positive learning environment (see chapter 5).

Viewing Ms. Barker's lesson through the lens of chapters 2–5, you begin to see that any teacher, regardless of experience level, can enact this kind of instruction and learn strategies to support students as they build connected knowledge of mathematics.

Logic suggests that if you spent enough time planning a lesson, enacting the lesson should be a snap: You have identified a learning goal and chosen tasks and tools to support your students' attainment of it. You have developed questions to assess their progress toward that goal and thought about difficulties they may have along the way. What could go wrong?

Guiding Principles

>> Teaching is complex and unpredictable; effective instruction requires planning and routines.

>> Your primary work is attending to, and supporting, students' interactions with mathematics.

>> Have a toolbox of moves to support mathematical thinking.

In reality, however, planning is necessary but not sufficient to enact an effective lesson. Even the best plan requires that you pay attention to your students' thinking, decide what to do in response, and then actually do it. Even with the best plans your students will surprise you and you will have to make adjustments.

Despite teaching's complex and often unpredictable nature, pivotal ideas and moves exist that will enable you to support students' gaining connected mathematical knowledge. This chapter explains moves to help you go from effective planning to effective teaching.

EFFECTIVE INSTRUCTION REQUIRES PLANNING AND ROUTINES

When we think of effective teachers, we often picture a smoothly running classroom, where everything goes according to plan and the teacher knows what will happen long before it actually does. In fact, teaching is complex and unpredictable. Students react in ways that you do not anticipate. They come up with ideas and interpretations that are difficult to deal with or understand. Although effective teachers with years of experience can better predict how students will act and think, they still encounter this complexity every day. Throughout your career you will have to make many decisions each day, often with incomplete information and in the service of conflicting goals and agendas. For this reason, prominent researchers and educators have likened teaching to "managing dilemmas" (Lampert 1985, p. 183) and have called for teacher education programs to prepare teachers for a career of uncertainty (Floden and Clark 1988).

ATTEND TO AND SUPPORT STUDENTS' INTERACTIONS WITH MATHEMATICS

Students develop connected knowledge of mathematics—the hallmark of deep understanding—by representing, communicating, reasoning and proving, solving problems, and making connections. Observe how they interact with mathematics and with each other, and push them to engage in those processes.

This approach is a shift in what many of us think of as the job of teaching. Instead of always doing mathematics ourselves, our primary task is to make sure that our students interact with mathematics to support their learning. Doing so often means shifting students' attention away from our actions to their own thinking and to the task at hand. We may spend more time observing and asking questions, and less time explaining and demonstrating. We may work to give students opportunities to struggle with difficult mathematical ideas, and discuss them with others, supporting them with moves designed to get them to make connections or engage in reasoning and problem solving. However, our job is not to make important mathematics easy by doing the work for them. This approach actually can prevent students from engaging in the thinking that allows them to make connections and develop understanding.

HAVE A TOOLBOX OF MOVES TO SUPPORT MATHEMATICAL THINKING

Developing pedagogical moves can also reduce the complexity of teaching. In addition to being good at enacting these moves, effective teachers know what moves to use when. These moves can buy you time when students react in unanticipated ways. These moves can also reinforce norms while supporting student thinking. They can create access for students and push them to reason mathematically and make sense of the mathematics they are learning. Over time these moves can become almost intuitive, but as a new teacher you will have to work to develop expertise in how and when to enact them.

Habits of Practice

>> Center your focus on the mathematics and on students' thinking.

>> Work to establish and support productive mathematical discourse.

CENTER YOUR FOCUS ON THE MATHEMATICS AND ON STUDENTS' THINKING

Recall that in the triangle of instruction, the teacher attends to and supports students' interactions with mathematics. This chapter's strategies will help you focus on the mathematics and how students are thinking about the mathematics.

Enact your plan

Enact the plan that you so carefully crafted to support student learning. Many beginning teachers' plans go off course because of various distractions during class. Although being flexible is important (remember Ms. Barker's decision to follow up on Jill's solution strategy and go "off plan"), beginning teachers should stay with the plan.

Attend to processes and answers

Although having the correct answer is important in middle and high school mathematics, all too often teachers concentrate on the answer at the expense of mathematical thinking. By increasing your focus on the thinking behind how students arrive at their answers, you will learn much more about students. You will also send the message that mathematics is a sense-making activity, where justification and reasoning are as important as precision. When you ask about and attend to student thinking, rather than just the answer, students will often discover their own mistakes and correct themselves.

Ask persistent questions

In chapter 7, we urged you to plan for asking different kinds of questions during instruction. Some are specific to your content (such as "How does the quadratic formula connect to the graph $ax^2 + bx + c = 0$?"). Other questions are more persistent and should become part of your everyday practice:

- Will that procedure always work? Why/why not/under what conditions?

- Does that relationship always hold true? Why/why not/under what conditions?

- How is today's math connected to what you learned yesterday/last week/in a previous chapter?

- Can you represent your thinking in a different way?

- Can you solve it by using a different method?

Consistently (and persistently) asking such questions will support your students to make mathematical connections, communicate their thinking, learn through problem solving, and think across multiple representations.

Teach your students to ask persistent questions

To create a culture of sense making, teach your students to develop the practice of asking persistent questions—of each other, of you, and of themselves. You can incorporate this practice in several ways. For example, after a student(s) has shared a solution with the class, all students in the class could write a persistent question in their notebooks that they would ask about what the student(s) shared. Or, if students are working individually on tasks, have them turn to a neighbor, share a solution, and then ask each other a persistent question. Displaying and referring to a poster with persistent questions would also be helpful.

Attend to students' mathematical thinking

Although students' overt behavior is easier to notice, work to tip the balance toward noticing mathematical thinking. The more deliberate and dedicated you become in attending to student mathematical thinking, the more you indicate that behavior that distracts from mathematical thinking has no place in your class. Chapter 11 gives strategies to shift the focus from students' behavior to attending to mathematical thinking.

Maintain a high level of cognitive demand

Chapter 5 mentioned the QUASAR project, the goal of which was "to provide students with opportunities for thinking, reasoning, problem solving, and mathematical communication. Student learning could not be expected to deepen or become more conceptually rich, it was argued, unless students were regularly, actively, and productively engaged with cognitively challenging mathematics" (Stein et al. 2009, p. 14). The QUASAR project yielded a list of classroom factors associated with the maintenance or decline of high levels of student thinking and engagement in challenging mathematics. These factors (fig. 8.1) have direct implications for instruction that supports students in building connected knowledge. For more about these factors, as well as narrative cases of mathematics classrooms where these factors play out, see Stein and colleagues (2009).

Factors associated with the maintenance of high-level cognitive demands
- Scaffolding of student thinking and reasoning is provided.
- Students are given the means to monitor their own progress.
- Teacher or more capable students model high-level performance.
- Teacher presses for justifications.
- Tasks build on students' prior knowledge.
- Teacher draws frequent conceptual connections.
- Sufficient time is allowed for exploration—not too little, not too much.

Factors associated with the decline of high-level cognitive demands
- Problematic aspects of the task become routinized (e.g., students press the teacher to reduce the complexity of the task by specifying explicit procedures or steps to perform; the teacher "takes over" the thinking and reasoning and tells students how to do the problem).
- The teacher shifts the emphasis from meaning, concepts, or understanding to the correctness or completeness of the answer.
- Not enough time is provided to wrestle with the demanding aspects of the task, or too much time is allowed and students drift into off-task behavior.
- Classroom-management problems prevent sustained engagement in high-level cognitive activities.
- Task is inappropriate for a given group of students (e.g., students do not engage in high-level cognitive activities because of lack of interest, motivation, or prior knowledge needed to perform; task expectations are not clear enough to put students in the right cognitive space).
- Students are not held accountable for high-level products or processes (e.g., although asked to explain their thinking, unclear or incorrect student explanations are accepted; students are given the impression that their work will not "count" toward a grade).

Fig. 8.1. *Classroom factors associated with the maintenance and decline of high-level cognitive demands (Stein et al. 2009)*

Think back on a recent lesson that you taught. Which factors of maintenance and decline can you identify in your instruction? Although using this lens to "see" your instruction through reflection might be difficult, you could use these factors to examine and improve your instruction in the following ways.

To analyze your instruction
The factors of maintenance and decline serve as useful tools to analyze your own teaching. One approach is to record a class and then, during playback, put a check by the factors that occurred during the class. Then reflect on what went well—on ways that you maintained a high level of cognitive demand. Think about how often you enact those factors. Are they typical in your instruction, part of your classroom norms? Then reflect on the factors of decline that you checked. Again, are some more typical than others? Do

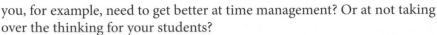

you, for example, need to get better at time management? Or at not taking over the thinking for your students?

You and your mentor (or another trusted colleague) could also use the factors to guide observations. Your mentor could check off and make notes about factors observed during a classroom visit and then you could debrief together. Alternatively, if you observe colleagues' classrooms, use the factors as a checklist to focus your observation.

As targets for improvement

Choose a maintenance factor that you want to get better at. Then plan for and enact instruction to incorporate that factor. For example, to get better at pressing for justifications, choose tasks that require your students to make justifications, plan questions that press for justifications, and develop persistent questions that you can ask to press your students for justification. Focus on this factor for a couple of weeks, until it becomes more normal than abnormal in your teaching.

Alternatively, you may have identified factors of decline that you want to minimize. Focus on one of those factors for a couple of weeks. First, recognize when you are enacting the factor. You can enlist your students to help with this. Say to them, for example:

> I am trying to get better at not always telling you exactly what to do to solve a problem. I think that you can do a lot more than I've been giving you the chance to show me, and I want to get better at giving you a chance to show me what you can do. But I need your help. So, each time you ask me a question and I start telling you exactly what to do, I want you to point it out to me. I'm going to start an "I've been telling too much" jar and put a quarter in for each time you help me recognize that I'm telling you too much. At the end of the month, I'll buy us a treat with the money in the jar!

By enlisting your students to help you, you can identify when you are enacting the factor in the moment. You could also ask anyone observing you to keep track of when you do something from the decline list. Once you get better at self-identifying, you can work to do something different. In this example, you could try to counter too much telling by asking a question so that you could listen to what a student is thinking, determining why the student is stuck, and then working with the student to determine a next step in the solution process.

Dealing with the unexpected

Although we advised you earlier to stick closely to your plan, sometimes deviating from it to respond to students' mathematical needs is appropriate. Think about Ms. Barker's deviation from her plan in chapter 1. When Jill presented an unanticipated solution strategy, Ms. Barker quickly assessed how Jill's strategy fit with the lesson's learning goals. After determining that more examination of the strategy would benefit her students, Ms. Barker decided to spend class time unpacking Jill's strategy. Ms. Barker kept her focus on the identified mathematical learning goal and used it to gauge the utility of deviating from her original plan. You can do the same when you encounter something unexpected that might cause you to deviate from your plan. Will deviating to follow a particular line of thinking help your students achieve the learning goal? If so, then it may well be worth the time to follow a different path. If not, find a way to acknowledge a student's contribution, question, or suggestion and then carry on with your plan.

WORK TO ESTABLISH AND SUPPORT PRODUCTIVE MATHEMATICAL DISCOURSE

Fostering productive discourse between students about mathematics is one of the most important things you can do to help them gain connected knowledge. Although you will work on this complex, difficult task throughout your career, the subtleties of doing so lie beyond the scope of this book. However, you can establish productive discourse from the beginning of your career in several ways.

First, recognize and plan for different discourse formats. Students can communicate with each other in small groups, in whole-class discussions, and individually with the teacher. Similarly, discourse can take the familiar form of talking but can also include writing, drawing pictures, and such subtle things as gesture, body language, and facial expression. Second, as discussed in the planning chapter, different questions, or discourse moves, can serve different purposes.

Moves that encourage participation and access

Getting all students to participate is a major challenge to establishing productive mathematical discourse. By the time students get to middle and high school, they may have often observed that students who talk the most in math class are those who can come up with correct answers quickly and accurately. Their teachers may have followed a discourse pattern known as IRE: the teacher *initiates* discourse by asking a question, a student *responds*, and then the teacher *evaluates* that response. This discourse pattern is recognizable in mathematics classrooms:

Teacher: And the area formula for a parallelogram is?
    [Three students' hands shoot up in the air.]
Teacher: Jamie?
    Jamie: Base times height.
Teacher: Good.

This type of classroom discourse limits students' opportunities to learn and tells the teacher little about what students know and can do (Franke, Kazemi, and Battey 2007).

The following teacher moves give all students the opportunity to think about the question being posed and to formulate a response. The moves afford equitable access to engage with the mathematics and increase the opportunity to participate in the mathematical discourse. Chapter 5 presented some of these moves; we revisit them here to focus on establishing and supporting productive mathematical discourse.

Wait time

Some students take longer to think through something mathematically—weighing different strategies or trying different approaches, or trying to remember a definition or reconstruct a mathematical formula. After you ask a question, give enough time to think so that more students have a chance to formulate an answer. Using wait time effectively allows all students access to the mathematics at hand. When you pose a question to the whole class, ask students to not raise their hands when they have an answer. Rather, say explicitly that you want to give all students time to think about the question.

Say that you expect all students to think about the question and their response—and then have strategies to hold all students accountable for doing the mathematical thinking. For example, you can ask students to either write their response in their notes or, if they don't have a response, write down a question about what you posed. Alternatively, if you have a classroom set of individual whiteboards, students can write their responses (or questions) on those to prepare for sharing with the whole class.

Wait time is useful not only after your questions or prompts but also after students' comments and questions. When you move on too quickly, or evaluate a student response as in the IRE discourse pattern described above, some students do not have time to think about the response and may even get the message that their responses are not worth thinking about.

Turn and talk

Turn and talk (sometimes called "think, pair, share") is a powerful move to get students to talk about their mathematical thinking. This move is relatively easy to enact: pose a question or topic for discussion, allow wait time for individual thinking, and then have students turn to a classmate to talk about their response. You can use turn and talk in several ways. Have students turn to their partner and—

- explain what they think the directions are for the task;

- explain what they understand about Suzy's comment; or

- say whether they agree or disagree with Tyvon's statement and why.

Turn and talk also allows you to assess student thinking. Listening to the small conversations gives you a sense of what students are understanding and where they are still struggling.

Turn and talk also encourages participation by allowing students to formulate their ideas in a more private space, which for some students will feel safer than sharing their thinking with the whole class. Also, while students are talking with their partners, you can easily identify ideas that you want students to share with the whole class and then let them know ahead of time that you will call on them to share. This move can give students a chance to rehearse how they communicate their mathematical thinking before sharing with a larger group.

Turn and talk is also useful when you ask a question and a long silence follows. Instead of filling the silence some other way (such as answering your own question), ask students to turn to their neighbor and talk about it. Once they have, you can ask a specific person to share or ask for a volunteer.

Write first

Before you have students answer a question orally, have them write their answer in their notebooks. Some students may need to see the mathematics that they are doing on paper—they may need the paper as an organizational tool, for example. For students who can do the mathematics in their head, writing down their thoughts may help them to articulate their thinking. For others, writing their thinking may serve as a necessary reference for working on later problems. After they have written for a few minutes, ask them to share their mathematical thinking by reading what they have written. Like turn and talk, this move allows you to assess students' mathematical thinking and strategically choose which students you will ask to share with the whole group. Reading something they have written also gives some students essential support to participate in whole-class discourse.

Cold call

In cold calling, your students do not raise their hands in response to a question you pose; rather, after using wait time to allow for mathematical thinking, you call on students—either through conscious choice or randomly. You can use several strategies to call on students randomly:

- Draw from a bag (or jar or basket) of popsicle sticks (or slips of paper), each with a student's name written on it.

- Assign each student a number and use a random-number generator.

- Use spinners, dice, or the like.

- Avert your eyes and point blindly to names in your grade book.

Cold calling sends the message that you expect all students to think about your questions and have a response. At first, cold calling may intimidate students not used to sharing their thinking with the whole class (perhaps they fear being wrong in front of their peers). If you have established the usefulness of all kinds of thinking (including getting wrong answers), then students may be less intimidated to share their thinking in front of their peers. Early in the school year, you must make clear that for students to ridicule or make fun of each other is unacceptable. One way to integrate cold call into your instruction is to use it with turn and talk or write first, enabling you to overcome some of this initial reluctance.

Moves that elicit student thinking

In addition to encouraging participation, ask students questions to help them verbalize their mathematical thinking, such as the following:

- How did you get that answer?

- How were you thinking about the problem?

- What have you done so far?

- What part(s) do you understand?

- What part(s) of the problem are you struggling with?

- Can you tell me what the problem is asking?

- What are you trying to find out?

You should routinely ask these questions in response to both correct and incorrect answers. Questioning both valid and invalid mathematical thinking shows that you are interested in how your students think about the mathematics (recall the triangle of instruction). It also emphasizes to students that they are responsible for knowing how they arrived at an answer and for communicating that thinking to others.

Eliciting student thinking is also important for you to assess what students know and their challenges with particular mathematical content. Smith, Bill, and Hughes (2008) call these kinds of questions "assessing questions" and argue that before a teacher can ask "advancing questions" (those meant to help move students toward a solution; see next section) that are connected to how a student is thinking, the teacher must first understand how that student is thinking.

You should also pose mathematical questions in writing to elicit student thinking and require that your students respond in writing. You can achieve this move through, for example, warm-up exercises (sometimes called "bell work"), exit slips (they hand you their written response as they exit the classroom), or mathematics journals.

Moves that advance student thinking

Especially when you give students demanding tasks, they will often feel stuck and need your help. You can use several moves to support them without taking over the mathematical work for them (recall fig. 8.1). First, assess what they know and understand. Getting them to clarify their own understanding often helps them figure out a path to take; other times, you will need to know what they have been thinking in order to build on that thinking. So, begin by asking questions that elicit students' thinking and then pose questions (or statements) such as these:

- What is the problem asking? How is that connected to what you've tried already?

- What have you been doing that is not working? Why do you think it isn't working?

- What do you need to find out?

- What do you know that can help you solve the problem?

You could also refer students to something in their textbooks or notes—to help them connect what they are having difficulty with to previously learned mathematical content. Perhaps they are struggling because they have forgotten a definition or theorem that applies to this situation; you can suggest revisiting a definition or theorem list in their notebooks. Perhaps the problem they are working on is similar to one they have worked on before, but they are not making that connection.

The key to advancing students' mathematical thinking is to use what you know about them as mathematical thinkers in combination with what you know about the mathematics at hand (think about the triangle of instruction), and then make suggestions that move students toward solving the problem they are working on. This practice is one way to scaffold students' learning: giving just enough information and support to move students in a positive direction, but not taking over the mathematical thinking for them by telling them exactly what to do.

Moves that push for clarity, meaning, and sense making

You can use other questions and discourse moves that specifically push students to make connections and reason. Earlier we advised using persistent questions in attending to both mathematical processes and answers. Posing persistent questions is also a powerful way to support students in reasoning, representing, communicating, solving problems, and making connections.

Chapin, O'Connor, and Anderson (2009) suggest four "talk moves" (in addition to wait time) to support students' mathematical learning.

Revoicing
Revoicing clarifies (for both the student who speaks and other students) mathematical thinking that a student has verbalized. The move entails repeating what a student says (echoing back what you heard) and then asking the student whether what you stated fairly represents what the student verbalized about his or her mathematical thinking. In the following, a geometry teacher uses revoicing as a talk move:

Mr. Chester's students are sharing solutions to the following problem, which they have been working on in small groups:

Draw three different triangles that have an area of 18 in^2.

Penelope is at standing at the board. She points to her group's poster and says, "So, we started with the first triangle, and just thought, 'what number' times 'what number' divided by 2 equals 18?"

Mr. Chester waits for a moment and then says, "So let me see whether I understand what you were thinking. I heard you say that you were looking for two numbers that, when you multiplied them together and then divided by two, the result would be 18. Is that right?"

Mr. Chester doesn't parrot what Penelope said; he doesn't simply repeat back exactly what he heard. Instead, he rephrased Penelope's statement (revoicing), clarifying her statement. Mr. Chester's use of revoicing supports Penelope with mathematical language (using *multiplied* instead of *times*) as well as to clarify for others what quantity is divided by two (in Penelope's statement, it could be that only the second factor is divided by 2).

Repeating

In using the repeating talk move, the teacher asks another student to repeat or rephrase what someone else said. For example, after Penelope's statement in the example above, instead of revoicing, Mr. Chester could have asked another student, "Can you restate what Penelope said in your own words?" Having other students repeat what they have heard serves several purposes. Used consistently, this move emphasizes the importance of students listening to one another's mathematical thinking. Like revoicing, it also clarifies the speaker's thinking and gives the speaker opportunity to further explain his or her thinking (if the repeater gets it wrong).

Applying one student's reasoning to another's

Asking students to apply their own reasoning to someone else's reasoning is different from the teacher asking questions to support a student's reasoning. With this talk move, the teacher asks a student to respond to another student's reasoning. In our example above, Mr. Chester could have used this talk move after Penelope's explanation by asking another student, "Do you agree or disagree with the method that Penelope used? Why?" or "Does Penelope's method make sense? Why?" or "How is Penelope's method connected to your group's method? How are your methods similar? How are they different?"

Adding on: Prompting students for further participation

In adding on, the teacher asks for ideas from students to extend the mathematical thinking being discussed. In our example above, after using one of the other talk moves (do not use this talk move first), Mr. Chester could have prompted his students for further participation by saying, "Thank you, Penelope, for sharing your group's method and how you were thinking about this problem. Who would like to add to this discussion?" or "Who would like to share additional insights about this problem?" Adding on is particularly powerful when you know that your students have used several different strategies to solve the same problem and you want to give them an opportunity to share their strategies with peers.

Moves that nurture discussion and shared mathematical authority

Some moves explicitly make students responsible for their own thinking and for the conversation at large. These moves focus the attention on the student–mathematics side of the triangle of instruction rather than on the teacher vertex. Further, they emphasize that mathematical authority does not reside in the status of a particular speaker, but in the mathematical reasoning of the argument.

Have students lead the discussion

Having students lead the discussion takes practice and nurturing, but this move can focus the mathematical authority on the mathematics being discussed rather than having the focus always be on the teacher.

Teach your students to facilitate talk moves

You do not have to be the only person in the room who facilitates talk moves. For example, when students are sharing strategies for solving a problem, the student presenter can ask an adding-on question, prompting another student to present the next solution. Students can also ask each other, "Do you agree or disagree with my thinking about this problem? Why?" Cultivating your students' abilities to use talk moves will support your classroom's discourse community.

Respond by asking, "What do others think?"

Responding to students' questions by asking the class, "What do others think?" will help your students see that you do not consider yourself the ultimate mathematical authority in the room.

Use focusing, not funneling

Teachers commonly ask questions intended to scaffold the work for students, but the questions do nothing to help the student understand. Imagine that a student is given the following problem:

Convert the following equation for a line to slope–intercept form:
$$3y + 5 - x = 5x - 7$$

Li:	Ms. Jones, I don't know how to do this.
Ms. Jones:	Well, what do you know about the slope–intercept form?
Li:	[Silence]
Ms. Jones:	Well, do both sides of the slope–intercept form have x's?
Li:	No?
Ms. Jones:	That's right. So we need to get all the x's on one side. What do we have to do to get rid of the x on the left side of the equation?
Li:	Subtract?
Ms. Jones:	Well, the x is already being subtracted. What's the opposite of subtraction?
Li:	Addition.
Ms. Jones:	That's right; we have to add the x to both sides.

Ms. Jones's questions do not help Li make sense of the problem. They are designed to get Li to give the correct answer. Li does not have to think and make sense of the math—if Li waits long enough, Ms. Jones will ask her a question she can answer without having to think about the math at all. Without Ms. Jones asking Li a series of cuing questions, Li would have no way to do the problem, and Li will probably not be able to take anything from this conversation to help her convert other linear equations to slope–intercept form.

Wood (1998) named this pattern of interaction "funneling." Teachers engage in funneling by asking questions that are not designed to push student thinking or assess their understanding, but to elicit the right answer.

In "Enhancing the Learning Environment through Student-Led Mathematical Discussions," a chapter from *Mathematics for Every Student: Responding to Diversity, Grades 9-12* (National Council of Teachers of Mathematics 2009a), high school mathematics teacher Patricia Avery describes using this move in her classroom.

Funneling is common in mathematics classrooms. Students and teachers are reassured in the short term by correct answers, but in the long term funneling prevents students from making sense of mathematics and engaging in the processes that lead to connected knowledge.

By contrast, focusing is an effective teaching move that does support students in making sense of mathematics (Wood 1998). Focusing mathematical talk involves listening to students and asking questions that do not take the thinking process away from the students.

Consider the same scenario as above, except this time Ms. Jones uses focusing instead of funneling:

Li: Ms. Jones, I don't know how to do this.

Ms. Jones: Well, let's begin with your telling me what you notice about this equation as it's written here.

Li: *[Pauses]* I notice that the problem has two variables, x's and y's.

Ms. Jones: What else do you notice?

Li: That x's are on both sides of the equals sign.

Ms. Jones: OK. Those are important things for you to notice. I also wonder whether you noticed that this is a first-degree equation—that the exponent on the x's and y is 1. Do you know what that means?

Li: I think it means that this is the equation of a line—oh, it actually says that in the problem, doesn't it?

Ms. Jones: It sure does! Now, what does the problem ask you to do?

Li: Convert this equation to slope–intercept form. Oh. I know what that is—we did something like this last week. Let me look back in my notebook.

Ms. Jones: While you are doing that, I'm going to go see what Bart needs. I'll be back here in a couple of minutes. Once you have found what you're looking for in your notebook, I want you to strategize about a first step that's going to help you complete this task.

Ms. Jones helps Li focus on what is important in a way that will not only help Li solve this task but also support her when she faces similar tasks: Li could ask herself the kinds of questions that Ms. Jones just did. So, focusing not only supports students to solve the problem they are working on but also helps them develop metacognitive abilities.

CONCLUSION

Even though previous chapters addressed planning as an important element of successful teaching, teachers still must call on skill and judgment to enact a plan amid complex and often unpredictable classrooms. You also need to learn specific moves to stay focused on students' interactions with mathematics. By keeping the focus on mathematics, and learning moves to establish and maintain positive and productive mathematical discourse, you can enact lessons in which students routinely represent, reason, communicate, solve problems, and make connections. Incorporating these moves consistently will help you better respond to the unexpected and better manage the complexities inherent in teaching for connected mathematical knowledge.

SUCCESS
from
the START
Your first years
teaching SECONDARY
MATHEMATICS

chapter **nine**

Reflecting on the Mathematics Lesson

M r. Mario was one of the first teachers author Rob Wieman met when starting to work with beginning teachers in their classrooms. Rob and Mr. Mario worked to create interesting tasks that would support students to communicate with each other and make sense of mathematics. They worked hard to teach students how to have respectful conversations that connected to important ideas. They saw progress during the year: Students talked with each other about math. Certainly, these conversations were not always ideal—often they were about procedures without justification. However, Rob and Mr. Mario saw this as tremendous progress; students were beginning to interact with each other and with the math in ways that could lead to connected mathematical knowledge. When students worked on problems, there was a steady hum of conversation and students were not depending on Mr. Mario to help them every step of the way.

But then a new problem arose. Generally, after students worked on a problem(s) for a while, Mr. Mario wanted to bring the whole class back together so that groups could share ideas and make connections between different solutions. This whole-group discussion was an essential part of the lesson: students would make sense of new and different ideas, and the class as a whole could summarize the important new mathematics. Getting the smaller groups to stop talking, however, was problematic. Mr. Mario found himself repeating that it was time to stop talking in groups and to start paying attention to the whole group. This transition took several minutes, and even when most students paid attention to the large-group discussion, small groups of students kept chatting.

Mr. Mario and Rob set out to solve this problem. After Mr. Mario identified the problem, they decided that Rob would sit next to a couple of groups and simply observe what happened when Mr. Mario called for everyone's attention. Rob wrote down what group members did and said. The students chatting after Mr. Mario asked them to be quiet were usually talking about the math. In a larger sense, they were doing exactly what Mr. Mario wanted. The conversations sounded like students were discussing an important idea. They kept talking because they had more to say about the mathematics.

Rob and Mr. Mario then thought about how Mr. Mario's actions aligned with what he wanted his students to do and what they understood. They also thought about exactly what Mr. Mario was doing and saying. Through this reflection, they realized that Mr. Mario was asking his students to stop talking and then expected them to do so immediately. This clarification caused Rob and Mr. Mario to think about their own experiences in large-group settings where they had been asked to talk in small groups or with a neighbor. They realized that those transitions generally took a while as well, because they were often in the middle of saying something and wanted to finish the thought. Rob and Mr. Mario agreed that having a leader insist on instant silence would have struck them as rude and unprofessional. Perhaps, they thought, Mr. Mario's students were not ignoring his request but were instead still engaged in mathematical thinking.

Then Mr. Mario and Rob discussed what they wanted students to do when moving from a small-group to a large-group discussion. Having students stop talking immediately was not as important as giving them time to finish vocalizing their thoughts. Instead of saying some version of "Everyone needs to stop talking now," Mr. Mario would say, "I need you to bring your conversations to a close so that we can have a larger discussion in a minute." A subtle change, but it seemed both much closer to what they wanted and more respectful of students engaged in meaningful discussion.

Mr. Mario was excited to try this new approach. When Rob checked in later that week, Mr. Mario reported that the transitions were going somewhat better, but students still took a long time to quiet down. Perhaps, he thought, when students were paying attention to each other in their small groups, they could not hear his requests to end their conversations. If he wanted them to focus their attention on each other in their small groups, he realized, he should not expect them to also pay attention to some announcement he was making. So Rob and Mr. Mario decided to try having Mr. Mario go around the classroom a minute or so before he wanted to pull the class together for a full-group discussion and tell each group to finish up their conversations in a couple of minutes.

When Rob observed Mr. Mario's class later that week, Mr. Mario was doing as they had planned. Some groups wrapped up their conversations, but others kept talking, as if Mr. Mario were not there. Talking with Rob about it later, Mr. Mario agreed that with some groups his new strategy had little effect. Once more, they thought about what might be going on when

Mr. Mario told groups to finish their conversations. Watching the next period, Rob noticed that members of some groups still had difficulty attending to Mr. Mario: they were concentrating on listening to the group member who was speaking. Mr. Mario and Rob decided that before asking the students in these groups to end their conversations in a couple of minutes, Mr. Mario would lean over and put his hand in the middle of the group of desks and wait until all the students looked at him. Then he would tell them he was planning to have a whole-group discussion and that they needed to finish up their conversations in a couple of minutes.

Ten years later, Mr. Mario is an experienced teacher. He still sometimes moves from small to large group discussion by going to each group, putting his hand in the middle of their table, and telling them that they need to finish their conversations in a minute or two. Observers often comment on how well students talk to each other and how well he manages the class. People sometimes marvel at his "way with kids"—how students seem to listen to him so well. Visitors often learn that Mr. Mario did not start out that way, that his way with kids is the result of methods that he worked on with others through trial and error. That careful thought about what he wanted, what he did, and how his students reacted led to changes that became improvements that he could incorporate into his teaching.

* * *

To begin a chapter on reflection with this story may seem strange. It seems to be about so many other things: planning, management, establishing routines. For us, however, reflection is a central element in how Rob and Mr. Mario turned a teaching problem into an opportunity both to learn and to improve teaching. Certainly, in improving how he managed transitions, Mr. Mario had to clarify goals and plan how to move toward them. He had to enact his plans not just once, but over time. He had to observe how and whether those plans moved him closer to his instructional goals.

What made all this possible, however, was careful, collaborative, and systematic reflection. Mr. Mario and Rob engaged in reflective processes that enabled them to move from having an intuitive sense of a problem to having a clearer vision of the interactions that gave rise to that problem. Their reflection allowed them to clarify the precise behavior they wanted. It helped them create conjectures about why students were acting the way that they did, and how teacher actions were affecting those behaviors. This analysis, in turn, enabled them to plan new teacher moves to more directly address the problem and support students in positive interactions with mathematics and each other.

People in general, including teachers, believe that experience improves performance. Although this is true, improvement does not come from experience alone. Experience leads to improvement through reflection. If we systematically examine our experiences and think about how our actions related to what we expected or planned, we can build knowledge about how teaching moves and tasks are likely to support students to develop deep, connected knowledge of mathematics.

Guiding Principles

>> Reflection allows teachers to learn from teaching.

>> Effective reflection is based on evidence.

>> Effective reflection connects teaching and learning.

REFLECTION ALLOWS TEACHERS TO LEARN FROM TEACHING

Reflecting on their work is how teachers learn best from their experiences. When reflecting on teaching and learning in the context of specific lessons, teacher moves, and student outcomes, teachers can begin to identify and clarify their own assumptions and expectations, they can learn to identify the big mathematical ideas that undergird the content that they teach, and they can begin to connect specific teaching moves and tasks with student outcomes. Reflecting on a good lesson helps teachers identify effective moves and tasks. Reflecting on a lesson that did not go as planned helps teachers identify student misconceptions or patterns of interaction that do not support students to learn mathematics.

If teachers do not reflect on their teaching, in contrast, each lesson is brand new. Good lessons feel good, bad lessons feel bad, but neither acts as a learning experience. Without reflection, each new lesson plan is, essentially, a stab in the dark.

EFFECTIVE REFLECTION IS BASED ON EVIDENCE

When we teach, we often react to situations on the basis of gut feelings and intuitions. Because of the complexity of teaching, this is not only understandable but also necessary; if we paused to think through every decision, we would never get anything done. However, gut feelings and intuitions can also obstruct learning and growth. Our intuitions are based on our own beliefs and experiences, and to grow and learn we need to move beyond what we already know and are comfortable with. Our intuition can also lead us astray: It may tell us that students who can complete procedures quickly and accurately have deep conceptual understanding of mathematics, but decades of mathematics education research tell us that this is often not true. It may tell us that a student is not engaged because he is slouched in his chair, but he may be listening intently. Without some reality check, our intuition can reinforce and perpetuate our existing beliefs and knowledge.

The antidote to unchanging beliefs supported by untested intuitions is evidence and a desire to discover surprises in our teaching and our students. So if we want to reflect on how a particular task supported students to achieve a learning goal, we need to gather evidence to determine whether they achieved it. If we want to reflect on how students are working in groups, we need to collect evidence of how they are working in groups. If we do not, our understanding of our students may have more to do with our own mood on any particular day than with our students' behavior and knowledge.

Effective teachers always look for surprises in the data and evidence they collect. These surprises give them opportunities to learn more about student understandings and motivations, mathematical content, and how teaching affects learning. So when Mr. Mario and Rob decided to collect data about students who were not getting quiet, they found that the students were often talking about math. This finding was surprising and helped them reconsider the problem that they needed to solve. The problem was not about getting the students on task; rather, it was about giving them time to finish their talk in a structured manner. If Mr. Mario and Rob had not gathered that evidence, their initial intuition—that the students were simply being too social and not paying attention—might have led them to institute counterproductive changes as a way to solve a problem that did not exist.

EFFECTIVE REFLECTION CONNECTS TEACHING AND LEARNING

Reflecting on what happens during a lesson can teach you much about students, what they are thinking, how they are acting, and how they interact with each other and mathematics. Reflecting on student thinking and student work can teach you about mathematics. Even students' mistakes or difficulties—even if they can do procedures—can show you the big conceptual ideas and connections that will help them create more connected knowledge.

As a teacher, however, you want to learn whether and how specific teacher moves or decisions (including what tasks to give or questions to ask) support student learning. Noticing and reflecting on how students make sense of a recursive representation of a linear function is interesting, but reflecting on how the question you asked focused them on the difference between successive terms allows you to hone your questioning for the next lesson. The point of reflection is to improve your teaching, to learn things that you can use to solve teaching problems, and to evaluate how well your plans and actions worked to support student learning.

Sometimes reflection connects teaching and learning by using evidence and reflection to inform future planning. Students might focus on the common difference between terms when dealing with a linear context, which keeps them from understanding the explicit formula. For example, they may see buying a given number of hats at $5 apiece as adding 5 to whatever a customer had to pay for the previous number of hats. Each new hat is five more dollars, so their rule is +5. This may make others' rule of $y = 5x$ difficult to understand. So the next time you teach this lesson, you may decide to ask each group how much 400 hats would cost, rather than just 1, 2, 3, 4, and 5 hats. This problem will push students who are thinking additively to find a different method, because adding up 400 fives would be tedious and inefficient.

Reflection sometimes connects teaching and learning by evaluating whether moves you already made had the desired effect. Mr. Mario implemented each teacher move, gathered evidence, and compared the results with his expectations. When students did not respond exactly as hoped after the first adjustment, Mr. Mario and Rob acknowledged that the teaching move needed more refinement.

ENGAGE IN A REFLECTION CYCLE

Learning from reflection requires deliberate and systematic efforts. The following six-stage reflection cycle can guide you in reflection that improves teaching:

Habits of Practice

>> Engage in a reflection cycle.

>> Learn from surprising or unpredicted events.

>> Engage in document reflection.

1 Identify and describe the problem of practice.

2 Clarify desired outcomes.

3 Hypothesize teacher moves that may produce outcomes from step 2.

4 Plan for and implement a move from step 3.

5 Collect and analyze data.

6 Repeat steps 1–5 (if necessary).

Step 1: Identify and describe the problem of practice

Focusing reflection on specific problems of practices moves you from general statements about what is happening in your classroom (for example, "my kids don't understand anything I teach them") to identifying problematic elements of teaching and learning (such as "my students are having a hard time understanding what *limit* really means"). Focusing on specific problems of practice will help you generate concrete, usable knowledge to inform future teaching.

Further, to change something in your classroom, you first need a clear understanding of the problem and to be able to describe it specifically. Mathematics teachers' problems of practice typically fall into three categories: (1) students' understanding of mathematics, (2) specific teacher moves, and (3) students' behavior or patterns of interactions. The strategies below can help you identify and describe problems of practice in each category.

Focus on students' (mis)understandings of mathematics
Often, students who can do the procedures or techniques you have taught show some misunderstandings about the underlying concepts. Clarifying for yourself what concepts they understand and misunderstand will help you strategize teacher moves to advance their learning. Several types of evidence are useful to describe students' (mis)understandings about mathematics: samples of student work (from class activities, exit slips, homework), conversations with students (during class, in tutoring sessions), and notes you or an observer took during class. Once you have evidence to consider, ask yourself questions such as these:

- What do students understand about the mathematics?

- What misconceptions or misunderstandings do students have? Did they work through these, or do they still have them?

- What did students spend time thinking about during the lesson?

Focus on specific teacher moves

Have you ever wondered about the quality of the questions you ask? Perhaps you wonder about the clarity of instructions on activity sheets that you design or whether the homework you assign really helps students. Such problems of practice may be less problematic than students' misunderstandings, but reflecting on these aspects of teaching can improve your students' experiences in math class. For example, you may want to reflect on how well a task and its context illustrate how rate of change is represented in a graph, an equation, or a table. Teachers may also reflect on more general elements of instruction, such as moves to invite more extensive discourse or to get students to work as they come in the door.

Perhaps you need to gather more information about this type of problem of practice before you can describe it well. For example, if you feel that the questions you ask during whole-group discussion are not particularly effective, video or audio recordings of the lesson would help you better describe what is problematic about your questions or how students respond to them. Questions such as these can help you clarify and describe this type of problem of practice:

- What move or decision did you make?

- What did you expect to happen?

- How did you expect students to respond to this move or task?

- What actually happened?

- What caused the difference between what you expected and what actually happened?

Focus on students' behavior and patterns of interaction
Some problems of practice, such as Mr. Mario's, are not about student difficulties in learning particular mathematics, but about how students interact with you and each other. Especially when you are a new mathematics teacher, students will behave in ways that you did not predict or are uncomfortable with. Reflecting on these problems of practice will help you develop teacher moves that support students to adopt more positive behaviors.

Mr. Mario benefited from having Rob collect evidence about student behaviors during transitions. Enlisting a colleague or mentor to help you collect evidence will help you describe student behavior. Such evidence includes observer notes, video or audio recordings of student interactions, journal entries that you write, and descriptions of your conversations with students.

Once you have evidence to consider, ask yourself questions like these:

- What were students doing and saying?

- What was positive about their behaviors and interactions?

- What behaviors were problematic?

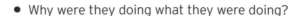

● Why were they doing what they were doing?

Describing your role in problems of practice

Part of clearly describing the problem is to also hypothesize about your role in the situation. For example, after describing how students had difficulty completing a set of problems, evaluate your role in their difficulties. Were the directions you gave unclear? Did you allot enough time for students to complete the problems? Did students have access to appropriate materials and tools? How did you react to their behaviors? Were your actions aligned with what you wanted, and if so, how? Consulting the list of factors of maintenance and decline (fig. 8.1) may help you describe your role in the problematic situation.

Step 2: Clarify desired outcomes

Clarify exactly what you expect as an outcome. After describing what students actually did, ask yourself questions such as, "What did I want them to do? How is that different from what they did?" Understanding that difference will help you in step 3.

If you are working on a problem of practice about students' (mis) understandings, be able to describe how you expect them to know the mathematics: what connections they should make, what representations to use, and how they should reason about the mathematics. You can look to your own understandings about the mathematics, talk to other math teachers about their understandings, or consult the textbook or supplementary materials for indicators of understandings. Standards documents (such as *Principles and Standards for School Mathematics* [National Council of Teachers of Mathematics 2000] and the Common Core State Standards for Mathematics [National Governors Association Center for Best Practices and Council of Chief State School Officers 2010]) can also help identify specific mathematical goals and outcomes.

If you are working on a better understanding of the impact of a particular teacher move (such as a specific set of questions), then in this step you will identify outcomes that you desire as a result of performing that teacher move. Let's say you are focused on improving your questioning, because often you ask a question only to be confronted with silence and blank stares. You do not want that outcome; now is the time to articulate the outcome(s) you do want. For example, you may want the outcome to be that when you ask a question, students spend a minute thinking about and writing down an answer in their notebook. Or that students hold up their pencil when they have an answer. Or that you want students to think for thirty seconds before raising their hands.

If you are working on a problem of practice about students' interactions, then again, you have identified what you do not want them to do in step 1. Now is the time to identify what outcome you want. Other chapters of this book offer options for positive behaviors and ways to redirect (mis) behaviors (such as chapter 11). If you are teaching for connected mathematical knowledge, you want students to always interact with the mathematics they are learning.

Talking with a colleague or mentor might help when you clarify desired outcomes, as in Mr. Mario's case. Having Rob to talk with helped him clarify what he wanted his students to do during the transition from small-group to whole-group discussions.

Step 3: Hypothesize teacher moves that might produce outcomes from step 2

Once you have described the problematic situation and clarified desired outcomes, consider teacher moves to try that might produce these outcomes. Use the table of contents to identify a chapter that has strategies for you to consider. As you reread the habits of practice in that chapter, consider each one through the lens of your problem of practice and desired outcomes. Consider a few practices or teacher moves that you hypothesize might work, and choose one to try.

Step 4: Plan for and implement a move from step 3

Two types of planning occur in this step: planning for instruction and planning to gather evidence. First, incorporate the teacher move that you identified at the end of step 3 into a plan for an upcoming lesson (see chapter 7 for lesson planning strategies). Be deliberate and specific about when you will use the teacher move and the outcome you expect. Envision what implementing the teacher move will look and sound like as well as what your expected outcome will look and sound like (see chapter 4 for more about envisioning effective instruction).

Second, make a plan to gather data. Chapter 7 included planning to gather evidence as a habit of practice. If you leave the collection of evidence to chance, other demands of teaching will draw your attention. Planning for what evidence to collect also helps us analyze the data (step 5). In thinking through a lesson, we make several predictions that can then become the basis for making sense of what actually happens. For example, in looking through examples of student work we can sort responses according to different solutions we anticipated in our planning. Or if we planned a specific teacher move to help students attend to their peers' reasoning, we could see whether their responses to this move resulted in closer attention to that reasoning. Planning gives a purpose to our tasks and moves, and it can serve as a helpful lens for looking at what happened in class.

Step 5: Collect and analyze evidence

Step 5 parallels step 1 in the ways that you should now collect and analyze evidence of the teacher move you are trying. In step 4 you planned what evidence to collect and how to do it; now you need to implement that plan.

Step 6: Repeat steps 1–5 (if necessary)

Like Mr. Mario, the first teacher move you try might not produce the outcomes that you desire. If so, learn from what you did, how it worked (or did not work), and begin the cycle again.

LEARN FROM SURPRISING OR UNPREDICTED EVENTS

Sometimes you do not need to engage in a full reflection cycle to learn from your teaching. Although minimizing surprises and unpredicted events may feel safer, paying attention to and reflecting on surprising moments can prepare you for when those moments replay themselves. For example, you ask students to take out a pencil on the first day and are surprised that most students do not have something to write with. If you later reflect on that surprise and make note in your plan that your students did not have writing utensils on the first day of class, you will be less surprised if the same thing occurs at the beginning of the next semester. You could also take this information and design a lesson for the first day of the next year that does not require a writing instrument, or you may plan to provide one on the first day of class.

You may also be surprised by several things during your first years of teaching that can influence your perceptions of students. You may have a student who does not do homework consistently but scores highly on a test, which may surprise you the first time it happens and result in your having a higher opinion of the student than you did before. Or you may overhear a student who rarely speaks in class offer an insightful mathematical connection in a small group, which surprises and impresses you. Surprises or unexpected events rarely fluster effective teachers, who let these unplanned moments serve as learning opportunities.

ENGAGE IN DOCUMENT REFLECTION

Finally, when you reflect on your teaching and adjust tasks, lessons, and teacher moves, document what you have learned and tried. Recording what you have learned helps you avoid relearning the same lesson every year. You could make notes in your planning papers, attach sticky notes to textbook pages, keep a reflection journal, or make audio recordings to remind you of what did and did not work. The method of documentation is not the main point here; find a method that works for you and use it.

CONCLUSION

Although teaching is complex and difficult, you can learn to do it more effectively. To improve, treat your teaching as an opportunity to learn and engage in regular, systematic reflection. This chapter has shown you ways to identify problems, plan solutions, collect data, and analyze those data in light of your plans and actions. Through reflecting, your normal planning and teaching can become a site for learning, and you can move past intuitive understandings of teaching, students, and mathematics to more thoughtful understandings based on sound evidence and experience.

IV More Elements of Effective Teaching

As the day began at Middleville High School, Mr. Jones was excited. In his third year of teaching, he was developing a repertoire of teaching moves to push student thinking. His students talked to each other about the problems he gave them, asked questions when they did not understand, and pressed for justification if they disagreed with each other. He also was getting better at assessing what students knew and understood, and he was less surprised at their performance on unit tests. He had planned interesting lessons for today.

Before going to his classroom, Mr. Jones stopped to check his faculty mailbox. Today's haul was fairly typical:

- A reminder from the assistant principal that this year's state test would require students to use a graphing calculator and that math teachers should integrate calculators into their instruction

- A note from a parent whose child received a D on the last test

- A form from the teacher who oversaw detention the previous day, describing how one of his students had insisted that he had done nothing wrong in math class

- Several homework papers from students who, for various reasons, had not handed their homework in during class

Mr. Jones was gratified that he had a response to each "problem," even if it was to simply let it pass:

- He had already integrated calculators into his classes.

- He was confident that his policy of communicating with parents during the first few months of the year would mean that the disappointed parent would see him as an ally, not an adversary.

- A short conversation with the student in detention would resolve that problem.

- He placed the homework papers in his bag to check later, knowing exactly which problem he would look at to see whether his students understood important ideas.

Heading to his classroom, Mr. Jones thought about his first year of teaching, when a trip to the mailbox like this would have overwhelmed him. Back then, he felt like he was making progress in the most important aspects of his teaching, but so many others seemed to sneak up on him. He was always reacting and trying to catch up. He wondered whether learning how to handle some of these situations better as a first-year teacher was possible. Then he decided to check in with Angie, a new teacher in the math department, to see how she was doing and how he could help.

* * *

So far, this book has focused on everyday aspects of teaching central to your effectiveness. Every day, you will have to—

- decide what tasks and activities to engage your students with, and how you will support them;

- interact with students, and watch them interact with mathematics and each other;

- plan lessons, even if briefly, and reflect on how they went.

This section shifts the focus to other aspects of effective teaching— such as grading systems, working with technology, dealing with parents, and student misbehavior. Although these may not be central to your daily work, having efficient strategies to deal with them, and that align with your goals, is important. However, not having efficient ways to address these aspects can create problems. These chapters will help you think about these aspects of teaching in the context of larger issues of teaching and learning. This, along with our suggestions, should help you deal with the constant stream of demands in ways that support your larger goals and leave you time and energy to plan and support student learning.

chapter **ten**

Establishing and Maintaining Effective Group Work

Greg Hainsbury is a second-year mathematics teacher at a middle school outside the small southeastern city where he earned his master's degree. For two years, new teachers must work with a mentor for support and guidance. Greg's assigned mentor is Angela Goodhugh.

Greg observes in Angela's math class a twice a month. These observations drive fruitful discussions. Recently, Greg has been especially interested in how Angela managed small groups of students while they worked on math problems. Groups worked differently in Angela's class than in his. In Angela's class, everybody in the group worked on the problem, and students often stopped to ask each other questions or make sure that other group members understood what was going on. Students did not need so much help or prompting from Angela; they worked together effectively on their own. When they did ask for help, they used Angela as resource to get back on track rather than monopolize her for long periods.

Greg did not know how Angela did it. At first he thought that she had better kids, that her students were more motivated or socially skilled. But Angela assured him that at the beginning of the year, these students had just as much difficulty working in groups as those in his classes.

In Greg's classes, students often strayed off task or worked independently despite sitting in groups. Many groups had trouble getting started without him and often spent much of the class waiting for help. He suspected that some weaker students simply waited until stronger students did the work and then had the stronger students show them how to do it. He wondered, how was this different from copying answers? Having students work in small groups was not promoting the deep understanding that Greg wanted for them.

Because Angela had helped with other problematic situations in his classroom, Greg was excited to talk to Angela about how she set up and ran her groups.

* * *

A generation ago in the United States, an observer would have hardly ever seen students working in groups in math class, at any level. Students generally worked individually and would call on the teacher for help if needed. Over the last twenty years, this situation has gradually changed. More teachers put their students into small groups to work on mathematics, believing that group work affords opportunities for learning with understanding that individual work often misses.

Having students work in small groups supports them to build connected mathematical knowledge. But group work for its own sake is not an appropriate goal for math class. Rather, group work should give students opportunities to engage in representing, reasoning, communicating, solving problems, and making connections. Group work requires students to engage in these processes in many ways and, with good teacher facilitation, supports them in doing so.

Establishing and maintaining the conditions for effective group work is difficult. Furthermore, group work is not an appropriate for all lessons (see chapter 7 for more about lesson structures). This chapter gives basic principles for why and when group work helps students and offers strategies to get the best out of students working in groups.

GIVE STUDENTS OPPORTUNITIES TO DEVELOP CONNECTED KNOWLEDGE

Effective group work puts mathematics in a social context and pushes students to make sense of one another's ideas and arguments. Effective group work to solve rich problems naturally engages students in the processes that lead to connected knowledge: reasoning, communicating, representing, solving problems, and making connections. For groups to make decisions, individuals must communicate their ideas through pictures, symbols, or speech. To work on a problem together, students must evaluate the statements of their groupmates; they must decide whether the strategy or interpretation of the problem makes sense and is consistent with what they already know.

SUPPORT EFFECTIVE DISCOURSE AND INDIVIDUAL RESPONSIBILITY FOR LEARNING

Simply putting students in groups does not guarantee that they will engage in reasoning, representing, communicating, solving problems, and making connections. Students working in groups need a classroom culture that

Guiding Principles

To promote effective group work—

>> give students opportunities to develop connected knowledge (to reason, communicate, represent, solve problems, and make connections); and

>> support effective discourse and individual responsibility for learning.

supports individual responsibility for learning and student interactions that foster mathematical thinking. Students need to feel safe to ask questions or make statements that they are not sure of. Students need to be willing to hear critiques of their reasoning or to slow down if a groupmate needs more time to follow their reasoning. All students should consistently focus on mathematics, not on other academic and social concerns.

If students see group work as a way to avoid mathematics, or do not care about helping classmates, or do not speak up when math does not make sense, then being in a group does not support them. You need to convey clear expectations and use specific moves to create and maintain a culture that will support students to work well together.

Habits of Practice

>> Assign group-worthy tasks.

>> Create particular groups with specific purposes in mind.

>> Give explicit group norms and expectations.

>> Assign roles within groups.

>> Model the group dynamic when interacting with groups.

>> Encourage and structure self-evaluation of group processes.

ASSIGN GROUP-WORTHY TASKS

Group work is most effective when students work on tasks that require collaboration. Such tasks force students to share ideas, make judgments about which strategies to pursue, and take responsibility for their own understanding and that of others in their group. Ideally, each group member both needs assistance from peers and contributes meaningfully to a group goal.

If you use group work for tasks that individuals could complete more efficiently, students who know how to do the problems may see the group as a detriment to their learning, or students who struggle may simply allow the stronger students to do all the work. Avoid this dynamic. For groups to support learning for all students, each member must solve problems, communicate, reason, represent, and make connections. This can happen even if the tasks do not require collaboration. Students can work individually and stop to check on their peers' understanding, or ask each other questions when needed. However, the engagement we want is most likely to occur consistently when tasks require all group members to engage in making sense, thinking, and reasoning.

To ensure group-worthy tasks, assign rich tasks that no student can solve right away and that are not immediately comprehensible. Such tasks may have many possible solution paths, none immediately obvious. Some textbooks put these problems at the beginning of units to get students to put the mathematics they will be learning in context and to motivate them to learn specific techniques. Other textbooks place such problems in supplementary materials or at the end of chapters. Creating these problems on your own is difficult; you should not expect to be able to do so. For rich problems such as these, look in your curricular materials or consult other resources (see "Recommended Resources" at the end of this book).

You can generate group-worthy tasks by taking problems that you are already working on and adding constraints that force group interaction and accountability. Below are two ways to achieve group-worthy tasks by adapting existing tasks.

Constrain information

Giving out pieces of information about the problem to individual group members, rather than the whole problem to everyone, will force group members to share the information and make sense of it together. A classic example is simple logic puzzles. Imagine giving your groups this problem:

Five students ran a race. Freddy did not come in first; Ninette did not come in fourth. Stu beat Amy but lost to Betsy. Two girls were between the boys. What place did each student come in?

If you gave each group member all the information, this would not necessarily be a group-worthy task. Individual students could solve it without having to ask others questions or reason with them about their solutions. They would not need to communicate their thinking.

Now imagine giving individual group members just one piece of information above and telling them that they may read each piece of information aloud to the group—but they may not show it to other group members. Now to complete the task, each group member needs information that others have. Formulating a group answer also increases the likelihood that group members will have to explain how they got their answer and why it works so that other group members can come to a consensus.

Require collaboration

Many teachers find that when they give problems to groups, individual students simply do all the problems on their own. They do not stop to check whether others have questions or to check their work against one another's. They do not explain their reasoning or how they are stuck to other group members. Two strategies that, when used together, can counteract this dynamic:

1 Change the goal of the task from completing the problem to being able to explain or communicate something about the problem.

2 Give one problem at a time and require a satisfactory explanation before giving the group a second problem.

The first approach is especially effective if you designate one explainer for the group. The group goal, then, is to make sure that the explainer can explain how to solve the problem and justify each aspect of the solution to your satisfaction. This strategy forces students to work to support the explainer and communicate their own understanding to the explainer.

The second approach prevents students from racing ahead, oblivious to the understanding or questions of their groupmates. Satisfactory communication, representation, and reasoning are essential prerequisites to moving on to the next task.

When using these two strategies, change the explainer with every new problem. Listen to explanations only from the explainer, not a groupmate, and hold the explainer to a high standard of clarity and justification. In upholding high standards for the explainer, you hold the whole group accountable to helping their peers explain well.

CREATE PARTICULAR GROUPS WITH SPECIFIC PURPOSES IN MIND

When you create groups, think about individual students and their strengths and weaknesses as well as their particular issues. You will need to balance several factors, each of which can affect students' ability to get the most from group work.

Social concerns

Social concerns may weigh strongly in your group assignments, especially at the beginning of a semester or school year. Less confident students may benefit from having a friend in their group. Other students may need to be separated from friends who distract. Students with histories of antagonisms or unhealthy competition may need to be kept in different groups. Students prone to impulsive behavior or social distraction may need to be in groups near the front of the room, where you will be standing or sitting more often. Given the diversity of many contemporary classrooms, you should be aware of mixing your groups on a variety of dimensions, including sex, race and ethnicity, and any other affiliation relevant for your school. Beyond pushing mathematical behaviors, one benefit of group work is the opportunity for students to interact with a great range of fellow students, often peers whom they might not otherwise come in contact with. As the semester progresses and you have established norms around how students behave in class and treat one another in groups, you may have more leeway in these issues, but they will always be something to pay attention to.

Special needs

Some students will need to sit in particular groups because of specific needs. Students with vision or hearing issues will need to sit near the front of the room, where they can see and hear more of the group discussions. Students who struggle with English may benefit from having a classmate who speaks their native language in the group, if possible. (Try not to rely too heavily on one student to translate but to spread that role around over the semester.) Other students may have conditions for learning identified on their individualized education plans. Be aware of special needs and work to accommodate those students in grouping decisions.

Academic strengths and concerns

Groups should allow students to engage in communicating, reasoning, representing, solving problems, and making connections. Many teachers assume that putting the high-achieving students with low achievers is the best approach. That way, the thinking goes, the high achievers can help the low achievers. This practice sometimes backfires, however. Being in a group with high achievers often makes it even more difficult for low achievers to take on the role of leader or explainer. The high achievers continue to explain and represent, and the low achievers continue to act passively in math class.

Group your students so that the maximum number of students can be an expert within their group at some point during the semester. This often means grouping low achievers with other low and medium achievers and working hard to support them in making their own explanations. This way, instead of getting overshadowed by high-achieving, confident students, less advanced students can create and explore their own solutions.

Consider specific students' strengths or experiences in the context of the mathematics you will study. If you are doing a unit on statistics, and you will collect data on some aspect of student experience (say, number of hours of TV watched or hours worked per week), having students who vary along this dimension would be especially helpful. If you will work on a problem that involves auto mechanics, it might be helpful to spread among the groups the five students who you know are interested in cars.

GIVE EXPLICIT GROUP NORMS AND EXPECTATIONS

Before you have students work in groups, become clear in your own mind about how you want those groups to work. Clarify the following important aspects of group work for your students.

Everyone must learn and know the mathematics

All group members must learn and know the mathematics. Be explicit that working in groups does not mean that students are not responsible for the material; the group is not done just because one student in the group understands or can do the math. Students cannot use group work to shirk the responsibility of learning.

Everyone needs to help a group member when asked

A member of a group may not refuse to talk to another member of the group or help other members who ask for it. Group members who need help also should understand that learning mathematics is hard work and that fellow group members may need time to complete their thoughts before helping a peer.

No member may ask the teacher a question unless all members have the same question

Allowing questions only from entire groups, not individuals, is a powerful way to get students to interact and ask questions of one another. If you set up this expectation, you must adhere to it every time a student asks a question. Some teachers use the following strategy: When a student wants to ask you a question, ask someone else in the group what the question is. If the second student does not know, remind the group of the rule and tell them you will check back in a minute to see whether everyone has the same question. When you check back, ask a different student what the question is and repeat the process. This process often results in a group member's knowing the answer to the question, which helps to confirm that group members can and should help one another.

No talking between groups

Unless specifically asked to, students from one group should not consult with students in another group. Students within each group must talk to and use one another as a resource.

ASSIGN ROLES WITHIN GROUPS

Many teachers assign roles within groups to help a wide range of students participate in group activities. But every student, regardless of role, must learn mathematics by reasoning, representing, communicating, solving problems, and making connections. Fulfilling any role does not absolve students of this primary responsibility.

To facilitate work on the mathematics at hand

Some teachers assign each group member a different role, such as reader, recorder, and reporter. When assigning different roles, think about the mathematical activity that students will engage in during the group work. If students need to make a poster and then report out during whole-group discussion, then appointing a recorder and a reporter—two different students who are in charge of two different aspects of communicating the group's work—might make sense. You could also assign a group member to be the reasoner, who pushes group members for mathematical justifications. Be creative with assigning roles, but keep the focus of the roles on reasoning, communicating, connecting, representing, and problem solving.

For logistical purposes

Students need to take care of many purely logistical tasks, such as gathering materials, collecting papers, and returning calculators to the case. Assigning those roles to specific students helps classrooms run efficiently and saves valuable time and effort.

To monitor and cultivate group processes

Some teachers assign a student to the role of facilitator to make sure that everyone contributes or understands. This function can be valuable insofar as it helps students become aware of group dynamics and puts the responsibility for the smooth functioning of the group in students' hands. However, students in this role must not ignore their primary responsibility: learning mathematics.

Rotating roles

If you assign roles, rotate them so that all students play all roles. If one role is to assess the group process, the role should rotate so that each member of the group gets to do that, not just one. This way, no student gets stuck in one role, and all students can engage in every role's particular thinking.

MODEL THE GROUP DYNAMIC WHEN INTERACTING WITH GROUPS

Ideally, groups in your class should be able to work independently, allowing you to spend most of your time observing them, and perhaps asking clarifying questions so you can get a better sense of their thinking. Of course groups will struggle, both with the mathematics and with how to work together effectively. How you interact with the group can either reinforce dependence on you or scaffold their own ability to work independently.

By talking with individual students while the rest of the group is otherwise engaged, you undermine the idea that groups should work together with a common purpose. You can use several strategies to ensure that you treat the group as a whole. As mentioned, one way is to answer a question only if everyone in the group has the same question. Here are two other strategies.

Ask members what they have tried or what they know that can help them

Asking students what they have already tried, or what they already know that could help them solve the problem, shows your interest in their ideas and forces them to become more aware of their own thinking. Often this will prompt further thinking from them. It will also help you figure out other questions you might ask them to scaffold their thinking.

Model the kind of talk you want in the group

When you answer questions or make explanations, check for understanding by asking different members of the group to explain what you said. Have members explain to one another. If they have difficulty, ask them to create a specific question to help you explain more effectively.

ENCOURAGE AND STRUCTURE SELF-EVALUATION OF GROUP PROCESSES

Students should know that they are responsible for the functioning of their group and, by extension, for their own learning and that of their peers. Having them evaluate both their performance as an individual and the group as a whole will help them become more aware of your criteria for effective group work and of their own role in their group.

Have students fill out checklists

Creating checklists of the group behaviors that you want students to engage in, and then asking students to check off the behaviors that they engaged in, has three benefits:

> 1 It forces you to clarify the exact behaviors that you want to see in groups.

2 It clarifies those behaviors to students.

3 It forces students to become aware of how they interact with others and how those interactions support or hinder their own learning.

Having students rate themselves on a scale forces them to think about how much they are engaging in those behaviors. Your checklist could include the following items:

- I asked a clarifying question when I did not understand something a groupmate said.

- I explained my thinking about a problem to the group.

- I checked to see whether a groupmate understood my explanation by having her repeat what I said in her own words.

- I used reasoning to decide whether a groupmate's explanation made sense.

- I disagreed with a groupmate and used evidence and reasoning to support my argument.

- I changed my mind when a groupmate made an argument that made sense.

- I worked to include everyone in the group.

- I learned the mathematics I was supposed to learn.

- I followed the group rules.

- I asked others in the group when I had a question before asking the teacher.

Give written reflection prompts

Having students write about their own performance, using language that echoes your own, will help them become more aware of their own role and of their ability to interact more positively with peers and mathematics. You can ask them to respond to questions such as these:

- How did working in a group help you understand the mathematics we are studying?

- How well did your group work together? How could you improve the way your group works?

- How aware were you of what other people in your group understood? How did you learn that? How could you learn more about what other people in your group understand?

- Do you generally sit back and listen and observe in your group, or do you take a more active part? What would happen if you changed this?

Having students evaluate their own work in groups will contribute to more effective group work.

CONCLUSION

Students develop connected knowledge of mathematics through reasoning and proving, representing, communicating, solving problems, and making connections. Working in groups to make sense of problems and agree on solution strategies can give students many opportunities to engage in these processes. However, setting up and facilitating group work so that it offers those opportunities takes more than simply placing desks together. When having students work in groups, clarify and support the interactions you want students to have with one another and the mathematics. Following this chapter's advice will help you to create and communicate norms for group behavior, choose tasks for groups to work on, and use teacher moves when interacting with groups to help your students work effectively in groups.

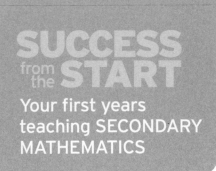

SUCCESS
from the START
Your first years
teaching SECONDARY
MATHEMATICS

chapter **eleven**

Classroom Management

While writing this book, Rob also worked with teachers who wanted to improve their teaching. The group met at one of the teacher's schools, planned a lesson together, and then observed Rob or the host teacher teach the lesson. Group members then shared their *perceptions*, looked at student work and other evidence of student learning gathered during the lesson, and evaluated the effectiveness of their plan.

One time the team was to meet at Katy's school. Katy had planned to have the team observe her second-period class. Rob's train was delayed, so the team decided to observe second period and use what they learned to help plan for fourth period. Rob arrived at the beginning of second period and was able to observe the class.

The team debriefed the second-period class and then planned for and observed fourth period. The group considered Katy's goal of getting students to talk to each other about math and discussed what seemed to stand in the way in previous classes. They planned moves to address these issues (such as assigning partners instead of just saying, "talk with a partner," and giving them specific time limits for their talk; telling them explicitly what they should talk about before letting them talk; and praising specific discourse behaviors). Katy asked Rob to teach fourth period. She did not have confidence in her ability to control the class and wanted to see the moves a more experienced teacher would make. Rob agreed.

One of the most interesting things about the day was Katy's reaction to the two lessons the group observed. Katy was a new teacher, having come to this school in the middle of the year and inheriting classes and students that had suffered from poor instruction. She struggled with classroom management, and her students were poorly behaved. She had difficulty getting students to work or to treat each other well enough to have constructive discussions.

After teaching the first lesson, Katy shared her thoughts with the group. She believed that the students were completely out of control. She had seen behaviors that she did not like and felt that the students simply did not respond to her or behave constructively. In contrast, the three observers felt like the students were generally well behaved and were engaged in interesting, important mathematical work. They gave many examples of student thinking that showed understanding and student interactions that demonstrated reasoning and communicating about mathematics. Katy made moves that had a positive effect on students' behavior, and the team could describe both the moves and the effects. Katy's impression of her students' behavior and her ability to manage the class did not align with the impressions of the observers.

When Rob taught the second class, Katy again had interesting reactions. As with the first class, she seemed to concentrate on students who were not behaving how she wanted, and she had difficulty seeing examples of positive behavior and interactions with mathematics that other observers could describe in detail. Katy also ascribed her students' good behavior to things she could not control, such as their mood or the presence of observers. Even though we had plans to address problems and those problems had shown up, and our moves worked precisely as planned, Katy had great difficulty seeing her students' behavior as resulting from teacher actions.

Katy's perceptions of her teaching and her students, and her beliefs about her own effectiveness, are familiar to people who work with new teachers. Certainly her classroom management techniques were not perfect, and she did struggle to influence her students' behavior. However, her failure to attend to positive behaviors and her belief that she could do little to affect her students acted as barriers to her own effectiveness. Her perceptions of her class were more a function of her emotional state (worry that she was a bad teacher) than of an objective view of the evidence. Her penchant for concentrating on negative behaviors gave her a false view of what her class was like, blinded her to the limited success she was having, and made it difficult to build on the positive behaviors that her students did routinely demonstrate.

STOP+REFLECT

>> Is this story familiar?

>> What behavior problems do you consistently face?

>> What positive behaviors do you observe?

>> Do you feel like you can affect your students' behavior?

>> Have a more experienced colleague observe your class.

>> How does what you notice compare to what your colleague notices?

For most new teachers, the greatest emotional job stress is students who misbehave. Student misbehavior can derail plans, interrupt learning, and shatter a new teacher's sense of control and confidence. When confronted with undesirable behavior, you naturally want to react to it effectively. Although reacting well is important, effective teachers prevent undesirable behavior from occurring in the first place. This is why other chapters have devoted so much time to describing how you can set up routines and patterns of interaction that support mathematical learning. The best classroom managers spend much more time creating routines and establishing norms (see chapter 5) and selecting and enacting engaging, appropriate tasks during lessons (see chapters 6–8) than they do reacting to bad behavior. The most effective classroom management strategy is to engage students in learning mathematics through interesting and challenging work designed so that they can succeed. Students engaged in intellectual work have little need to be disruptive.

Even if you establish positive interactions and choose engaging tasks, you will face students who do not behave the way you would like. You will have to decide how to react. This chapter will help you develop strategies to react in the moment and, more important, attitudes and ways to think about misbehavior that will help reduce unproductive conflict, minimize emotional stress, and help you improve your teaching.

MIDDLE AND HIGH SCHOOL STUDENTS NATURALLY PUSH BOUNDARIES

Even if you plan effectively and create clear routines and norms for behavior, students will not always act exactly as you wish. Preteens and teenagers are at a developmental stage where they routinely push against behavioral boundaries. They are trying to figure out who they are, how much power they have, and what boundaries are flexible. This does not mean that misbehavior is OK. But you will have to work to establish expectations and accountability over time, and students will test your boundaries. Their testing is not a personal indictment of you. They are, in a sense, doing their developmental job. Once you know this, you can be better prepared to deal with it and can design and enact strategies that meet them where they are.

STUDENT BEHAVIOR AND TEACHER ACTIONS CREATE A CYCLE OF INTERACTION

One way to think about classroom management is to see teachers and students engaged in a cycle of interactions around behavior: A student action prompts a teacher response, which prompts a student response, in turn prompting another teacher response, and so on. In this cycle, student–teacher interactions are most prominent, and those interactions focus on negative behaviors (fig. 11.1). Note how the mathematics becomes secondary in this kind of cycle of interaction.

Guiding Principles

>> Middle and high school students naturally push boundaries.

>> Student behavior and teacher actions create a cycle of interaction.

>> Teacher actions affect student behavior.

>> Effective teachers notice the full range of behavior and understanding.

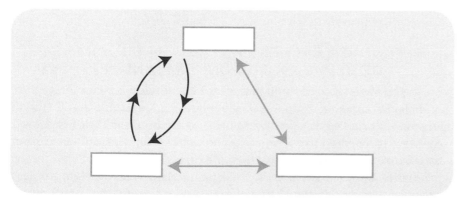

Fig. 11.1. *A student–teacher interaction cycle that displaces mathematics*

Such negative cycles of interaction are unproductive and often upsetting. Engaging in them makes it appear that you and your students are opponents locked in a conflict over authority, control, and respect. And where conflict occurs, the natural tendency is to want to win—but no one wins in such situations. You, as the teacher, want to win to maintain your authority and control. Students want to win to maintain credibility with their peers (and because they are teenagers, testing boundaries). Indeed, this desire from both parties to win generally simply reinforces the cycle and keeps students and teachers stuck in unproductive conflict.

As upsetting as these negative cycles can be, you control how you engage in them. You can initiate contact with students in ways that support their mathematics learning, regardless of their behavior. You also can choose whom you interact with and how. Effective teachers spend their time initiating positive cycles of interaction and minimize time in negative interactions. Through thinking about how you interact with students, and by taking the initiative to engage with students differently, you can break these negative cycles over time, or at least avoid getting trapped in them.

TEACHER ACTIONS AFFECT STUDENT BEHAVIOR

Many beginning teachers, like Katy, feel that they can't control student behavior. Family life, moods, social conditions, school culture, and the popular media all contribute to students' behavior (both positive and negative) and are beyond the control of any one teacher. Nevertheless, teacher actions affect student behavior. Students who struggle to focus in one class can do extremely good work in another. As teachers, we have worked to change what we do, what we say, and how we interact with students. Over time our own students changed how they interact with mathematics, with us, and with each other. Sometimes, like Katy, we could not readily see the effects of our actions. When we moved past our initial perceptions, however, and examined what we did and how students reacted, we learned that we do affect students' positive and negative behaviors.

Not that affecting student behavior is easy. It can be difficult and takes time and effort. But your actions, how you interact with students, and your ability to articulate clear expectations and follow through on them can profoundly affect your students' conduct and the classroom environment. Furthermore, you can learn to affect student behavior; the ability is not some intangible personal gift that only some people are born with. This book explains techniques that we hope will result in well-behaved students who learn effectively.

EFFECTIVE TEACHERS NOTICE THE FULL RANGE
OF BEHAVIOR AND UNDERSTANDINGS

Noticing students who are not doing what they should be doing is important. Many teachers, however, especially new ones, spend much of their energy monitoring what is going wrong but fail to register all that is going well. Many teachers will concentrate on two off-task groups and not register what is going on in the five groups that are on task.

This tendency to attend to the negative poses several problems. First, teachers often get a skewed picture of their students and their classroom, and consistently feel like they and their students are doing a bad job. This negativity does not feel good to teachers or students and contributes to conflict that does not support students to learn mathematics.

Second, attending to the negative can keep teachers from seeing their positive effects on students. Like Katy, we may engage in effective teacher moves that result in good conversations in ten of thirteen student pairs. However, if we notice only the three pairs not having good conversations, we dismiss our teacher moves as ineffective. By attending only to the negative, we risk feeding our belief that we have little effect on students, and we would miss an opportunity to add effective teacher moves to our toolbox.

Third, when we emphasize the negative, we miss opportunities to build on positive ideas and behaviors. When we pay attention to positive behaviors, we can point them out to students and thus build community based on what seems to be organic behavior stemming from the students themselves. (This move is called "recognize and reinforce." See chapter 5 for more about this move and about building a learning community in your classroom.) If we tell students only what not to do, they have few models for what they should do.

STOP+ REFLECT

>> Think of a time when you and a student were trapped in a conflict. What was the interaction like? What were you and the student talking about? What would you have preferred to be talking or interacting about?

>> What do you notice and look for as you teach? Do you spend more time noticing negative behaviors than noticing positive behaviors?

Habits of Practice

>> **Maintain a balanced focus of attention.**

>> **Establish positive interactions.**

>> **Establish the primacy of mathematics.**

>> **Build on your students' strengths.**

>> **Establish consistent expectations and accountability.**

MAINTAIN A BALANCED FOCUS OF ATTENTION

Teaching involves paying attention to many things. Beginning teachers often attend to only a narrow range of things during lessons. For example, they may pay too much attention to an individual student to monitor his behavior or to support his learning. In paying attention to that one student, they may not notice other students' off-task behavior or may fail to register other students' interesting and important mathematical thinking. Teachers may be especially attentive to student errors; in noticing only the errors, they may lose opportunities to build on interesting and important mathematical ideas that other students voice. Effective teachers work to balance their attention to register a range of students and behaviors. Effective teachers seek to balance how much attention they pay (1) to individual students versus the whole group and (2) to negative versus positive behaviors.

Attending to individual students versus the whole group

Although supporting and responding to individual students is important, also be aware of the group at large. This is especially true at the beginning of a semester when you are trying to support students in meeting your expectations for how they treat each other and how they interact with the mathematics. For example, experienced teachers often talk of an ability to "scan the room"—to look at the class as a whole to assess how effectively students are working and whether specific groups may need redirection or the class as a whole may need more support. But do not let scanning the room keep you from paying attention to individual students. Consider two strategies to balance your attention to the whole group while working with individuals or small groups:

1 Position yourself so that the front of your body faces most of your students. If you are talking with a small group on one side of the classroom, position yourself on the side of the group so that your back is to the wall. That way you can look up quickly and see the whole room. If you are talking with an individual in the middle of the classroom, squat down instead of bending. Squatting to get to the students' level allows you to use your feet as pivot points so that you can quickly and easily turn your body to scan the classroom.

2 Be aware of how much time you spend with a small group or individual. Sometimes teachers spend a lot of time with a particular individual or small group and do not make it around to others in the class who may need support. If you find yourself spending a lot of time with a small group, for example, give them a small task to accomplish and tell them that you will return on your next pass around the room. If you are spending a lot of time with one individual who needs extra support, pairing that individual with a classmate who can help would both support his or her learning needs and free you up to attend to others.

Attending to positive versus negative behavior

New teachers, especially, notice poor behavior much more readily than positive behavior. Although you must be on the lookout for disruptive and dangerous behavior, strive to find examples of positive behaviors and to name them publicly and explicitly. Doing so sets a positive tone for the class as a whole. It also helps you and your students get explicit and specific images of how people in your class should act. To the extent that the positive behaviors that you attend to are mathematical (representing, communicating, reasoning, solving problems, and making connections), it also allows you to concentrate on mathematics rather than social interactions.

ESTABLISH A POSITIVE TONE OF INTERACTION

When teachers and students interact positively, students are more likely to feel known, respected, and empowered. Over time this feeling makes students feel much safer and much less likely to confront you over a perceived slight or unfairness. Use the following strategies to ensure a respectful, humanizing tone when interacting with students.

Address students by name and use "please" and "thank you"

When you use students' names, you signal that you know them and notice what they do, say, and think. Using their names is a powerful deterrent to misbehavior and a powerful incentive to engage in mathematical discourse. It also signals respect and civility that helps set a tone for the class. Consistently using "please" and "thank you" also shows that you respect your students as people. Somewhat surprisingly, teenagers react positively to simple courtesies.

Get down to the students' level (physically)

When addressing an individual student, first move to where the student sits and then get down at her level, by kneeling or bending over, so that your faces are on the same horizontal plane and you are not physically talking down to her. By speaking with students on the same physical level, you reduce the emphasis on the power relationship. If you do not assert your power publicly and physically, they will feel less compulsion to resist your power. Being on the same physical level also creates a more welcoming space for students to share mathematical thinking or converse about the mathematics.

Engage in specific praise both publicly and privately

Praising students for specific behaviors or mathematical ideas is a powerful way to indicate that you notice and value what they do and how they think. Public praise, in which you describe positive behaviors or ideas that you saw and heard, also models the behaviors you want for students. Give specific praise, so that students know what kinds of things you want to see. You could say things like, "I liked the way that Hailey's group all waited until Jim was done thinking on his own before they started talking. That really gave Jim a chance to figure some important things out," or "I liked the way that in Remy's group they were all looking at each others' papers and pointing at the things they were talking about." This praise tells students much more than "I really liked the way you were working in groups."

Using public praise effectively takes some thought. For example, if students are generally working well, do not interrupt them to praise particular students; wait until the end of the activity. If students are generally not working well, specific praise during the activity can give them a better sense of what they should be doing. However, overusing public praise will diminish its impact on student behavior. Finding the "just right" line between too much and too little public praise may take some practice for beginning teachers. You can enlist your mentor to help you by making public praise the focus of a series of observations.

Praising in private also serves important goals. First, it helps you foster a positive relationship with individual students. Second, early in the school year if you ask individual students to join you for a minute in the hall and praise their work, your students will learn that being asked into the hall is not a punishment. This will make it easier to take students into the hall if you need to have difficult conversations later. You can also praise individual students who struggle with content or behavior. Establishing a positive tone of interaction positions you as an ally and makes it less likely that they will engage in negative cycles of interaction later.

Have difficult conversations in private, not public

Often, teachers discipline students from across the room, using their "teacher voice." Doing so not only distracts other students but also makes the offending student more likely to react poorly. If you need to address a student's misbehavior, do so individually. When speaking to students one on one, move next to them, talk quietly, get down at their level, and use their name (remember how Ms. Barker, in the chapter 1 vignette, interacted with Maggie about being tardy). De-escalating conflict signals both strength and caring. By keeping the conversation private, you maintain control. Other students will notice that you respond to behavior calmly and in ways that do not upset the flow of the classroom.

Interact with students outside class

When students feel that you really know them, they are much more likely to behave well. Noticing which students are involved in (or also attending) school events such as plays, concerts, and games, and then saying something to them, shows that you know who they are and pay attention to what they do.

ESTABLISH THE PRIMACY OF MATHEMATICS

Too often, most talk between teachers and students is about behavior, not mathematics. Interacting around negative behavior often locks students and teachers into negative cycles of interaction. The best way to avoid this trap is to respond to student misbehavior by asking them about their mathematical thinking. Some teachers call this "redirecting," because you redirect students' attention to the task at hand. For example, if you notice that a group of students is off task, walk over to the group and ask something like, "What problem are you on?" or "What have you done so far?" or "How are you thinking about this problem?" Redirecting their attention to the mathematics says, "I know that you have not been doing what you're supposed to be doing, and I want you to get back to work," thus stopping a negative cycle of interaction before it can begin.

When you ask the question that redirects their attention back to the mathematics, students may not be able to answer it (because they have not been on task). If that happens, tell them that you will be back in a minute or two to see what they are thinking. Then make sure that you get back and ask them again. If they respond that they do not know what to do (a common response), counter by asking them what they do know and understand about the problem.

Responding to low-level misbehavior by asking students about their mathematical thinking is your most powerful tool to shape their behavior and create a positive intellectual environment. It accomplishes several important goals at once: It tells students that the focus of the class is mathematics. It asserts your interest in their thinking and establishes that your relationship is based on their mathematical thinking, not their behavioral compliance. Finally, it gives you something positive to do when facing a potentially difficult emotional situation.

BUILD ON YOUR STUDENTS' STRENGTHS

In every math class, many students are doing exactly what you want: learning mathematics. These students rarely misbehave or disrupt class. Paying attention to these students' positive behaviors and using them to build a more positive culture is a powerful way to create a culture of positive interactions around mathematics. Chapter 5 presented several strategies to establish and maintain a positive learning community in your classroom. Let's revisit one in light of building on your students' strengths (recognize and reinforce) and then consider a strategy to use in your class (identify and use natural leaders).

Recognize and reinforce

Imagine that you have your students working in groups of four for the first time. You begin their work time by circulating around the room and noticing how they are working together. Most groups are having a difficult time getting down to work. Some students are chatting about nonmathematical things. Other students are working individually and not talking to other members of their group at all. However, in one group, students are working in the way that you envisioned. The students started by reading the problem and then one student asked, "What are we supposed to be finding out here?" Another member then explained what she thought the problem was asking and then asked the questioner whether he understood. Others members were looking at the speaker and nodding their heads or looking back at the problem.

For managing behavior, this situation presents the perfect opportunity to "recognize and reinforce" (Lemov 2010). Instead of telling groups that were not working well to get to work, stop the whole class and describe what the functioning group was doing well. Ask for your students' attention and, once they are quiet, say something like, "I really like how one group started with everyone reading the question, and then one person in the group identified something he did not understand about the problem and asked a question. After he asked the question, one of his group members answered it and everyone else was looking at the speaker, checking whether they understood the problem in the same way. When you get back to work in your groups, I would like all group members to make sure that they understand what the problem is asking or come up with a question to ask their group. I will be walking around listening for good questions." (Chapter 5 gives more information about this strategy.)

Identify and use natural leaders

Natural leaders emerge in most groups of people, including classrooms. Natural leaders can have great influence on other members of the group. They often set the tone of group interactions, and others look to them for cues of what to do, how to act, and what to think. As early as possible, figure out who the natural leaders in your classes are. (These leaders may not be model students. Natural leaders can have a positive or negative influence on others.)

Then figure out ways to have positive interactions with the natural leaders and to empower them to lead positively in your class. Options include giving them some important responsibility, or highlighting an answer that they give, or mentioning that you saw them play soccer over the weekend. This does not mean that you favor these students or have different behavioral expectations for them. Rather, it means that you see them as a resource to create a positive climate in your class. If you can get natural leaders to act in ways that you want, other students will follow more easily. At the beginning of a semester, when you choose students to hold up as examples of positive behavior, find opportunities to notice the natural leaders. Their social power will become an asset for you rather than a liability.

MAINTAIN CONSISTENT, CLEAR EXPECTATIONS AND ACCOUNTABILITY

Remember, adolescents often react to your expectations by pushing against them. They are figuring out that things are not always as they seem and that adults may not always mean what they say. They need to learn to what extent you actually mean, and will follow through on, what you tell them. Let students know clearly, consistently, and repeatedly what your expectations are and that you will hold them accountable for those expectations.

Although this endeavor sounds simple, in practice it is actually quite subtle. Beginning teachers, as well as more experienced teachers, often undermine the very expectations they try to set. By adopting several relatively simple moves, you can become clearer and more consistent, and avoid many of the ways that new teachers typically undercut their own authority. Let's revisit moves from chapter 5 in light of managing classroom behavior.

Stand still and do not talk over students

Giving directions while you and your students are distracted by other things can undermine your authority. Giving directions while handing out papers or while your students are still unpacking their backpacks or chatting about the weekend sends the message that your directions are not that important. You will have to repeat directions, having inadvertently taught students that they do not have to listen the first time. Stand still when telling students what to do—do not do anything else—and wait until the students are also not doing anything else. Though it may take some time, the effort is worthwhile and shows that you expect students to listen to and follow your directions.

Give directions in multiple ways and clarify

Even if you stand still and wait for students to be attentive, they may not understand your directions the first time. Giving directions in several different ways (on the board, written on an assignment, orally) makes students more likely to understand without your having to repeat yourself. If you give written directions as well as oral ones, and students request that you repeat your directions, simply direct them to look at the board or their activity sheet.

Often, students may not follow directions because they are not clear about what to do. Clarifying your directions will help. You could say (standing still and after getting their attention), "Maybe I wasn't clear enough. When I said, 'Take out your homework and go over it with your partner,' I meant that you should have your homework paper on your desk and you should begin by comparing your answers to your partner's. I should be seeing you looking and pointing at your partner's paper, and I should be hearing things like, 'I got a different answer for number 6,' or 'How did you do number 13? I didn't get that one.'" Clarifying directions for the whole class is also a powerful way to address specific students who are not following directions without putting those students on the spot or creating a conflict.

Align words with actions

Acting in ways that do not align with what you say can also undermine your authority. If you say that doing mathematics is the focus of class, but you begin class by asking students about their weekend or by telling a story about your childhood, you have undermined your own message. You have shown that talking about other things in math class is OK. Similarly, if you say that you expect students to begin working when the bell rings, but you are talking with a student or organizing papers when the bell rings, you indicate that you are not ready to pay attention to their work and that they, too, can take a while to get started. You need to not only "talk the talk" but also "walk the walk." Teenagers are particularly sensitive to when adults' words and actions do not align. Consistently check to make sure your words and actions are not in conflict.

Address obvious misbehavior directly and consistently

Sometimes a student is simply behaving badly. Although you want to concentrate on positive behaviors, you do need to address obvious, nontrivial misbehavior. Letting it go will simply allow students to think that you are not noticing and that you do not mean it when you tell them what is not allowed.

When addressing misbehavior, keep the conversation quiet and private. State what they should be doing, and move the conversation away from behavior as quickly as possible. By asking them what they have done on the math problem, for instance, you address their misbehavior indirectly. You can also walk away once you correct their behavior, allowing them a little time to comply. By saying you will be back in a minute to see how they are doing, you walk away from conflict but keep them accountable.

> ## STOP+ REFLECT
>
> » Think of how you give directions to your students. Do you have to repeat them? What strategies from this section could begin to solve that problem?
>
> » Do your actions and words conflict in other ways? Do you send mixed messages about goals and expectations? How? How can you become more consistent?
>
> » Try asking off-task students about their mathematical thinking for a week. What happens to their behavior? What happens to what you notice? How does this move affect the way you feel while teaching?
>
> » Try noticing positive behaviors and commenting specifically on them at least once in each class. Does doing so affect student behavior or what you notice and feel while teaching?

WHAT IF ALL THIS DOES NOT WORK?

Certainly, there will be times when none of these strategies affect students' misbehavior or when dangerous, threatening student misbehavior requires an immediate, forceful response. For example, you should have a response to consistent misbehavior that is a natural consequence of the behavior and serves to correct it with minimal punishment. If a student remains off task by chatting with her neighbor, even after you have asked her several times what problem she is on and directed her to the mathematics, a natural consequence could be that she changes her seat. Work to develop consequences that are closely connected to different misbehaviors and then apply those consequences consistently.

Sometimes you may need to remove disruptive students from the classroom. Doing so gives them and you time to calm down. Follow these suggestions to increase the likelihood of a positive outcome for both you and your students.

You are in control of the conversation with the student in the hallway. Such conversations have only two goals: (1) you clearly state your behavioral expectation, and (2) the student decides whether he or she can come back into the class and meet that expectation. Do not let the conversation shift to whether you are fair or whether the student broke a rule—focus only on the goals. Save longer conversations about what went on for later. If the student is not ready to have the conversation on your terms, he or she may not return to class.

Attempting to remove a student from class may force a conflict. You can call for support from administration before you ask the student to leave, and have an administrator present when you speak with the student.

Finally, know your school's policy about removing students and getting help from others when serious behavioral issues arise. In some schools, administrators frown on requests for help with student behavior, and you will not be able to call on them often for support. In other schools, administrators work hard to support teachers in this way. Often, the presence of a higher authority will compel the student to have the kind of positive interaction that you seek. Find out from more experienced colleagues what the norms are in your school and strategize with them about ways to briefly remove a student from class.

CONCLUSION

In the opening section of this book we described teaching as managing interactions between students, content, and teacher. When facing student misbehavior, return to this framework—both to understand how misbehavior can lead teachers and students astray, and to figure out how to respond in ways that support students in learning mathematics.

Misbehavior often leads to negative cycles of interaction that distract students and teachers from the primary focus of mathematics classrooms: solving problems, reasoning, representing, communicating, and making connections. Classroom management seeks to avoid those negative cycles when possible and to break them once they have started. The moves here should help you control your interaction with students to avoid a negative cycle of conflict and control, as well as establish the primacy of students working to make sense of mathematics and your own role in supporting them.

chapter twelve

Teaching Struggling Students

Before taking Ms. Bonham's class, Maria dreaded math class. Starting in third grade, where she had struggled to learn her times tables, she fell further and further behind. She squeaked by somehow, year after year, but how was she supposed to understand this year's math when she didn't understand it last year or the year before that? She always worried that the teacher would call on her and that the class would discover how stupid she was in math. She worked to be as invisible as possible.

Somehow, Ms. Bonham's class was different. They worked on more interesting problems and dealt with things that Maria understood and had experienced. She still struggled sometimes, but she had time to relate what she knew about the situations in the problems to the solutions. Even if she could not solve the problems right away, she got time to understand what the problems were. She had begun to ask questions in her group, and some members told her that her questions helped them figure things out. In Ms. Bonham's class, asking a question was not a sign of stupidity; it was an important part of being good at math.

For the first time, Maria felt like she could succeed in math class—which was funny, because she still struggled with her times tables and fractions. But she also thought that her work on problems would pay off, even if it took a long time. Sometimes, even though she still had a hard time with all the x's and y's, the students who

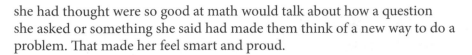

she had thought were so good at math would talk about how a question she asked or something she said had made them think of a new way to do a problem. That made her feel smart and proud.

* * *

As with all teachers, some students will struggle to succeed in your class. You may think that these students simply lack some essential set of skills or are not motivated to learn. And yet some teachers, like Ms. Bonham, are better at teaching struggling students than other teachers. How do they do it? How do they teach statistics to students who cannot add fractions? How do they teach geometry to students who cannot solve simple equations? How do they teach algebra to students who seem to hate school?

To teach struggling students, let's redefine the "problem" of struggling students into one that we have more power to solve: Concentrate on what they can do over what they cannot. Concentrate on making content more accessible. Finally, define success more broadly so that a wider range of students can succeed.

The challenges of teaching struggling students are the same as for teaching all students—namely, how to create opportunities for students to reason, represent, solve problems, communicate, and make connections in the context of meaningful mathematics, and how to remove barriers that make it difficult for them to do so. Ms. Bonham created a classroom where Maria's deficiencies did not block access to important mathematics or prevent making sense of it. This chapter will help you do that for your struggling students.

STOP+ REFLECT

Think about Maria's story. Now think about a student you teach who does poorly. How do this student's prior experiences compare to Maria's experiences in math classes?

Guiding Principles

>> All students can make sense of mathematics with connected knowledge.

>> Identify barriers to learning.

>> Adjust your instruction.

>> Teaching well for struggling students = teaching well for everyone.

ALL STUDENTS CAN MAKE SENSE OF MATHEMATICS WITH CONNECTED KNOWLEDGE

Many Americans believe that, beyond simple arithmetic, mathematics is a difficult subject that fewer and fewer people understand as they progress through school. From that belief comes the related belief that teaching for understanding is especially problematic for struggling students. We emphatically disagree. For students who struggle, having the opportunity to build connected mathematical knowledge is especially important because simple rote memory of meaningless procedures is precisely what they often find so difficult to achieve.

Connected mathematical knowledge is more robust and effective for all students. Procedures alone, divorced from larger conceptual understandings, are harder for students to retain and apply in new situations—especially for many students with a history of failure in school mathematics. Many have difficulties with memory and retrieval. Mathematical work that depends solely on memorizing rules and mastering procedures without greater conceptual understandings plays to their weaknesses and deprives them of powerful tools to overcome or compensate for some of their deficits in memory and organization. Although gaining connected mathematical knowledge takes effort, once it is gained it is more secure and takes considerably less effort to retain and use.

Math knowledge is not just the result of natural talent and ability, which no one can control. Although some students have more natural talent and ability in mathematics, well-directed effort is the main ingredient in success. Students control such effort, and teachers can encourage and support it. With enough effort on the right task and in the right environment, all students (except those with severe cognitive disabilities) can reason, represent, communicate, solve problems, and make connections in mathematics.

IDENTIFY BARRIERS TO LEARNING

You can think about struggling students as having barriers that inhibit productive engagement with mathematics. Though you can adjust your instruction to remove barriers that are not necessary and to help students negotiate unavoidable barriers, you first need to understand and recognize the barriers to productive engagement that students experience.

Three basic types of barriers block students' engagement with mathematics:

1 Barriers of skill and knowledge

2 Emotional barriers

3 Physical barriers

In barriers of skill and knowledge, students may lack specific procedural fluency. They may not know how to solve simple algebraic equations or how to operate on negative numbers. Students might lack mathematical understanding, such as not understanding the meaning of division or the relationship between an equation and a graph. Students could also lack specific social skills, such as listening carefully to a peer or responding to criticism. Students could lack specific experiences, such as understanding the context of a problem. Or they could lack other academic skills that may affect their performance in math class, such as having reading difficulty or not understanding spoken English well.

In some emotional barriers, students may struggle to feel engaged or motivated in math class. They may resist group participation or may continually push up against your authority. Students may feel tremendous anxiety in the face of assessments or having to share their work publicly. They may simply not see the usefulness or purpose of working to learn math.

With physical barriers, students may have difficulty seeing or hearing or may have trouble sitting still for extended periods. Whatever their barriers may be, getting to know your students includes finding out what barriers they may have experienced in math classes and how to overcome them.

ADJUST YOUR INSTRUCTION

When students struggle, adults often assume that the students need to change—to be more motivated or get better at basic math skills. A more productive way of thinking about struggling students is to consider their struggle as a problem of instruction: what teachers are currently doing is not working for struggling students. We can best support struggling

STOP+ REFLECT

>> Think of students in your classes who are not succeeding. What do you think the problem is? To what extent have you determined that the problem is in them?

>> Think about how the instruction that they receive may not work well for them. How might you change that instruction to support them without making the math trivial or too easy?

students by making what we are doing more effective. Such an approach, though difficult and challenging, empowers teachers: we can do something to help struggling students. This approach also helps us avoid blaming struggling students for their own failures, a dynamic that ultimately causes resentment and disengagement.

TEACHING WELL FOR STRUGGLING STUDENTS = TEACHING WELL FOR EVERYONE

Although some students have cognitive issues that require special interventions, most strategies in this chapter help all students, struggling or not, to engage productively with mathematics. For example, you might supply calculators so that students who struggle with simple computation can concentrate on the structure of mathematical problems. This practice actually helps all students move beyond an obsession with calculation and can help them attend more explicitly to, for example, structural features of equations and graphs or the relationship between two variables when looking at correlations in statistics.

Habits of Practice

>> Identify barriers to learning mathematics.

>> Remove unnecessary prerequisites for learning goals.

>> Remove or alleviate social barriers to learning.

>> Expand the definition of, and avenues to, success.

>> Teach metacognition.

>> Find ways to remediate.

IDENTIFY BARRIERS TO LEARNING MATHEMATICS

Thinking about students' struggles as the result of barriers to engaging with math allows you to support students by removing unnecessary barriers and by helping them negotiate unavoidable ones. However, you first need to identify the barriers that your students face. Consider the following strategies when identifying students' barriers to learning mathematics.

Research students' "typical" struggles in mathematics

Much research addresses how and why students struggle in school and in mathematics in particular. Reading this research will help you know what to look for when students are not achieving. (See the Recommended Resources section at the end of this book.)

Ask experienced colleagues

Your colleagues will have a wealth of knowledge about what difficulties students might have in math class. Find colleagues who have successfully taught struggling students. Ask them about students' barriers to learning and strategies to overcome them. Teachers who have taught your students before will have firsthand information about struggles and about strategies to help students overcome them.

Consult curriculum materials

Many curriculum materials have extensive teacher notes that discuss student thinking and what things students may struggle with. Studying these resources will help you understand typical barriers to student learning.

Consult school records

Looking at past reports of your students, especially special education students who have individualized education plans, will yield important information about their struggles. You can then adapt your instruction accordingly to compensate for these challenges.

Talk to students and their parents/guardians

To gain information about students' barriers to learning, talk about their struggles with them and with their parents/guardians. Asking them what keeps them from learning, and what helps them learn, will give you insights about what they may need from you. (See chapter 15 for ways to gather information from parents or guardians.)

Observe and reflect

Perhaps the best way to identify barriers is to observe how students interact with each other and with the mathematics in your classroom. Doing so will yield the most information about individual students and their needs. In addition to your regular classroom observations while teaching, have a colleague observe students whom you are especially interested in learning about, or videotape your class and attend to specific students while watching the tape.

REMOVE UNNECESSARY PREREQUISITES FOR LEARNING GOALS

Some mathematical skills or knowledge become unnecessary barriers to students' access to important mathematics. One widespread barrier is procedural knowledge with no connection to a lesson's learning goals. For example, the goal of your lesson may be that students understand the meaning of the solution to an algebraic equation (the value that when substituted for the unknown will make the equation true). If you begin class

> ### Working with Special Education Teachers
>
> Some barriers to learning stem from cognitive difficulties. Without specific knowledge of learning disabilities, identifying and working with students who have cognitive disabilities is difficult. Trained special education teachers can help you understand these barriers; these teachers have expertise both in what barriers students have and in how to adapt instruction for different learning disabilities.
>
> However, special education teachers may not have expertise in what it means to learn and know mathematics with understanding. Some special education teachers see mathematics as rules and procedures to be memorized, with strategies geared mostly to that end. When working with special education teachers, be clear about what you want students to be able to do and understand. The clearer you can be about your goals, the more special education teachers will be able to help you meet them.

with an example like $(2/3)x + 5 = 19$, students who struggle with operations on fractions will have much less access to your mathematical goal, solely because of the numbers involved. Yet being good with fractions is not necessary to understand the meaning of the solution to a linear equation.

Similarly, in statistics, standard deviation is an important and useful idea, but computing it can be tedious and difficult for students. If your mathematical goal for students to reason about how "typical" a specific occurrence is (say, a batter hitting 50 home runs in a major-league baseball season or an American adult female standing over 6 feet tall), calculating the standard deviation is not necessary. Just knowing the standard deviation of a set of data about the occurrence is sufficient, because the point is to reason using the standard deviation.

In the next few sections, consider the following strategies to remove unnecessary prerequisites to your learning goals.

Change the numbers in the problem

Changing the numbers in a problem can often reduce procedural demands while preserving the mathematical structure. Making numbers friendlier often allows all students to see relationships more clearly and to concentrate on connections between mathematical ideas rather than on the calculations. For example, if a problem asks how "typical" it is for a man to be 191.3 cm tall if the mean is 178.3 and the standard deviation is 11.3, the mathematical reasoning is the same if you make the height 195 cm, the mean 180, and the standard deviation 10.

Give students access to technology

Letting students use technology to simplify calculations also removes unnecessary procedural barriers. Such technology can include hardware (graphing calculators, tablet computers), software, and Web-based activities to enhance learning.

Chapter 15 has more information about using technology to support learning.

Give students formulas and definitions

If you want students to reason about the relationship between surface area and volume, for example, giving them the formulas for surface area and volume allows them to engage in the thinking that you want them to do. Having formulas and definitions may make memorizing unnecessary and allow students to engage in the problem—to make important decisions, for example, that involve reasoning and justification. If you have a shape made up of several smaller shapes, and you want students to find the area of the larger shape, students still must figure out what the smaller shapes are and how they fit together. Having access to the formulas for area does not diminish the problem's level of mathematical thinking.

REMOVE OR ALLEVIATE SOCIAL BARRIERS TO LEARNING

Your students may face barriers to learning that have nothing to do with math. Some students may have physical disabilities that prevent engaging in mathematics. Consider these strategies to remove or alleviate nonmathematical barriers to learning.

Accommodate special needs

For a student with a physical disability, think about and adapt aspects of your instruction that may obstruct his or her learning. For a student with a sight disability, you may need to adjust your practice of using different chalk or whiteboard marker colors to indicate important mathematical content. Or, for a student with a hearing disability who reads lips, be aware of any tendencies you have to speak while facing the board. (Remember advice from earlier chapters to stand in one place and not do other things while speaking to your students.) Students with difficulty seeing or hearing may need to sit near the front. You can give students with difficulty sitting for long periods opportunities to stand up and move around (such as by handing out papers).

Establish effective classroom norms

Other techniques to remove nonmathematical barriers to learning are intimately connected to envisioning and creating norms to support students in reasoning, representing, communicating, solving problems, and making connections (see chapter 5). Establishing effective norms in your class will support students who struggle with many of these processes. For example, you can support students who hesitate to share their thinking by fostering a classroom culture that encourages and values student thinking.

Make strategic decisions about student seating

Making strategic decisions about where students should sit and whom they should work with can alleviate many social barriers. If students cannot stay on task with a distracting friend nearby, seat them far apart. If a student who traditionally struggles in mathematics habitually defers to more accomplished peers, consider grouping that student with others who have struggled so that they all are more likely to participate. (See chapter 8 for more on student groups.)

Remove contextual barriers to access

Problems of context represent another nonmathematical barrier to learning. If students are learning mathematics by solving problems but the context is unfamiliar, then the context could become a barrier rather than a support. Imagine introducing linear equations to children in New York City with the following problem:

> Frank has a sawmill. His sawmill can produce 142,000 board feet of lumber in a day, which he stores in his lumberyard. His lumberyard has room for 994,000 board feet of lumber, and right now 284,000 board feet are stored there. How many more days can he operate his sawmill before he needs the trucking company to come deliver his lumber to his buyers?

The context of this problem would mystify many New York City middle school students. They probably will not know what board feet are and will have no experience with trucking companies and buyers or with storing things in yards. They may have limited experience with such large numbers even in realistic contexts. Imagine giving, instead, this problem:

> Barry owns a café. He knows that on Wednesday mornings he usually sells about 360 bagels. He also knows that he can make 48 bagels in a batch. At 6 a.m. he has made 108 bagels. How many more batches of bagels will Barry have to make to have enough for his customers?

This context is much more familiar for many New York City schoolchildren. They have gone to bagel stores, have seen bakers putting bagels in the oven and taking them out. They have watched bakers bringing fresh bagels to the front of the store and replenishing depleted stocks. This context offers scaffolding for students so that they can solve the problem. The mathematics is the same, but changing the context removed unnecessary barriers.

When working with struggling students, use familiar contexts that will highlight the mathematics. Look at the tasks from your curriculum and make sure that the contexts make sense to your struggling students. If not, change the context so that students can access the mathematics of the problem with more ease.

* * *

Identifying and removing barriers to learning can be subtle work and depends on your goals for students' learning. Sometimes you may want students to struggle by identifying familiar mathematical structures or patterns in unfamiliar contexts. Then the lumberyard problem would be good to use with students in any urban center. The point of that problem would be having students realize that the linear structure was similar to the structure in the bagel shop problem, even though they did not know the context well. Similarly, you may want students to engage in procedural practice and see the connection between procedures and greater ideas. For example, when having students graph a linear equation by creating a table of x and y values and then plotting points, you may want them to solve for y in terms of x several times and have them think about what is changing and why. In this case, doing the procedure may take time, but it is intimately connected to the mathematical connections you want them to make. So even if students struggle with the procedure, you do not want to eliminate it because it is an essential element of the mathematics.

EXPAND THE DEFINITION OF, AND AVENUES TO, SUCCESS

When students have more ways to succeed, more students will succeed (Boaler and Staples 2008). Americans have traditionally defined mathematical success in narrow terms. Being good in school mathematics has meant, almost exclusively, being able to perform increasingly complex procedures quickly and accurately. This paradigm not only fails to acknowledge and value important mathematical goals and processes but also creates artificial barriers to success. Consider these strategies to redefine what success means for your class.

> **STOP+REFLECT**
>
> Think of a mathematics topic you will soon teach. Identify a procedural or contextual barrier not connected to the learning goal. How can you remove that barrier without changing students' access to the mathematics?

Identify skills that indicate and lead to success

Expanding the definition of success helps all students make progress; it gives them things to do, rather than ascribing their struggles to simple lack of ability over which they have no control. One approach is to identify a wider set of skills and dispositions that constitute mathematical achievement and knowledge. Reasoning and proving, representing, communicating, solving problems, and making connections is a good place to start. Chapter 2 (p. 16) described success built around students' abilities to engage in these five mathematical processes. Revisit that list and consider how adopting this characterization of success will support students who traditionally have struggled in mathematics.

Assign tasks requiring broad skills and prior knowledge

If all your tasks require speedy and accurate procedural knowledge, you will never convince your students that they can be good in math in many ways. Give tasks that require students to solve problems by reasoning, communicating, connecting, and representing. (Chapter 6 describes how to choose and adapt tasks for various purposes.)

Praise effort and ability

When children are praised only for their ability, they see failure as evidence of a lack of talent and they avoid challenging situations (Mueller and Dweck 1998). When students are also praised for their effort, they are much more likely to see failure as a temporary setback that more effort can overcome—and as an essential stage of learning. They are much more likely to seek out and engage in challenging activities and subsequently have the opportunity to learn more. So instead of saying, "Look at how smart you are.

You solved this problem without my telling you what to do," you could say, "I am impressed with how many different methods you tried when solving this problem. You really stuck with it for a long time, and that helped you finally get an answer."

Assign status to struggling students

Make sure that struggling students are seen as competent and smart in your class. Look for important and interesting thinking by struggling students, and publicly acknowledge those—revoicing if necessary—so that everyone can see these important contributions and good ideas. Cohen and colleagues (1999) call this assigning status: an important aspect of making sure that all students can engage in discourse and make sense of mathematics.

Ask, rehearse, call on

For struggling students (or any students) who are reluctant to share their thinking in front of others, tell them ahead of time that you will ask them to share. You can rehearse what they might say, in their small group, letting groupmates give suggestions or encouragement. Then you can call on them to share their thinking. Rehearsal allows shy students or those with little confidence to be more sure of success in what feels like a risky activity.

TEACH METACOGNITION

One key to effective learning with understanding is metacognition: monitoring one's own understanding and sense making (Bransford, Brown, and Cocking 2000). Successful mathematics students, and experts in any domain, can assess how well they understand something and can identify problems they are having and ask questions. All students should learn this concept, and you can build components into assignments to foster metacognition.

Have students think about their understanding and formulate questions

While students work on problems, periodically stop their work and ask them to evaluate how well they understand the mathematics. Ask them to identify the parts they understand and the parts that they do not, as well as when they began experiencing difficulty. Having them then create questions to address their areas of misunderstanding and weakness will help them improve their ability to communicate about mathematics and can lead to beginning to understand on their own. A great irony of mathematical thinking is that getting clear about what the question is often makes the answer much more evident.

Have students evaluate their own performance

Creating ways for students to think about and communicate their confidence in their thinking helps them learn to monitor their understanding. Ultimately this process can show them that understanding is the goal of learning. Doing this publicly shows struggling students that successful students are not necessarily brilliant, but rather are conscious of their own understanding and work hard to get support when they do not understand.

This, in turn, can demystify mathematical success and build a sense that math is something that they can succeed in with enough properly directed effort.

Used properly, this device can decrease emphasis on right answers as the sole criterion for mathematical success. Students can learn that getting clearer about what they do not know, instead of simply knowing everything, is a hallmark of good mathematical thinking.

Have students explain strategies to get "unstuck"

Asking students to describe what they do when they initially cannot do a problem reinforces that you expect them to struggle and that you believe they can persist and succeed. It also forces students to think about how they can persist through struggle and can reinforce strategies you discussed in class, such as reviewing notes, asking a friend, and skipping the problem and returning to it later. When successful students model this habit of thinking, struggling students can gain strategies to use when having difficulties. Displaying posters of strategies that students commonly use when stuck can help all students who encounter confusion or difficulty.

FIND WAYS TO REMEDIATE

Thus far, these suggestions to have been ways to support struggling students socially and emotionally or ways to work around their mathematical weaknesses. They do not address a central dilemma of teaching middle and secondary school mathematics: You may have students who lack essential skills and knowledge needed to succeed in middle or high school mathematics. Yet you do not have the time or support to teach them what they should have already known. How can you support them to learn math they should already know, without breaking too much from the curriculum you need to teach them? Though this question has no easy answers, we have two suggestions to help students who have holes in their mathematical understandings.

Use games

Playing number games can help students who need remediation with numbers and mathematical ideas, especially if the players explicitly attend to their thinking processes (metacognition) and to the numerical relationships within the games themselves. Many effective math games can be played without much planning and for as little as a minute or two. They are ideal to fill in downtime, such as the last five minutes of class (not enough to introduce a new problem) or the time waiting for a last group to finish making their poster. Many games target fraction concepts, basic number sense, and calculation shortcuts that will give students new ways to develop facility with number and operations. Talking about strategies for these games will also help students develop skills in discourse and can take much of the pressure and embarrassment out of working on "basic" mathematics.

Appendix 1 contains several games, easy to learn and to play, that help students develop fundamental number sense and strategic competence. Besides the rules of play, we offer suggestions to extend these games' rules to make them more challenging and to facilitate discussions about the games that help students see and use important mathematical relationships.

Design activities that allow student choice

You can support students who struggle with basic skills and knowledge by developing tiered assignments with problems organized by level of challenge and difficulty, and then allowing students to choose which activities to do. Students who find the first few problems relatively easy can move to a harder section. Using this approach ensures that all students have appropriate tasks and encourages metacognition.

If you use this strategy, students must not treat choice as a way to avoid doing work. Choice needs to be connected to a genuine self-judgment of mastery; otherwise, it does not work as designed. Also, do not connect choice activities to weighted grading schemes, where harder problems are worth more points. The criterion for choosing tasks should be the student's self-evaluation, not some external reward system.

CONCLUSION

The key to supporting students with difficulty succeeding in math class is to meet those students where they are and adapt your instruction to give them the opportunity to solve problems, reason, represent, communicate, and make connections. Instead of seeing the problem as student deficiencies, which you cannot control, see it as one of removing barriers to participation and enlarging the definition of success to reflect the engagement with mathematics that you envision for your students. These strategies not only help struggling students but also support all students to build connected mathematical knowledge.

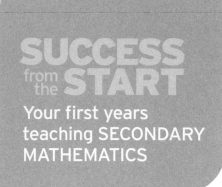

SUCCESS
from
the START
Your first years
teaching SECONDARY
MATHEMATICS

chapter **thirteen**

Effective and Engaging Homework

Ms. Perez was concerned that some of her students did not do their homework consistently. A colleague asked what her homework assignments were like and what she expected her students to do in homework. Reflecting on this question, Ms. Perez realized that every homework had two types of questions, practicing procedures and more challenging problems that required explanation, application, or transfer. She also realized that she did not expect students to do any problems completely by memory. She assumed that students would look in their notes or textbooks for examples to replicate. She believed that when students looked at examples and practiced replicating procedures, they would develop fluency with the mathematical techniques. For harder problems, she expected that students would probably not know how to solve them right away, and she hoped that they would work to see the connections between these situations and the techniques learned in class.

Once Ms. Perez clarified her goals and expectations for homework, she wondered, "Do my students know and share these expectations?" Perhaps they thought that they were supposed to simply remember how to do all the problems. Perhaps when they did not remember immediately how to do a problem, they did not realize that they were supposed to look back at the book or their notes. This might explain their lack of consistency in doing homework—maybe they gave up because they were frustrated with not knowing what to do.

Ms. Perez decided to talk to her students about how to engage with homework. She deliberately includes relatively straightforward problems, where they had to practice a mathematical procedure, and harder problems, where they had to figure out how to solve the problem and then decide on ways to do so. She planned to dedicate part of an upcoming class to have students work on homework—to practice using their notes and books as resources and to share successful homework strategies with classmates. (A version of this story, by Veronica Vazquez, appeared in the Winter 2010 newsletter of the Delaware Council of Teachers of Mathematics.)

* * *

Homework is nearly universal in American schools, yet the effects of students engaging in mathematics homework are not well studied or understood. For teachers, homework poses a challenge. How can teachers create opportunities for productive learning outside the classroom without control over the environment where students do their homework or the ability to respond to difficulties and needs while completing homework? As if this were not enough, homework also is a perennial center of conflict between teenagers, parents, and teachers. Too often, homework is more about struggles over authority than about learning mathematics. Despite these challenges, strategies are available to both increase the likelihood that students learn from doing homework and decrease the likelihood that students, parents, and teachers engage in negative interactions around homework.

HOMEWORK SHOULD FOSTER PRODUCTIVE INTERACTION WITH MATHEMATICS

Just as in class, mathematics homework should emphasize thoughtful and productive interaction with mathematics. This point is worth repeating because often mathematics homework is not connected to productive mathematics learning. Many teachers give homework for reasons not immediately connected to learning math; they see homework as a way to engender discipline, or to have fun, for instance. Although these goals may be admirable, and could be a by-product of effective homework assignments, they should not be the primary goals for math assignments. The primary goal of homework in mathematics should be that students build connected mathematical knowledge: represent, reason, communicate, solve problems, and make connections.

Guiding Principles

>> Homework should foster productive interaction with mathematics.

>> Be clear about goals and expectations for homework.

BE CLEAR ABOUT GOALS AND EXPECTATIONS FOR HOMEWORK

Do not assume that students have the same ideas as you do about homework's purposes and value. You probably see homework as an opportunity for students to solidify or expand understanding. Although some students may also see it this way, many students may see homework as a task to be completed in exchange for a good grade or as an imposition on their time.

You may envision students looking back at their notes or asking a friend for help on homework problems. Your students may assume that they should already know how to do all the homework problems and that any obstacle or sign of confusion means that they simply are not equipped to complete the assignment. When you and your students have different understandings of the goals of homework, you may end up working at cross purposes.

Because of this danger, be as clear as possible about your goals and expectations for homework. This clarity serves two purposes:

1 It helps you align homework assignments with learning goals and with what students can do. In getting clear about purposes and homework, you can detect and correct inconsistencies.

2 It allows you to give students clear, consistent directions and signals—increasing the probability that students will engage with homework in the ways that you want.

Habits of Practice

>> Identify and articulate clear goals for homework.

>> Create assignments that require deep thinking.

>> Encourage metacognition.

>> Teach explicit strategies for success.

>> Create structures and routines that support engagement and success.

>> Use homework to gather information about students' understanding.

>> Start small.

STOP+REFLECT

>> What are your goals for homework? How does it connect to productive interactions with mathematics that require and support solving problems, reasoning, representing, communicating, and making connections?

>> How do you envision students working on homework? What do you expect them to do when they do not immediately know how to approach a problem or exercise?

IDENTIFY AND ARTICULATE CLEAR GOALS FOR HOMEWORK

Homework has many different valid goals. You must clearly articulate your goals for homework. As you read the following goals (listed in no particular order) for assigning homework, note the ones that coincide with your own:

- To develop procedural fluency

- To generate data and ideas that may become the basis for a discussion or activity in class

- To make connections between different types of problems and procedures

- To apply procedures to new contexts

- To give students the opportunity to work for long periods on nonroutine math problems, generating a variety of solutions for class discussion

- To expose experiences and ideas that may become part of a mathematics discussion

- To make sense of another student's ideas

- To reason mathematically

- To explain one's thinking

- To assess students' understanding or mastery of an idea or skill

All these goals, except the last, are mathematical. Each entails developing connected mathematical knowledge through problem solving, reasoning, representing, communicating, or making connections. Assessing students is not a mathematical goal, but homework becomes another instance of students interacting with mathematics and gives teachers opportunities to observe and assess that interaction, even if indirectly.

CREATE ASSIGNMENTS THAT REQUIRE DEEP THINKING

For students to learn from doing homework, you need to design assignments that require problem solving, communicating, reasoning, representing, and making connections rather than assume that students will do such thinking on their own. Furthermore, questions that elicit these processes need to be the centerpiece of your assignment, not an add-on or extra. Through homework, you can foster thinking like this in two ways: (1) have students think specifically about the mathematics they are working on, or (2) have them monitor their own thinking and understanding—what cognitive scientists call metacognition (see chapter 12). Below are suggestions for how to require students to think mathematically during homework.

Have students explain their thinking before practicing procedures

Some curriculum materials include questions that require students to explain their mathematical thinking. In deciding what to give students for homework, look for those questions and ask students to think about them at the beginning of the assignment. Typical textbook homework exercises might require students to factor several quadratic expressions and then explain their strategy for doing so. Ideally, you want students to think about different factoring strategies while doing the problems. Describing the strategies first and then using their work on the problems to refine their explanations forces them to think about their strategies as they work.

Give students "model answers" to correct or critique

Evaluating model answers requires that students interpret, understand, explain, and critique others' mathematical work, which supports mathematical reasoning. When students attend to others' reasoning, they must make sense of mathematics in a variety of ways. When students evaluate others' procedures, they must attend to precision, and when they critique mathematical mistakes, they must reason and justify. Your model answers should include a good mix of correct, incorrect, and partially correct reasoning, forcing students to attend to the mathematics to justify and critique the reasoning in the solutions.

Have students sort problems

Categorizing problems forces students to make connections between problems. You can establish the criteria for different categories of problems, or you can ask students to create the criteria as part of the assignment. You could give students a variety of equations, including some with x's and y's, some with d's and t's, some linear, some quadratic, some with only one variable, and some with two variables. You could then ask them to sort the equations into categories. To complete this assignment, students must look at mathematical structure and decide which equations are similar in structure and which are not.

Have students create problems with particular features

Creating their own problems is a great way to get students to think about the structure of the mathematics they are learning. By asking students to create a problem that you could solve using the definition of tangent, for example, you require students to attend to general and important features of the tangent ratio and to connect those features to a particular context. Try making this the first problem of a homework assignment on calculating trigonometric ratios, and then direct them to think about refining the problem as they calculate the ratios. In this way you prompt them to think about what features of the problems they are doing make them connected to the tangent ratio, rather than to the sine or cosine ratios.

ENCOURAGE METACOGNITION

Chapter 12 described the importance of metacognition. Just as you can help students learn by having them regularly stop during class and evaluate how well they understand the material and monitor the effectiveness of their problem-solving strategies, you can help students develop metacognition on homework assignments. Here are several strategies to help students develop awareness of their own learning and problem solving while they do homework assignments.

Have students evaluate their performance or indicate problem difficulty

You can foster metacognition by having students indicate how confident they are of their answers to problems. Students can place a *C* next to problems they are sure they got correct, a *U* next to problems they are unsure of, and a *W* next to problems they are sure they got wrong. Or they can indicate their confidence on a 1–5 scale, with 1 being confident that they are right and 5 being confident that they are wrong. The particular scale is not important; students must have a system to indicate their confidence in their answers that forces them to evaluate their own understanding.

Students can also become more metacognitive by indicating how difficult they found the problems on the homework, again using a scale that is clear and forces them to make distinctions. This approach is similar to having them evaluate their performance, but it differs in some ways. There may be problems that are difficult for students but that they are confident that they answered correctly. For students, this ability to pinpoint what is difficult and what they do not understand is often the first step to greater understanding—and, in itself, forces students to communicate and make connections.

Have students explain what strategies they used when they got stuck

Asking students to describe what they did when they initially could not do a problem reinforces the idea that you expect them to struggle, that you have confidence in their ability to persist and succeed. It also forces students to think about how they can persist through struggle and can help reinforce strategies you discussed in class, such as reviewing notes, asking a friend, or skipping the problem and coming back to it later.

Give students choices based on their self-evaluation

Choice, another tool we described using for struggling students, can also be an effective way to create homework that both is accessible to a wider variety of students and gives them opportunities to assess their own understanding and facility. Just as we suggested for problems in class (see chapter 12), you could arrange homework problems in sections that differ in difficulty and have students choose which section to start with. If students find the first few problems relatively easy, they can move to a more difficult section. This approach allows students to pay attention to and evaluate their efforts, and it helps prevent the all-too-common phenomenon of students finding homework boring and routine or too difficult.

Just as in class, when you do use these strategies for homework assignments, students need to know that choice is not a way to avoid work. Choice needs to reflect students' sincere judgment about their understanding, and they should be able to justify the choice they made in terms of their mathematical understandings.

TEACH EXPLICIT STRATEGIES FOR SUCCESS

Often, teachers and students think that successful homework completion comes from personal qualities such as persistence and independence. We think that students who consistently complete their homework at a high level exhibit strategies that all students can learn. By teaching these strategies explicitly, you will support your students in completing, and learning from, their homework. Following are several moves you can use to teach these techniques.

Name successful homework strategies

Before you can teach specific strategies, you need to name and describe them. Figure 13.1 lists strategies to help students learn effectively from homework. Consider posting these strategies in your classroom.

Fig. 13.1. *Successful homework strategies*

- Use examples from notes or from the textbook:

  - Look at notes to see how to do the problem.

  - Try the problem on your own; use notes to check your method.

  - Try problems without referring to notes at all.

- Try a problem, leave it, and come back to it later after doing other problems.

- Identify exactly what you are confused about; formulate a specific question.

- Get help from others.

Model homework strategies

Just naming and describing homework strategies in class is not enough; you need to model them. Take class time to show your students how you would do a homework assignment, using and naming each strategy as you go.

Give students class time to practice homework strategies

After you model homework strategies in class, give your students class time to practice them. While they do homework in class, walk around and notice specific students using the strategies. If students ask for help, ask whether they have used any strategies that you modeled. If they cannot remember the strategies, refer them to the poster with the named strategies.

Assign homework buddies

To simply tell students that they should ask for help when they run into trouble while doing their homework is not enough. You can assign students

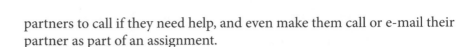

partners to call if they need help, and even make them call or e-mail their partner as part of an assignment.

Use these strategies in class, not just on homework

Students will be much more likely to use effective strategies on homework if they also use them in class. If students are working on problems in class, have them think about and use the same strategies that you would encourage them to use on homework.

CREATE STRUCTURES AND ROUTINES THAT SUPPORT ENGAGEMENT AND SUCCESS

Having to think about all aspects of homework can overwhelm both teachers and students. Structures and routines create a culture in which positive interactions with mathematics become habitual, and they can offer consistent responses to more mundane aspects of homework so that teachers and students can concentrate on the mathematics. Routines also help prevent spending valuable class time on answering questions about grading, having students rummage through their backpacks, or discussing a litany of excuses for uncompleted homework. You need routines for the following tasks.

Assigning and recording homework

Students should know how they are going to find out what the homework is and have a regular way to record that homework assignment in their notebooks or calendars. As much as possible, this procedure should be the same every day or class meeting. Establish this routine early in the semester, and make sure that students adhere to it. Here are some ways to establish this routine:

- Post the homework at a specific place in the classroom (on a blackboard or bulletin board) every day. Have students write down their homework for the evening when they first sit down in class.

- Create a weekly assignment sheet and hand it out at the beginning of the week.

- Reserve the last few minutes of class every day to assign homework. Students may not leave until they have written down the homework.

Collecting, checking, and returning homework

Develop a consistent way to collect, check, and return homework papers. Though you need not collect every homework assignment, you need a consistent mechanism to let students know whether you will collect a particular homework assignment:

- Have a tray for homework, and announce at a set time in class (at the end of class, after correcting it, or as they enter) that students should put their homework in the tray.

- Have students pass the homework up to the desks nearest to you during class.

- Have students put their homework on their desk at the beginning of class; you can check to see whether it is completed while you walk around as they begin work.

Whatever system you implement, be consistent. Practice it with your students so that it takes minimal time and creates minimal disruption.

Going over homework

Many secondary math classrooms begin with the teacher asking whether students have any questions about the homework. This is a routine of sorts, but not a particularly thoughtful one. A better routine would entail the teacher making some sort of survey of what difficulties the students had so as to make an informed decision about whether to dedicate class time to that problem. Here are some ways to do this:

- Know ahead of time which homework problems are especially important. During the first five minutes of class, while students are discussing the homework with partners or in groups, look at students' answers to these questions to assess whether reteaching or a discussion about a particular question is necessary.

- Have students work together to check their homework regularly, asking them which problems they, as a group, have questions about.

- Collect homework and look over a few important problems and then decide what you need to reteach or explore.

Which routine you have is not as important as the fact that it allows you to decide what problems to go over on the basis of a good assessment of what students know and understand, and that it gives you time to think about the best way to address common problems.

Dealing with work for absent students

Absent students can wreak havoc on carefully designed homework routines. Having a clear way for students who were absent to find out what the homework assignment is, do it, and hand it in is extremely helpful:

- Have student folders in your classroom; put graded homework assignments in each student's folder. Homework stays in the folder until absent students return.

- Have homework folders in a specific place in your room, with new assignments arranged in folders by date. When absent students return, they take the appropriate homework from the folder.
- Have a homework buddy be responsible for contacting the absent student and telling him or her the homework assignment.

Integrating homework responses into class discussion

Integrating student responses into class discussion can be a powerful motivator and can give students opportunities to reason and communicate about mathematics. Giving out a student solution and asking others to make sense of it indicates that their thinking is valuable and that making sense of others' ideas is essential to studying mathematics. It also shows that you notice what they do and take it seriously. Here are some ways to do this:

- Use student data generated from homework assignments as the basis for statistics investigations.

- Show specific student responses to a particularly important question and have the class discuss those responses.

- Use two or more different student responses to the same problem. How are they the same? How are they different? Are both correct? How do you know?

- Sort student responses into categories.

In response to dismal homework completion rates, one science teacher read student responses to a question he chose ahead of time in every class. He named the student and included as wide a variety of students as possible. After a few days, more students began doing their homework, and his classes were more animated and engaging.

A note about routines: consult with your colleagues. If teachers at your school have effective routines for any of the preceding tasks, think about using them. Your colleagues can help you set up the routines, deal with logistical requirements, and troubleshoot. If some of your students have had that teacher, they will already know the routine, making it easier to teach it to others.

USE HOMEWORK TO GATHER INFORMATION ABOUT STUDENTS' UNDERSTANDING

Your primary focus should be on observing and learning from students' interactions with mathematics. Looking at student homework can be a valuable way to learn about students and their mathematical understandings. Assessing homework, however, can also become time consuming; you must find ways to gather useful information from homework quickly and efficiently. Below we present effective and efficient strategies to assess students' mathematical understandings through homework.

Focus on one or two key problems

Look at one important question that gives information about students' understanding. Have clear markers you are looking for in their answers and a systematic way to record information about their understandings.

Analyze student choice or self-evaluation

If you give students choice, or have them evaluate their confidence in their answers, use this information to see how much they think they understand. Again, focus on a few key problems and assess whether they accurately evaluated their own understanding. You can see whether they find the material generally easy or generally hard.

Look at only some students' work

Instead of looking at every student's work, look at only some students' homework. Assessing a quarter or a third of the students' homework should give you a good sense of the thinking students exhibit, as well as typical problems they encounter. If you adopt this technique, choose which students' work to look at in an unpredictable way; by the end of the semester you need to have looked at all students' work equally.

START SMALL

Homework is a complex part of teaching and learning. The challenges of homework can consume teachers, especially beginning teachers. Concentrate your energies on things that you can control and that will have the greatest benefit for your classes and students. This may mean that homework has lower priority than planning for classes, because you are more in control of the class environment and how students interact with mathematics in that environment. Training your students to approach homework in new ways is not as important as training them to approach math class in new ways. Ultimately, the best way to have students interact with homework productively is to create a classroom where they interact with mathematics productively.

This chapter gives many ways to design and support effective homework. Do not try to implement all these suggestions at once. Begin with routines that students are already used to, routines that they may have learned from previous teachers. Enacting familiar routines requires much less effort from everybody involved. You then might want to introduce just one suggestion from this chapter and work to get good at implementing it. Although this chapter presents homework as an interconnected web of complementary practices, these practices are built incrementally, one at a time. So, choose one thing to work on to make it more likely for more of your students to engage with their homework in positive ways, or to lessen the time you spend on the logistical challenges of homework. Try it for a week and see what happens.

CONCLUSION

Homework, like all work you assign, should give students opportunities to solve problems, reason, represent, communicate, and make connections.

By creating clear expectations for homework, and being explicit about how students can work through difficulties in it, you increase the likelihood that homework will support their mathematical learning and that students will work on it productively. Creating opportunities for students to assess their own understanding and choosing appropriate tasks will also help them work productively and give you an opportunity to assess their understanding. Creating routines around homework will help you deal with logistical challenges more efficiently. Ultimately, teaching your students to interact independently and productively with mathematics in class will help them do so on homework.

chapter fourteen

Assessment, Feedback, and Grading

I t was Saturday afternoon, and Mrs. Abernathy smiled as she finished grading her students' algebra 2 unit tests. When she started teaching six years ago, grading unit tests would take all weekend. Now it took much less time, partly because she no longer minutely corrected every mistake and partly because she put fewer problems on tests. She also encountered fewer surprises while grading tests. This was partly because of her experience; she knew much more about the mistakes that students would make. But she suspected that it was mostly because she had gotten better at figuring out what her students understood before she gave the unit test. When she started teaching, she often thought her students all understood the material—only to find out while grading tests that some were completely lost.

Two years ago, after reading an article on formative assessment with some other teachers, Mrs. Abernathy started teaching her students to take a more active role in evaluating their own understanding. Instead of taking so much time grading, she had them assess their own work and see how well they had done on homework or in-class tasks. She thought that this practice was partly why she now argued less with students over grades: their grades did not surprise them as much, either.

Mrs. Abernathy and her colleagues had also experimented with ways to format and grade tests. She had been surprised how creative they had gotten, especially because she had never considered that tests and quizzes could look different from the ones she had taken as a student and given as a teacher. Although not all these new test formats were effective, a surprising number had resulted in increased achievement for her students.

* * *

For most of us, quizzes and tests were the only assessments we experienced as mathematics students. Assessment was what teachers did to find out who has learned and who has not, and to generate grades. This view of assessment is narrow and limiting, particularly if your goal is for students to build connected mathematical knowledge.

You assess student understanding constantly. Your primary job during mathematics lessons is to pay attention to how students interact with the mathematics and to then guide instruction and decide how to support students. When you view assessment from this perspective, you are much more able to make instructional decisions based on what your students do and do not understand. And for a bonus: conflict with students over grades is less likely.

Two different kinds of assessment exist: summative and formative. Summative assessment is what most of us remember from our days as math students. It indicates whether students have learned the material. Teachers use summative assessments to grade, sort, and evaluate students. Formative assessments take place during instruction to see how students understand the material. Teachers use formative assessments to improve learning and instruction (Black and Wiliam 1998).

You could view much of this book as an argument for the importance of formative assessment. Chapters suggest ways to create classroom conditions and design lessons to assess students and then use that knowledge to support their learning. Summative assessments are an important part of middle and high school math. You will need to spend time creating and grading summative assessments and interacting with students about them. Because this book has attended extensively to strategies for formative assessment, this chapter focuses on summative assessment and creating efficient grading systems.

Guiding Principles

>> Assessment does not take place only after teaching.

>> Assessment should reveal students' understandings.

>> Align assessments and grading with learning goals.

ASSESSMENT DOES NOT TAKE PLACE ONLY AFTER TEACHING

Although this chapter is about summative assessments, effective teachers spend much lesson time attending to how students interact with mathematics and what that indicates about student understandings. Teachers use what they learn in this kind of assessment to plan instruction and guide their in-the-moment teaching decisions. This process involves clarifying mathematical goals, anticipating solutions, observing and monitoring student work, and reflecting on how planning and instruction supported learning. Chapters 6–9 give advice about engaging in these processes to support students and contribute to your professional growth.

ASSESSMENT SHOULD REVEAL STUDENTS' UNDERSTANDINGS

Even though summative assessments often come after students are expected to achieve specific learning goals, classroom practice can incorporate these assessments to give students, teachers, and parents valuable information to support learning. Preparing for summative assessments can help students learn math with understanding, and their grades on assessments should send clear messages about what they need to do to improve.

In U.S. schools, assessment sometimes serves purposes that can undermine the learning this book advocates. Teachers often use grades on assessments to rank, motivate, or punish students, causing many students to disengage from learning. Regardless of your purposes, others will use the grades you give to rank and motivate students. Although you cannot counteract these cultural practices and pressures, you can minimize the negative effects of grading in your classroom and on your interactions with students.

ALIGN ASSESSMENTS AND GRADING WITH LEARNING GOALS

Grades are the subject of substantial controversy in U.S. education and a potential source of conflict between teachers, students, and parents. Grades should measure and reflect student mastery of mathematical learning goals, not other, nonmathematical behaviors. A good grade in math class should signify that a student has deep, connected knowledge of the mathematics and can solve problems, reason, represent, communicate, and make connections.

Our friend Matthew relayed a conversation he had with his fellow math teachers. They all had students who argued that a correct answer arrived at by an obviously incorrect procedure should receive full credit on tests. To such students, the goal of assessment was to get the correct answers. Matthew and his colleagues wanted to try different strategies for writing tests that would counter such beliefs. One suggested format supplied the answers to problems and asked students to describe how to arrive at that answer. Because the students already had the answer, their grade would be based on their knowledge of the process. By changing the assessments to ask students to engage in the desired processes, and explicitly assessing those processes, these teachers gained better information about students' learning, sent clearer messages about learning goals, and held students accountable for those goals more effectively.

Grading and assessing mathematical understanding can encompass positive behavior, but only if behavior is defined as dispositions and actions that support and indicate mathematical understanding. Defining the mathematical behaviors we want students to exhibit, and then creating ways to measure them, moves behavior from compliance to intellectual skill and engagement. So, for example, grades should not be about whether students sit still or do their homework in pencil, but instead about whether they ask insightful questions or communicate their ideas.

Furthermore, grades should not be based on relative student performance. Getting a B should represent a specific level of understanding of the content, not that the student is slightly less competent than a student with a B+. Thus, all your students could get an A if they all master the learning goals. Similarly, all your students could also get an F if they all fail to master any of the learning goals. Although you will probably get a range of grades in your class, creating a normal distribution so that others can identify the brightest or poorest students is not the goal of your grading system.

Habits of Practice

>> Align assessments with learning goals.

>> Create a transparent grading system.

>> Teach students how to study.

>> Enable students to self-assess and process feedback.

>> Create an efficient grading system.

>> Vary assessment tasks, formats, and grading.

>> Base homework grades on productive interactions with mathematics.

ALIGN ASSESSMENTS WITH LEARNING GOALS

Students often complain that what they were tested on was different from what they learned in class. If assessments should evaluate whether students have achieved learning goals, then assessments should align with those goals. The strategies below can ensure this alignment.

Create assessments first

Creating an assessment should be one of the first steps in planning a unit of study. When planning a unit, ask two simple questions:

1 What should students know and be able to do by the end of this unit?

2 How will they demonstrate this knowledge and skill?

The answers to the first question drive the answers to the second question, and the answers to the second question become the basis for your unit assessment. For example, in a unit that introduces sine, cosine, and tangent, you might want students to understand the relationship between these functions and the role of similar triangles. You may want them to understand that the sine, cosine, or tangent of a given angle is a specific number because all right triangles with that particular angle are similar, and that the ratio of corresponding sides in that family of similar triangles is the same and equal to that specific number. If this is your goal, how will students show that they understand? One way may be to present the problem in figure 14.1.

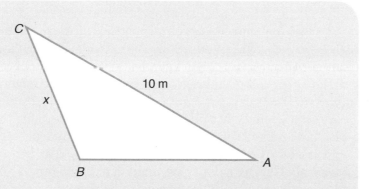

Suzy knows that the sine of 30 degrees is 1/2 and that the sine is the ratio of the opposite side over the hypotenuse. In this triangle, Suzy decided that x should equal 5, because x is the leg opposite the 30-degree angle, and the longest side of the triangle is 10. Do you agree with Suzy? Why or why not? Make sure that you explain the reason for any rule you use in your justification.

Fig. 14.1. *A problem to assess student understanding of trigonometry*

Beginning a unit by creating the final assessment forces you to become clear about the unit's learning goals and about the questions you want students to be able to answer to show mastery of the learning goals. In so doing, you become much more likely to align your instruction with these goals.

Assess a variety of skills and processes

Critics of U.S. education and schools have long derided "teaching to the test" as the antithesis of helping students gain deep content knowledge and the ability to think critically and creatively. Though we are sympathetic to these criticisms, the point is not to teach (or not teach) to the test but rather to ensure that the assessments and the instruction align with learning goals.

In mathematics, the learning goal for students is to gain connected knowledge of content, which they demonstrate through reasoning, representing, communicating, solving problems, and making connections. Assessments should include tasks that require students to engage in these processes, and completing these tasks will give you evidence of students' understanding. For example, asking students to solve a problem two different ways and explain how the ways are connected forces students to solve problems, make connections, and communicate.

Creating assessments that address the diverse skills and processes that make up connected mathematical knowledge of specific content is hard work. Luckily, most curriculum materials include assessments that you can use. Whatever they offer, analyze those assessments much as you would analyze tasks in your curriculum materials (see chapter 6). You may need to adapt those assessments to better align them with your goals.

Align goals, teaching, and activities with assessment

After designing your assessments, continually check that your learning goals, teaching moves, and classroom activities are aligned with the mathematics that you hope to assess. You may become clearer about learning goals in ways that make you rethink your assessment. That is fine; change your assessment. Your activities may be skewed toward one or two processes at the expense of the others or may emphasize one content element over another. Revise your activities or tasks to bring them back into balance. Your teaching moves may prevent students from reasoning (by rushing to explain, for example), or you might need to push students more to make connections so they can gain the connected knowledge to do well on the assessment. (Chapter 8 discusses common teaching moves that undermine student learning.) Plan different moves to address these issues.

Grade specific processes

Grades you give should align with the interactions you want students to have with mathematics. If the point of the assignment was to justify a solution, do not grade for just getting the right answer. If you keep track of the processes you are evaluating, then a good grade means more than just good work; it means that the student justified well, or represented clearly, or showed procedural fluency.

CREATE A TRANSPARENT GRADING SYSTEM

Transparency in grading forces you to be clear about your goals and criteria. Students will not have to guess at what they must do to get full credit on a test problem, or what constitutes a good explanation or sufficient work. Clarity and transparency also makes negative interactions with students about grades much less likely.

A grading system has two aspects. One deals with weighing components of student performance—how much each assignment, test, or problem is worth when computing a final grade for the quarter, semester, or year. The other is the criteria for measuring student performance—what constitutes good work. A transparent grading system makes both aspects clear to students before they engage in learning.

Create and use clear weights for different aspects of student work

Weighting different elements of student performance in their final grade is simply a matter of deciding what different aspects of student performance you want to measure and determining their value in the final grade. Some teachers make quizzes and tests worth 50 percent of the grade, homework 25 percent, and projects 25 percent. Other teachers weight these differently and may include class participation, short papers on particular mathematics, or mathematics journals.

Whatever you decide, your system has to be manageable and must yield grades that correspond to mathematical understanding. If you weight homework at 50 percent of a student's grade, but you merely check to see whether it is completed, half the grade does not correspond to mathematical behavior or understanding. Such a grading system does not align with connected understanding.

Create clear criteria for quality work

Much more important than weighting each aspect of your grading system is clarifying your criteria for quality work. Doing so entails more than simply stating what good work looks like, although this is important. It also involves creating rubrics for graded work that describe criteria for quality work and then spending time in class helping students understand the criteria (for example, have them "score" a set of work done by fictitious students and compare their scores with other students, working to come to agreement on any differences in scoring). If your grading criteria model the norms and habits of interaction that you want, making grading criteria clear is supported by, and becomes part of, your effort to create class culture and norms that support mathematical learning.

Also make sure that your criteria are balanced and reflect the elements of connected knowledge that mark deep mathematical understanding: representing, reasoning, communicating, solving problems, and making connections. With the procedural focus of much of school mathematics, this may be a challenge. Try to integrate these processes into your assessments a little bit at a time—for example, by having students solve one nonroutine problem for a quiz, or having one problem on a test involve critiquing the reasoning of a hypothetical peer.

TEACH STUDENTS HOW TO STUDY

Too often, middle and high school mathematics teachers assume that their students know how to study, when many students lack good study skills. Teaching students to study will help them improve. It will also help them become more active in their mathematical learning and in evaluating their understanding. Below are strategies to help your students better prepare for assessments.

Identify, name, and describe basic study techniques

Students cannot study effectively if they do not know what to do. Identifying, naming, and describing techniques that enable students to study effectively (such as in fig. 14.2) will help them succeed. Your students probably know some of these strategies; as a group, they can probably come up with all of them. Use class time to engage your students to create a list of study techniques, and then post that list in your room and make copies for their notebooks.

Practice study techniques during class

Offer students time during class to practice study techniques. Begin practice sessions by modeling a technique and then supporting your students as

- Predict what will be on the assessment, with specific examples.

  - Base this prediction on class notes, homework, and textbook.

- Look in your notes, homework, and textbook to identify important representations, techniques, ideas, problems, and contexts.

  - Create a study sheet with these important ideas, representations, techniques, ideas, problems, contexts, and so forth.

  - Think to yourself how these are connected to each other.

- Assess whether you can do what you predict will be on the test.

  - Attempt to do the kinds of problems you predict will be on the test.

  - Keep track of how well you do by checking answers in the back of the textbook or comparing your answers with a friend.

- Work to learn how to do the things you struggle with.

  - Ask a friend or a teacher.

  - Look in your notes.

  - Look in the textbook.

  - Look at homework problems.

- Create memory devices for remembering important ideas or techniques.

Fig. 14.2. *Effective study techniques*

they practice it. These practice sessions are much like the practice sessions for doing homework (chapter 13).

ENABLE STUDENTS TO SELF-ASSESS AND PROCESS FEEDBACK

You can make grading more transparent, make assessments opportunities to learn, and help students develop more self-awareness of their mathematical thinking by having them spend time assessing their work on tests and quizzes and strategically going over graded items. Below are some ways you can do that.

Have students self-assess on tests and quizzes

Help students develop self-assessment skills by having them assess how well they think they did on each test or quiz question. You could have them predict their grade before handing in the assessment or rate how confident they are in the response to each problem. These strategies not only make them pay better attention to their own sense of understanding and mastery but also give you a sense of how good they are at monitoring their understanding.

Give time for structured processing of feedback

Have students go over their tests, perhaps with a partner. Students could spend class time going over their quiz or test and write down things they need to work on and strategies for doing so. Or you could create a document that describes common mistakes or misconceptions that you found on the test. Have students check whether they made these mistakes, and if they did, have them make corrections. Whatever you do, the point of having students process feedback is to have them evaluate what they know and do not know so that they can find ways to improve.

Have students grade themselves

For more open-ended questions, have students grade themselves according to a rubric that you have created, and then have a partner grade their work under that rubric. Once the student and a partner agree on a grade, they could compare their evaluation to one that you gave.

CREATE AN EFFICIENT GRADING SYSTEM

In addition to supporting student success on good summative assessments, you also need efficient systems to record and communicate grades to students. Although approaches vary with teacher and situation, any efficient grading system enables you to—

- grade work efficiently and record grades easily;

- share grades with students efficiently and easily; and

- assess student understanding by looking at grades (the grading system informs you about students' strengths and weaknesses).

Here are some suggestions to develop a grading system that has these characteristics.

Have students find their mistakes

Instead of correcting all procedural and arithmetic errors, simply deduct points for procedural errors, note that the mistake was procedural or arithmetical, and give students time to find their own mistakes. This approach saves you the time of having to correct every little mistake and will give students the opportunity to look carefully at their own work.

Record exactly what you are assessing in your grade book

If your grade book has only a series of numbers, you cannot readily access information about students' mathematical strengths and weaknesses. An A and an F show that the student did well on one task but badly on another.

But if you had written "Justification/Prime Numbers" at the top of the column with the A and had written "Timed Test, Linear Equations" over the column with the F, you could tell at a glance that this student needed to develop procedural fluency with solving linear equations but was good at creating justifications. This practice will help you answer questions from students and parents about what they need to work on.

Have students track their progress

Some teachers have students keep track of how they are doing in class by providing a system with which students can record and easily access their grades. Teachers also then teach their students how to combine those grades to see where they stand at different times in the semester. Students' grades will be less of a surprise at the end of the semester.

Get ideas from experienced colleagues

Talk to more experienced colleagues about how they manage grades. Other teachers are a source of valuable information, and you can adapt their approaches as needed.

VARY ASSESSMENT TASKS, FORMATS, AND GRADING

All students can gain deep, connected knowledge of mathematics, demonstrated through solving nonroutine problems, reasoning, representing, communicating, and making connections. To assess whether students have this connected knowledge, you need to assess not only procedural fluency but also students' abilities to engage in these processes. Develop various assessments to evaluate these skills. When designing assessments, use a process similar to the one you use in choosing and designing tasks for classroom lessons (see chapter 5).

You can also vary the format of assessments. Nearly all mathematics summative assessments in the United States consist of students working for a class period, individually, on a relatively large number of problems that they have not seen before and that have relatively short answers. Consider the following alternative formats.

Create group assessments

Instead of making tests or quizzes an individual exercise, have students take them as a group. This approach lets you assess group dynamics and lets students draw on each other's knowledge and strengths. The simplest way is to allow students to work in groups to solve the problems on an assessment. To make sure everyone contributes, some teachers have all students still complete their individual tests. Others have the group hand in one test on which students took turns recording answers (in different ink colors, for instance).

Combine group and individual work

Try having students work on test problems as a group for the first part of the class period and then complete the test individually. During the group portion, students identify problems that they think they may have difficulty with and get advice from peers on ways to solve them. They can make notes on their test papers but cannot actually solve the problems while in the whole group. Students' grades are based on their performance during the individual portion.

Introduce or allow supports during quizzes or tests

Introducing or allowing particular supports during quizzes or exams has two advantages: It lessens the need for students to quickly recall memorized formulas, definitions, theorems, and the like. It also allows you to use more complex tasks on tests and quizzes so that you can evaluate students' ability and facility with organizing and using math resources and tools. Here are some suggested formats for this method:

- Allow students to use their notes or textbooks during tests or quizzes.

- Allow students to use a "crib sheet" for a test. This sheet should be a standard, small size, requiring students to decide what information will be most useful and helpful. Creating this crib sheet becomes an effective way to study.

- Create tests from a bank of questions that students have access to beforehand.

- At the beginning of the unit, give students a pretest that mirrors the final assessment, offering a preview of what you will test them on later.

Vary the kinds of answers you require

Similar to varying tasks, you can also vary the kinds of answers you require. Whatever form of answer you ask for, however, vary them from time to time, and align the format of the answer with the kind of question and what you are assessing. For instance, a multiple-choice question about the proper definition of a rectangle reveals nothing about a student's problem-solving ability, and having students work in groups to solve an open-ended question says little about their individual ability to remember important definitions. Here are some possible answer formats:

- Multiple choice

- Short answer (such as "solve this quadratic")

- Longer, open-ended responses (typically for more involved "word problems")

- Description of a problem solution

- Comparison of different given solutions

- Directions for executing procedures or solving specific types of problems

- Proofs or justifications

Vary grading

Changing how you grade is another way to diversify your approach. Below are several suggestions for strategies you can use when grading assessments.

Grading group assessments

On group assessments, you could randomly pick one person's quiz or assessment and make that student's grade the grade for the group. Theoretically, if they completed the assessment together and recorded their work individually, all group members should have the same thing on their papers. Or you could structure a similar method, except you grade Suzy's paper for question 1, Johnny's for question 2, Bobby's for question 3, Suzy's paper again for question 4, and so on. These grading practices hold students accountable for each other's learning and reduce your grading workload.

Grade group processes

You could also explicitly grade group processes, spending time during group quizzes observing and assessing groups on established criteria. Groups could also assess themselves, and you could then compare your assessment with theirs to gauge whether they aligned. (See chapter 11 for more about productive group processes.)

As you gain more experience, you can explore other ways to grade. Alternative grading formats should always align grades with learning goals and norms that you want to establish and reinforce. However, some of these grading formats may run counter to student expectations and desires. Some students might think that group grades will be unfair if they are working harder than others in their group. Before introducing unconventional grading formats, wait until you have established a relationship of trust and community in the classroom.

* * *

By following this chapter's suggestions, you will create efficient, informative grading systems. Furthermore, your grades will not surprise you, students, or parents and will help them figure out how to improve and achieve at higher levels in math class. Even so, students may sometimes question their grades. Consider the following suggestions to defuse conflict and support positive interactions, even around a potentially fractious topic:

- Discuss grades with individual students outside class time. If a student has a question or concern about a grade, say that you want to focus on his or her concern and ask the student to see you after class.

- If many students have similar disagreements with you about their grades, they may not understand your goals and how your activities and assessments align with your goals. It also may mean that they simply are not good at evaluating their own understanding. Work harder to align and clarify your goals and classroom activities. Integrate metacognition into homework and classwork, which over time will make students more aware of their own understanding and of the purposes of your activities and assessments. Conflicts over grades should decline as a result.

- Begin your semester by having students do math, not by discussing grading policy. Wait a few days to discuss specific grading policies, or discuss them as they come up (such as when you have your first quiz or when you give your first homework). This approach shows that your class is about interacting with mathematics in ways that develop connected knowledge. Students should learn that the surest way to a good grade in your class is to learn the mathematics.

- Grades should be based on students' ability to reason, represent, communicate, make connections, and solve problems. Using grades to punish or motivate, or giving grades for something other than mathematical purposes, undermines this fundamental purpose. Extra-credit assignments not requiring connected knowledge, but created solely to bolster grades (such as reports on the lives of famous mathematicians devoid of relevant mathematical content), also undermine this fundamental goal.

A last word on grading: these ways of looking at assessments and grades take time and effort. You need not use these techniques for all assessments or for assessments with many problems. Perhaps try a new approach for just a few problems on a test or the most important question on a quiz. You may want to give tests with fewer questions. You may want to mix up this kind of grading and assessing with more traditional ones. Throughout your career, you will balance efficiency, clarity, and the complexity of mathematical learning and teaching.

BASE HOMEWORK GRADES ON PRODUCTIVE INTERACTIONS WITH MATHEMATICS

For most teachers, homework counts for part of a student's grade in their class. Many of the suggestions about summative assessments and your grading system also apply to homework. Make sure that high grades reflect the interactions that you want, not merely right answers or task completion. Below are suggestions to incorporate into an efficient and effective system for grading homework.

Grade only one or two problems

Choose one or two problems that capture either the mathematics or the ways of thinking that you want students to know, and grade just those questions with clear criteria. You could look only at a question that asks them to

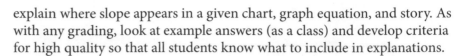

explain where slope appears in a given chart, graph equation, and story. As with any grading, look at example answers (as a class) and develop criteria for high quality so that all students know what to include in explanations.

Grade specific processes

Grades you give for homework should align with the interactions you want students to have with mathematics. For example, if the point of the homework assignment was to justify a solution, do not grade for just getting the right answer. If you keep track of the processes you are evaluating, then a good grade means more than just good work: it means that the student justified well, or created a clear representation, or showed procedural fluency.

Grade the homework of a subset of students

As mentioned in the homework chapter, you can look at a subset of papers and grade only those. If you adopt this strategy, choose papers in an unpredictable way, and look at students' papers equally over the semester.

CONCLUSION

Like all other aspects of your classroom, assessment and grading should help students develop connected knowledge of mathematics by solving problems, reasoning, representing, communicating, and making connections. Assessment gives teachers, students, and parents information to engage students more productively with mathematics. Your assessments should include a variety of tasks that align with your goals and instruction, and that mirror the thinking and activities that students engage in during normal class. Finally, create grading systems that are efficient and transparent so that your interactions about grades do not detract from discussions about mathematics but will become opportunities for students to learn about quality work and positive engagement with content.

SUCCESS
from
the START
Your first years
teaching SECONDARY
MATHEMATICS

chapter **fifteen**

Other Elements of Effective Teaching

Teaching is a complex endeavor. Thinking about all the elements of effective teaching at one time is nearly impossible, whether you are actually teaching or just writing about it. This book has presented ways to frame mathematics learning and teaching that can help you think about and begin to solve common problems you will encounter in your teaching, along with strategies and suggestions that align with those ideas. We have concentrated on those aspects of teaching most important for beginning teachers to think about and work to improve.

This chapter discusses three aspects of mathematics teaching that—though less prominent in day-to-day practice—nevertheless align with how students build connected mathematical knowledge:

1 Teaching with technology

2 Interacting with parents/guardians

3 Standardized testing and test prep

TEACHING WITH TECHNOLOGY

The technologies available for mathematics classrooms have grown exponentially over the past two decades. Middle and high school students and teachers now have access to handheld calculators (including four-function, scientific, and graphing) and computer software packages (such as The Geometer's Sketchpad, TinkerPlots, Fathom, Cabri, and GeoGebra). Many mathematics classrooms have a computer projector, SMART Board, or Promethium. Students often have access to computer labs or classroom sets of laptop or tablet computers offering access to a growing number of Internet math apps. Many students now carry smartphones that can calculate, take photos, and record video. These examples are just some of the technologies that can aid learning and teaching mathematics, and more are being developed.

The key to using technology to facilitate learning is to be thoughtful about its use. Used appropriately, technology can help students develop connected mathematical knowledge. You must find or design activities that require students to think mathematically while using technology. For example, having students use a graphing calculator to explore the impact of changing the values of a in $y = a \sin x$ is more effective than simply having students check their answers for the sine, cosine, and tangent for angles in a triangle. You must also think through the logistical demands of technology use just as you would about any tool your students use in learning mathematics.

Students need to learn how to use technology as a thinking and sense-making tool, not simply an answer-producing tool. They also need to take an active role in learning how to use technology. As with mathematics, students must work to make sense of their tools and figure out how to solve problems with them.

Defining technology

Because technology changes so fast, addressing specific technologies here would be futile. Nevertheless, a definition of "technology appropriate for use in middle and high school mathematics classrooms" is useful. *Focus in High School Mathematics: Technology to Support Reasoning and Sense Making* (Dick and Hollebrands 2011) argues that technology covers a wide spectrum of learning and teaching tools, some of which are electronic. These electronic tools, say the authors, enhance one's ability to—

- make and share representations (such as graphing calculators, document cameras, or projectors);

- make and manipulate mathematical or geometric objects (such as dynamic geometry software);

- make calculations and organize data (such as spreadsheets); and

- make and represent measurements (such as some computer-based recorders for graphic calculators).

The advice in the rest of this section is based on this definition.

Use technology for different purposes

Students in math classrooms use technology for several purposes. Incorporating technology into your lessons can support student thinking and help them build connected mathematical knowledge.

Give students access to multiple representations
Technology offers students access to multiple representations quickly and easily. Using a document camera, students can share a graph they sketched, a picture they drew, or an equation they solved. Technology can also generate representations, as when students can quickly graph points on a graphing calculator or create charts from data tables on a spreadsheet.

Explore mathematical relationships
Many technologies allow students to see multiple representations at one time. Students can easily make changes in one representation and see how it affects other representations. For example, students can change an equation in a graphing utility, or change the value of the coefficient in front of x in a linear equation by using a slider in an app, and observe what happens in the graph and table. With dynamic geometry software, students can drag the corner of a rectangle to double the length of opposite sides and then observe how the perimeter and area change.

Lighten students' calculation load
All too often, students can get caught up in manipulating numbers and lose sight of mathematical meaning. Onerous calculations can obscure underlying mathematical relationships or structure—especially for statistics, where calculating standard deviation, correlation coefficients, or lines of best fit by hand is untenable for any but the smallest data sets. With technology, students can calculate these statistical measures quickly and then use them to make arguments or analyze problem situations.

Offer students more flexible options in solving problems
With technology, students can often examine several cases or try things out to get a sense of problems and make multiple guesses. For example, to compare different cell phone rates, some students may make a table to find when plan A becomes more expensive than plan B. Features of a spreadsheet program make creating such a table relatively easy. Other students may graph equations that they developed for each plan. Using the graphing calculator allows for ease of graphing so that students can spend more time interpreting the graphs.

Give students instant feedback
Technology can give instant feedback. Students using a computer-based tutorial find out right away whether they have given the correct answer and can get help tailored to their procedural weaknesses. Students working to program an object to move in a preset direction in a dynamic geometry program get instant feedback on whether their geometric language was faulty.

Incorporating technology into lessons

Teaching with technology requires that you make several decisions when planning and enacting instruction. The advice below will support you and your students when incorporating technology into mathematics lessons.

Align technology use with goals and purposes
Technology in math class has uncounted uses. Finding the best use is less important than using technology in keeping with your goals and purposes. For example, if you want students to get better at recalling number facts, or at performing procedures quickly and efficiently, a computer program that generates exercises and evaluates student answers immediately may be appropriate. But if you want students to develop communication skills or be able to reason about multiple representations, this same technology may be a poor choice. While considering what you want students to think about in a particular lesson, you must decide whether the technology helps them think about those things or keeps them from achieving your learning goal.

Support students in thoughtful use of technology
Unfortunately, students often see technologies as magic problem-solving machines. For such students, "Which button do I push?" has replaced "Which formula do I use?" but they still think of mathematics as simply a set of procedures. Your students should think first about the mathematics and then use technology with a purpose in mind. Help your students in understanding that they solve problems by thinking mathematically and that technology is a tool that can help them (just as pencil and paper is a tool for solving problems).

Technology is a tool to solve problems and communicate ideas
Students should have a strategy to solve a mathematical problem before they begin pushing buttons or moving sliders. At its most basic level, this looks like students asking themselves whether they know 6×4 before they reach for the calculator. You can encourage this kind of problem-solving ability by asking students to come up with a plan before using technology. You can require that they tell you their plan before you let them use technology.

Students must also check that the answer technology produces makes sense. Prompt students to make predictions, evaluate whether their answers are close to their predictions, and interpret the answers that they get.

Support students in active learning of technology
As much as possible, students should learn how to use technology by using it, not following sets of instructions. As students use technology, they should think of what each command or button might do, or of what button or menu item they might want to use for a particular mathematical task. They should approach learning to use technology as a problem to be solved in itself. You can accomplish this by having them make predictions and by creating activities that involve exploring and playing with the new technology. As often as possible, have students model technology use, so that you can be free to observe, ask questions, and run discussions.

Have students work with partners and at their own pace
Instead of trying to have the whole class stay together, have students work off an activity sheet at their own pace, with a partner. If they do not know what to do with a piece of technology, encourage them to ask their partner for help (just as if they were stuck about something mathematically). Students are good at teaching each other to use technology. To prevent the more computer-savvy students from taking over, designate one "controller" in each pair who is allowed to touch the technology, thus requiring the noncontroller to talk to the controller. Switch roles often so that both partners stay engaged and learn about the technology. Appendix 2 has an example that demonstrates this approach with The Geometer's Sketchpad, a dynamic geometry software.

Avoid technical difficulties
Most teachers who have used technology in class have experienced technical problems that bring the class to a screeching halt or, worse, derail a lesson before it begins. Missing batteries, computers that won't boot up, and burnt-out light bulbs are the stuff of nightmares. The following suggestions can help you prevent some of these logistical snafus:

- Always have a backup plan that does not depend on technology. Especially if using a new technology, prepare an activity that does not depend on the technology working.

- Create systems and routines for handing out, handing in, storing, and turning on and off technology—especially calculators. You could store calculators in individual spaces and have students leave their ID in the slot when they pick up their calculators. If they forget to return it, you know who has the calculator out. Ask more experienced colleagues how they collect and hand out calculators and computers. Practice this system with your students so that they can do it quickly and efficiently.

- Always do a dry run of new technology before using it in class. If trying out a new document camera, or movement sensor, learn how to use it before you try it in class. Set it up in the classroom, and use it as you would with students, so you know what to do and what things may go wrong. Fiddling with toggle switches or power cords is a sure way to lose students' interest and attention.

INTERACTING WITH PARENTS/GUARDIANS

Although they want what is best for their children, parents/guardians must balance their support for their children's education with other important concerns. Parents can be valuable allies and collaborators, with important contributions that can improve the interactions in the triangle of instruction. They have legitimate concerns and needs regarding their child's math-

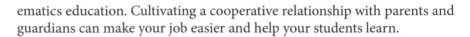

emratics education. Cultivating a cooperative relationship with parents and guardians can make your job easier and help your students learn.

Show parents that you are meeting their needs

Although parents want and expect many different things from schools, all parents share some basic needs. Many conflicts between teachers and parents stem from a parent's sense that these needs are not being met. Communicating to parents that you are meeting these needs helps establish productive partnerships. All parents need, and deserve, to know that—

- their child is safe;

- you are treating their child fairly;

- their child is learning mathematics;

- you know their child;

- they can take measures to support their child in learning mathematics; and

- they can easily communicate with you concerning their child.

Meeting parental needs by teaching effectively

You can best meet parents' needs by teaching their child effectively. The hard work of planning, assessing, and reflecting, as well as creating routines and a culture that supports student learning, is your best tool to forge productive relationships with parents. By creating a well-run classroom with engaging tasks and clear norms for behavior and interaction, you support students in building connected mathematical knowledge, and they feel safe, fairly treated, and known. This is your primary job. If you can do this, you will have fewer negative interactions with aggrieved parents and more opportunities for positive interactions about their child's success and growth.

Most parents will learn about you from their child, through what their children say and how they interact with homework. Effective teaching will ultimately yield positive reports from students. Creating effective homework will minimize student frustration and parental confusion. If you teach effectively, parents will gain confidence in your teaching and be more likely to see you as an ally when difficulties arise.

Communicating with parents effectively

Even with effective teaching, you must also establish direct lines of communication with parents. Unfortunately, many parent–teacher interactions are negative and conflict ridden—usually because the first time teachers and parents interact is when a teacher has a problem with a student. If you create a working relationship with parents before problems arise, parents will be more likely to see you as a partner rather than an opponent.

Establish early communication with parents as a group

Establish contact with parents as a group early in the semester to share information. Send a letter home with each student, or use electronic message boards or e-mail lists set up by your district. Whatever the format, this initial message should include the following:

- A description of the content their child will learn in your class

- What children will do in class, how you will assess them, and how much homework they can expect

- Suggestions for homework and helping struggling students

- How to contact you

Many curriculum materials have examples of such letters, in Spanish as well as English.

Avoid the temptation to include long lists of rules and materials, as well as detailed homework and grading policies, in this initial communication. Although that information is helpful, keep it to a minimum. More important is to communicate a sense of competence and organization, an enthusiasm for the subject, and an interest in students and their thinking.

Establish early, positive communication with individual parents

E-mailing or calling parents to praise a student is a small act that can pay big dividends. First, it shows that you notice and know their child and appreciate what he or she has to offer. This move is powerful, especially for students who have struggled with mathematics or behavior issues. Second, highlighting certain behaviors reinforces the interactions with mathematics and with others that you want in your classroom. Word will quickly spread among students that you notice what they do and value certain behaviors. Third, you put the parent–teacher relationship on positive footing, rather than start it off amid problems that may lead to conflict.

Be specific when praising a child to a parent. You are not simply praising, but showing that you notice details and that you have specific goals and behavioral expectations. You want parents and students to see success as a result of specific, named behaviors. For example, you can tell parents that their child asked a question in class that identified a problem many students were having and led to a discussion that clarified the meaning of slope for everyone. Or you can tell a parent that their child offered a picture to illustrate his partner's strategy, helping others in class understand the solution. Both examples name specific behaviors that not only represent good mathematical thinking but also help create an effective learning community.

Although you cannot do this with every student during the first weeks of class, doing it with just a few is helpful. Concentrating on students who have struggled with math or who are the most influential with classmates may leverage your praise even more.

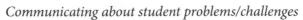

Communicating about student problems/challenges

Contact the parent if a student consistently has difficulties, either mathematical or behavioral. This communication should both inform the parent of the issue and problem-solve around the student's difficulty. When communicating with parents, strive to do the following:

- Emphasize that you want to help the child succeed.

- Describe behaviors or mathematical difficulties, not personal characteristics. Have examples of work or anecdotes of behavior ready to show or describe.

- Be ready to explain your explicit expectations and what the student can do to improve.

- Ask parents what they know about their child in relation to math class and school.

- Ask parents to help you make a plan to support the student; have some ideas about a plan yourself.

- Focus on the student, what the problem is and what might help her improve, not on your teaching.

- Thank parents at the end of the conversation and follow up with a phone call or e-mail to share progress or gather more information.

- Keep a record of the conversation.

These conversations go much better if they are not your first contact with a parent. Ideally, you will have already had a positive communication with the parent.

Responding to parent-initiated communication

Sometimes parents may contact you about concerns they may have or information they want to share. These communications are often fairly straightforward, requiring little more than sharing information or taking in information and thanking the parents. Sometimes, however, they may involve more substantive issues requiring more thought and engagement. When parents communicate with you, remember their needs and wants (see "Show parents that you are meeting their needs" earlier in this chapter). Most communications that parents start serve at least one of these needs, and showing that you want the same things is important.

When responding to parent communications, keep the following in mind:

- If parents want to meet with you, they need to set up an appointment; they cannot interrupt your teaching. Try to get them to describe the problem before the appointment, so you can think of important data/information you can bring to the meeting (such as student work or typical problematic situations).

- First, thank the parent for bringing this issue to your attention and then get more information. What is the problem?

- Listen; do not respond right away.

- Keep the conversation on the student and what the student is finding difficult. If the focus moves toward a critique of teaching, bring it back to the student.

- Do not judge; simply describe behaviors and student work.

- Work with the parent to come up with a plan for moving forward.

- Keep a record of the communication and follow up to see whether the plan is working.

If you find yourself in an intractable conflict with a parent, end the meeting and ask an administrator for support.

Making the most of school structures for parent–teacher communication
Most schools have structures and events designed to help parents get to know their child's teachers and how their child is doing in school. These are opportunities for you to communicate with parents in a way that invites them to trust you and see you as a partner in helping their child.

Back-to-school night/curriculum night. Back-to-school night is when parents come to their child's school. Although different schools have different formats for back-to-school night, here are some things you can do to foster positive relationships:

- Do some fun math together, ideally math their child has done. The best way for parents to get to know what your class should be like is for them to experience it.

- Mention a few things that individual students did in class that model behaviors or ways of thinking you want to reinforce.

- Gather information from parents about their children's needs and experiences in math (a 3-by- 5 card works well for this).

- Let parents know how they can contact you.

- Explain what you will be teaching and how you expect students to interact with mathematics in your classroom.

- Do not discuss individual children or recite rules and requirements.

Parent–teacher conferences. When meeting with parents individually, get information from them that will help you, and share information about their child. Conferences with parents also offer opportunities to show them that you know their child.

- First thank them for coming, and ask whether they have information that would help you or questions for you.

- Listen.

- Have an example of their child's work to share, and have specific things to say about it.

- Have examples of the student's behaviors and thinking.

Grades

People see grades as the most important way to communicate to parents, and the outside world, and yet they give little information. The most important thing to remember about grades is that they should be a surprise to nobody. Students should have a good idea of what they are doing well, and what they need to work on and how they can work on it. See chapter 14 for more on grades.

Another important element of creating productive partnerships with parents: avoid attributing negative motivations or personal characteristics to parents. Parents, like students, represent diverse expectations, experiences, and cultures. What may seem like a failure to invest in a child's education can, and probably does, have an altogether different explanation. Attributing a lack of caring or expertise to parents is unfair and destroys the trust necessary to create effective partnerships between parents and teachers.

A colleague who moved to the United States from Mexico as an adult described his experiences as the parent of an elementary school student. In Mexico, parents meet with the child's teacher only for problems, such as poor achievement or bad behavior. The idea of going to parent conferences when no such problems existed was completely foreign to him. Later he was shocked to learn that many teachers at his child's school assumed that he, and other parents from Mexico, simply did not care enough about their children's education to come to conferences. This made him angry and hurt, and it made him wonder whether those teachers were also making unfair assumptions about his child. The more you can become aware of and put aside your assumptions about what motivated behaviors or what behaviors may mean, the more likely you are to be able to work productively with parents and learn from them important lessons about their children.

STANDARDIZED TESTING AND TEST PREP

Standardized testing has taken on an important and, some would argue, highly controversial role in public educational policy and discourse. Standardized tests have become the instrument by which states determine which students graduate, which schools to restructure, and (if some would have their way) how much teachers get paid and whether they get to keep their jobs. Such tests are called "high stakes" with good reason. At the same time, many educators, researchers, parents, and political commentators argue that emphasizing such tests threatens to distort teaching and learning to the detriment of students and society as a whole. Whatever you believe about standardized testing, chances are that much is riding on your students' performance on these tests. Consequently, preparing your students to succeed on them is an important part of your job as a teacher.

Having deep, connected knowledge of mathematics is the key to success on tests, including standardized tests. The most successful students on such tests are those who approach tests as a series of problems to be solved, rather than as a series of high-pressure memory retrieval tasks. Successful test takers are used to applying the mathematics that they know to various settings and using a variety of representations. Effective teachers prepare students for high-stakes tests in the same way that they teach them mathematics: by having them solve problems, reason, represent, communicate, and make connections.

Several hurdles, however, may keep students from succeeding on high-stakes tests. Effective teachers integrate preparing for tests into their teaching in ways that help students overcome these hurdles and that reinforce other important learning goals. Effective teachers—

- know the test;

- familiarize students with nonmathematical aspects of the test;

- integrate test prep into everyday classes and regular assessments; and

- teach students to see the test as problems to solve by using what they know, not a series of memory retrieval tasks.

Know the test

To prepare your students for a test, you need to know the content the test will cover and the kinds of questions it will ask. Know the format, too: Will the test have short-answer, multiple-choice, or open-response questions? How will they be graded? How much will each question, or type of question, be worth? How much time will students have, and what will they be allowed to have with them during the test?

As much as possible, look to examples of the test to answer these questions, rather than standards documents, or official announcements describing what students will need to know. This may help you avoid the trap of spending several weeks on content that never appears on the test, even though it is in the official state syllabus.

Familiarize students with the test

To do well on math tests, students need to concentrate their mental energy on mathematics. When unfamiliar with the format of the test, they may become anxious and spend valuable energy trying to figure out what to do. First of all, students should know about the logistical, nonmathematical aspects of the test:

- What kinds of questions are on the test, and how much are they worth?

- What does the answer sheet looks like?

- How should they fill in their answers?

- What should they bring to the test, and what are they not allowed to bring?

Students should master all nonmathematical aspects of the test long before the test begins, so that they can concentrate on math during the test.

Students should also be familiar with how they will be graded and what counts as high-quality work. This is especially true for tests with open-answer questions, where students are graded on a rubric and must present more than just the correct answer to get full credit. Having students do sample questions from a previous test and then grade their answers according to the rubric will help them both become more aware of their own understanding and be more accurately attuned to what they need to do to succeed on the test.

Integrate test prep into everyday classes and regular assessments

Test prep is not something special that you do to cram information into students' brains right before the test. Familiarizing them with the content and format of the test, and teaching and modeling for them how to approach test questions, should happen all the time in math class. Give students problems or exercises in the format of the test and that mirror test content. Let students know that the work they have done is similar, in format and content, to what they will do on the test. This will help students develop confidence and see the test as normal mathematical activity rather than a special, mysterious ritual. If students are anxious about tests, do not tell them that what you are doing in class is similar to the test until after they have done it successfully.

Teach students to see the test as problems to solve by using what they know

Teaching students to approach the test as a series of problems to be solved by using what they know rather than as a test of what they have memorized combines the larger ideas of the book and the idea of integrating test prep into everyday lessons. We hope that in your classes, students work to make sense of mathematics by reasoning, representing, communicating, solving problems, and making connections. If they also do this regularly with problems that look like those they will see on the test, they will learn that the answers to test questions are things that students figure out. Emphasizing test questions as no different from other math questions that students can solve through persistence and applying what they already know will help students better approach tests. If students think that they should know all the answers right away, they could panic when they do not immediately know the answer to a test question.

CONCLUSION

This chapter could never answer all the potential questions new teachers might have about teaching mathematics or address all possible issues. Having a set of ideas about the learning and teaching of mathematics can help new teachers make sense of a wide range of issues and demands, and respond to them in ways that help students gain connected knowledge of mathematics. Your goal is to have students reason and prove, represent, communicate, solve problems, and make connections. You achieve it by planning the interactions described in the triangle of instruction. With this knowledge, you have a powerful way to think about testing, working with parents, using technology in your classroom, and whatever other aspects of teaching that may appear during your career. Ultimately we hope that, instead of reacting to demands and pressures, you can see various aspects of your job as opportunities to work with others to further support students in developing connected knowledge of mathematics.

Epilogue

As beginning teachers, we had high hopes for the effects we would have on our students and the classroom environments we would create. We envisioned ourselves as caring, dynamic teachers who would bring mathematics alive and inspire students to learn mathematics and the greater life lessons that come from hard work and intellectual engagement. We thought that the greatest teachers had a special gift, an innate ability to entertain, inspire, and empathize, and we longed to think that we might be like them.

But teaching is only sometimes like this vision. Certainly we have days when we connect with students or when a lesson lights a fire of understanding, but seeing ourselves as having some special gift is hard when such days are not the norm. Learning that teaching is more difficult and complex than any of us originally thought might be an unwelcome surprise. In retrospect, thinking that natural talent, kindness, intellect, and charisma could carry us through was comforting. When it took more than those characteristics, we often felt (and sometimes still do feel) discouraged and at a loss. Sometimes we wondered whether teaching was right for us.

Teaching is much more than enacting innate talents. Observing and talking with teachers showed us that effective teaching arises from knowledge and technique gained from years of directed inquiry and effort. Teaching is ultimately a quest to better support student learning. As a teacher, you can use your own teaching to investigate content, students, and teaching, and collaborate with colleagues to develop and enact better ways to support students. This is a rich and powerful understanding of what having a career in teaching means.

Ron Gallimore and Bradley Ermeling, educational researchers and teacher educators, and Swen Nater, a former professional basketball player, wrote about John Wooden, the legendary UCLA basketball coach whose teams won more national championships than any others (Nater and Gallimore 2010; Gallimore, Ermeling, and Nater 2012; Ermeling 2012). Many ascribed Wooden's success to the great players on his teams or to his talent to motivate and inspire. Wooden himself, however, often stated that his success came from something else altogether: At the beginning of every season, Wooden identified one aspect of his coaching to improve. He studied that aspect, read about it, watched other coaches, and talked with colleagues. He devised an improvement plan of approaches that aligned with his goal. He then carried out that plan and collected data during practices, documenting how his improvement plan was going. Finally he made adjustments based on what the data told him. By engaging in this process every season over his coaching career, he got better and better.

Think of a career in teaching the same way that Wooden saw his own career in coaching. Indeed, Wooden saw himself primarily as a teacher. He often said that his success came from what he learned as a high school English teacher in the 1930s. And he saw teaching as a constant process of improving one's instruction. Although perhaps less glamorous and flashy, this consistent effort to think about your craft, and to use your teaching as a site for learning, ultimately empowers you to become more effective. Instead of being a test of your fitness as a teacher, each day becomes another opportunity to learn and to think deeply with colleagues about the meaning of effective teaching and how to achieve it.

This is why so many teacher educators stress continued reflection and professional development. Teaching is an intellectual exercise, a career intimately connected to an endless quest to improve teaching through examining your own practice and working with others to gain knowledge and understanding.

As kids, we thought adults knew it all. Now as adults, we know better. But knowing it all seems less attractive than it once did. Continuing to learn is more fun—and more interesting. No matter where you are, you can always figure out ways to get better. We hope that this book has helped you begin that journey.

Recommended Resources

These resources are also available electronically on More4U.

We wrote this book to help new mathematics teachers lay a foundation for effective practice and long-term professional growth. Of course, the teaching and learning of mathematics involves more than we could cover. We recommend these resources to help you access further information and learn more.

The first four sections correspond to the sections of the book. For ease of use, we organized resources into smaller categories. We also included two other sections: Content Resources offers a starting point for planning units, lessons, or assessments, and Reflection and Further Growth gives resources for reflecting on your own practice.

We sought a balance between giving you a range of resources and limiting the list to the most helpful items. Some references appear in more than one section because they apply to more than one aspect of teaching. Also, some readings here address elementary mathematics instruction. Although this book is for middle and secondary mathematics teachers, these teachers can learn much from those who work with and study smaller children. Because elementary schoolchildren do not think like adults, elementary teachers and researchers work hard to discern what their students think and understand, and they work hard to make their goals and directions clear and explicit. These efforts stand as excellent models for the teaching and learning this book advocates.

SECTION I: THE BIG PICTURE

Examples of thoughtful teaching

Boaler, Jo, and Cathlee Humphreys. *Connecting Mathematical Ideas: Middle School Video Cases to Support Teaching and Learning.* Portsmouth, N.H.: Heinemann, 2005.

Chazan, Daniel. *Beyond Formulas in Mathematics and Teaching: Dynamics of the High School Algebra Classroom.* New York: Teachers College Press, 2000.

Lampert, Magdalene. *Teaching Problems and the Problems of Teaching.* New Haven, Conn.: Yale University Press, 2001.

Moses, Robert P., and Charles E. Cobb Jr. *Radical Equations: Civil Rights from Mississippi to the Algebra Project.* Boston: Beacon Press, 2001.

Learning mathematics with understanding and what that means for teaching

Boaler, Jo, and Megan Staples. "Creating Mathematical Futures through an Equitable Teaching Approach: The Case of Railside School." *Teachers College Record* 110 (January 2008): 608–45.

Bransford, John, Ann L. Brown, and Rodney R. Cocking, eds. *How People Learn: Brain, Mind, Experience, and School*: Expanded Edition. Washington, D.C.: National Academies Press, 2000.

Carpenter, Thomas P., and Richard Lehrer. "Teaching and Learning Mathematics with Understanding." In *Mathematics Classrooms That Promote Understanding*, edited by Elizabeth Fennema and Thomas A. Romberg, pp. 19–32. Mahwah, N.J.: Lawrence Erlbaum Associates, 1999.

Hiebert, James. "Relationships between Research and the NCTM Standards." *Journal for Research in Mathematics Education* 30 (January 1999): 3–19.

Hiebert, James, Thomas P. Carpenter, Elizabeth Fennema, Karen C. Fuson, Diana Wearne, Hanlie Murray, Alwyn Olivier, and Piet Human. *Making Sense: Teaching and Learning Mathematics with Understanding.* Portsmouth, N.H.: Heinemann, 1997.

Kilpatrick, Jeremy, Jane Swafford, and Bradford Findell, eds. *Adding It Up: Helping Children Learn Mathematics.* Washington, D.C.: National Academies Press, 2001.

National Council of Teachers of Mathematics (NCTM). *Focus in High School Mathematics: Reasoning and Sense Making.* Reston, Va.: NCTM, 2009.

Skemp, Richard R. "Relational Understanding and Instrumental Understanding." *Mathematics Teaching* 77 (December 1976): 20–26. Reprinted in *Arithmetic Teacher* 26 (November 1978): 9–15, and in *Mathematics Teaching in the Middle School* 12 (September 2006): 88–95.

SECTION II: LAYING THE GROUNDWORK

Charney, Ruth Sidney. *Teaching Children to Care: Classroom Management for Ethical and Academic Growth, K–8.* Turners Falls, Mass.: Northeast Foundation for Children, 2002.

Dweck, Carol S. "The Secret to Raising Smart Kids." *Scientific American Mind,* December 2007, pp. 37–43.

Fay, Jim, and David Funk. *Teaching with Love and Logic.* Golden, Colo.: Love and Logic Institute, 1995.

Lemov, Doug. *Teach Like a Champion: 49 Techniques That Put Students on the Path to College.* San Francisco: Jossey-Bass, 2010.

Wong, Harry K., and Rosemary T. Wong. *The First Days of School: How to Be an Effective Teacher.* Mountain View, Calif.: Harry K. Wong Publications, 2009.

SECTION III: THE LESSON CYCLE

Chapin, Suzanne H., Catherine O'Connor, and Nancy Canavan Anderson. *Classroom Discussions: Using Math Talk to Help Students Learn.* 2nd ed. Sausalito, Calif.: Math Solutions Publications, 2009.

Jackson, Kara J., Emily C. Shahan, Lynsey K. Gibbons, and Paul A. Cobb. "Launching Complex Tasks." *Mathematics Teaching in the Middle School* 18 (August 2012): 24–29.

Smith, Margaret S., and Mary Kay Stein. *Five Practices for Orchestrating Productive Mathematics Discussions.* Reston, Va.: National Council of Teachers of Mathematics, 2011.

Smith, Margaret S., Elizabeth K. Hughes, Randi A. Engle, and Mary Kay Stein. "Orchestrating Discussions." *Mathematics Teaching in the Middle School* 14 (May 2009): 548–56.

SECTION IV: MORE ELEMENTS OF EFFECTIVE TEACHING

Establishing and maintaining effective group work

Horn, Ilana Seidel. *Strength in Numbers: Collaborative Learning in Secondary Mathematics.* Reston, Va.: National Council of Teachers of Mathematics, 2012.

Classroom management

Fay, Jim, and David Funk. *Teaching with Love and Logic.* Golden, Colo.: Love and Logic Institute, 1995.

Lemov, Doug. *Teach Like a Champion: 49 Techniques That Put Students on the Path to College.* San Francisco: Jossey-Bass, 2010.

Teaching struggling students

Boaler, Jo, and Megan Staples. "Creating Mathematical Futures through an Equitable Teaching Approach: The Case of Railside School." *Teachers College Record* 110 (January 2008): 608–45.

Cohen, Elizabeth G., Rachel A. Lotan, Beth A. Scarloss, and Adele R. Arellano. "Complex Instruction: Equity in Cooperative Learning Classrooms." *Theory into Practice* 38 (Spring 1999): 80–86.

Cohen, Elizabeth G., Rachel A. Lotan, Jennifer A. Whitcomb, Maria V. Balderrama, Ruth Cossey, and Patricia E. Swanson. "Complex Instruction: Higher-Order Thinking in Heterogeneous Classrooms." In *Handbook of Cooperative Learning Methods*, edited by Robert J. Stahl, pp. 82–96. Westport, Conn.: Greenwood Press, 1995.

Fosnot, Catherine Twomey, and Willem Uittenbogaard. *Minilessons for Extending Addition and Subtraction: A Yearlong Resource.* Portsmouth, N.H.: Heinemann, 2007.

———. *Minilessons for Extending Multiplication and Division: A Yearlong Resource.* Portsmouth, N.H.: Heinemann, 2007.

Imm, Kara Louise, Catherine Twomey Fosnot, and Willem Uittenbogaard. *Minilessons for Operations with Fractions, Decimals, and Percents: A Yearlong Resource.* Portsmouth, N.H.: Heinemann, 2008.

Jansen, Amanda, and James Middleton. *Motivation Matters and Interest Counts: Fostering Engagement in Mathematics.* Reston, Va.: National Council of Teachers of Mathematics, 2011.

Assessment

Black, Paul, and Dylan Wiliam. "Inside the Black Box: Raising Standards through Classroom Assessment." *Phi Delta Kappan* 80 (October 1998): 139–48.

Black, Paul, Christine Harrison, Clare Lee, Bethan Marshall, and Dylan Wiliam. "Working Inside the Black Box: Assessment for Learning in the Classroom." *Phi Delta Kappan* 86 (September 2004): 8–21.

Hodgen, Jeremy, and Dylan Wiliam. *Mathematics Inside the Black Box: Assessment for Learning in the Mathematics Classroom.* London: GL Assessment, 2006.

Teaching with technology

Dick, Thomas P., and Karen F. Hollebrands, eds. *Focus in High School Mathematics: Technology to Support Reasoning and Sense Making.* Reston, Va.: National Council of Teachers of Mathematics, 2011.

Texas Instruments Education Technology. http://education.ti.com /calculators/downloads/us/activities/.

Interacting with parents/guardians

Delpit, Lisa D. *Other People's Children: Cultural Conflict in the Classroom.* Rev. ed. New York: New Press, 2006.

Mirra, Amy. *A Family's Guide: Fostering Your Child's Success in School Mathematics.* Reston, Va.: National Council of Teachers of Mathematics, 2005.

CONTENT RESOURCES

Teacher content knowledge/standards

Charles, Randall I. "Big Ideas and Understandings as the Foundation for Elementary and Middle School Mathematics." *Journal of Mathematics Education Leadership* 7 (Spring/Summer 2005): 9–24.

Driscoll, Mark. *Fostering Algebraic Thinking: A Guide for Teachers, Grades 6–10.* Portsmouth, N.H.: Heinemann, 1999.

Driscoll, Mark, Rachel Wing DiMatteo, Johannah Nikula, and Michael Egan. *Fostering Geometric Thinking: A Guide for Teachers, Grades 5–10.* Portsmouth, N.H.: Heinemann, 2007.

National Council of Teachers of Mathematics (NCTM). *Principles and Standards for School Mathematics.* Reston, Va.: NCTM, 2000.

National Governors Association Center for Best Practices (NGA Center) and Council of Chief State School Officers (CCSSO). *Common Core State Standards for Mathematics. Common Core State Standards (College- and Career-Readiness Standards and K–12 Standards in English Language Arts and Math).* Washington, D.C.: NGA Center and CCSSO, 2010. http://www.corestandards.org/math.

Content resources for unit planning, lesson planning, assessment

National Council of Teachers of Mathematics (NCTM). *Mathematics Assessment Sampler 9–12: Items Aligned with NCTM's "Principles and Standards for School Mathematics."* Reston, Va.: NCTM, 2005.

———. *Mathematics Assessment Sampler 6–8: Items Aligned with NCTM's "Principles and Standards for School Mathematics."* Reston, Va.: NCTM, 2005.

NCTM Focus in High School Mathematics Series: The Focus in High School Mathematics series helps teachers learn about issues involved in teaching for sense making in high school mathematics. Book content areas include algebra; geometry; statistics and probability; a more general book on activities from the NCTM journal Mathematics Teacher; teaching with technology; and equity. Available from NCTM: http://www.nctm.org/catalog/.

NCTM Navigations Series: The Navigations series includes grades 6–8 and 9–12 books on algebra, geometry, data analysis, probability, measurement, number and operations, reasoning, discrete mathematics, and mathematical connections. Each book offers activities to help students learn important concepts in that particular content strand at the appropriate level. The books also come with teacher resources, including written discussion of the important ideas, common student understandings and misunderstandings, and materials needed for the activities, such as student activity sheets. Available from NCTM: http://www.nctm.org/catalog/.

Content resources for struggling students

Fosnot, Catherine Twomey, and Willem Uittenbogaard. *Minilessons for Extending Addition and Subtraction: A Yearlong Resource.* Portsmouth, N.H.: Heinemann, 2007.

———. *Minilessons for Extending Multiplication and Division: A Yearlong Resource.* Portsmouth, N.H.: Heinemann, 2007.

Imm, Kara Louise, Catherine Twomey Fosnot, and Willem Uittenbogaard. *Minilessons for Operations with Fractions, Decimals, and Percents: A Yearlong Resource.* Portsmouth, N.H.: Heinemann. 2007.

Websites

NCTM Illuminations—Resources for Teaching Math. http://illuminations.nctm.org/.

The Math Forum at Drexel University. http://mathforum.org/

Texas Instruments Education Technology: http://education.ti.com/calculators/downloads/us/activities/.

REFLECTION AND FURTHER GROWTH

Ball, Deborah Loewenberg. "With an Eye on the Mathematical Horizon: Dilemmas of Teaching Elementary School Mathematics." *Elementary School Journal* 93 (March 1993): 373–97.

Boaler, Jo, and Cathlee Humphreys. *Connecting Mathematical Ideas: Middle School Video Cases to Support Teaching and Learning.* Portsmouth, N.H.: Heinemann, 2005.

Chazan, Daniel. *Beyond Formulas in Mathematics and Teaching: Dynamics of the High School Algebra Classroom.* New York: Teachers College Press, 2000.

Lampert, Magdalene. "How Do Teachers Manage to Teach? Perspectives on Problems in Practice." *Harvard Educational Review* 55 (May 1985): 178–94.

Lewis, Catherine, Rebecca Perry, Jacqueline Hurd, and Mary Pat O'Connell. "Lesson Study Comes of Age in North America." *Phi Delta Kappan* 88 (December 2006): 273–81.

Romagnano, Lew. *Wrestling with Change: The Dilemmas of Teaching Real Mathematics.* Portsmouth, N.H.: Heinemann, 1994.

Schön, Donald A. *The Reflective Practitioner: How Professionals Think in Action.* New York: Basic Books, 1983.

Websites

Annenberg Learner—Teacher Professional Development and Classroom
Resources across the Curriculum. http://www.learner.org/.
Inside Mathematics: http://www.insidemathematics.org/
The Math Forum at Drexel University. http://mathforum.org/.

References

Ball, Deborah Loewenberg. "Teaching Mathematics as an Unnatural Activity." Paper presented at the annual meeting of the National Council of Supervisors of Mathematics, Atlanta, March 20, 2007. http://www.mathedleadership.org/member/objects/resources/podcasts/2007/11_03202007_Ball.mp3.

Black, Paul, and Dylan Wiliam. "Assessment and Classroom Learning." *Assessment in Education* 5, no. 1 (1998): 7–74.

Boaler, Jo, and Megan Staples. "Creating Mathematical Futures through an Equitable Teaching Approach: The Case of Railside School." *Teachers College Record* 110 (January 2008): 608–45.

Bransford, John, A. L. Brown, and R. R. Cocking, eds. *How People Learn: Brain, Mind, Experience, and School.* Expanded ed. Washington, D.C.: National Academies Press, 2000.

Chapin, Suzanne H., Catherine O'Connor, and Nancy Canavan Anderson. *Classroom Discussions: Using Math Talk to Help Students Learn.* Sausalito, Calif.: Math Solutions, 2009.

Cohen, David K., and Deborah Loewenberg Ball. "Instruction, Capacity, and Improvement." In *Research Report Series No. RR-43.* Philadelphia: Consortium for Policy Research in Education, University of Pennsylvania, 1999.

Cohen, Elizabeth G., Rachel A. Lotan, Beth A. Scarloss, and Adele R. Arellano. "Complex Instruction: Equity in Cooperative Learning Classrooms." *Theory into Practice* 38 (Spring 1999): 80–86.

Cohen, Elizabeth G., Rachel A. Lotan, Jennifer A. Whitcomb, Maria V. Balderrama, Ruth Cossey, and Patricia E. Swanson. "Complex Instruction: Higher-Order Thinking in Heterogeneous Classrooms." In *Handbook of Cooperative Learning Methods,* edited by Robert J. Stahl, pp. 82–96. Westport, Conn.: Greenwood Press, 1995.

Dick, Thomas P., and Karen F. Hollebrands, eds. *Focus in High School Mathematics: Technology to Support Reasoning and Sense Making.* Reston, Va.: National Council of Teachers of Mathematics, 2011.

Driscoll, Mark. *Fostering Algebraic Thinking: A Guide for Teachers, Grades 6–10.* Portsmouth, N.H.: Heinemann, 1999.

Ermeling, Bradley Alan. "Improving Teaching through Continuous Learning: The Inquiry Process John Wooden Used to Become Coach of the Century." *Quest* 64, no. 3 (2012): 197–208.

Floden, Robert E., and Christopher M. Clark. "Preparing Teachers for Uncertainty." *Teachers College Record* 89 (Summer 1988): 505–24.

Franke, Megan L., Elham Kazemi, and Daniel Battey. "Mathematics Teaching and Classroom Practice." In *Second Handbook of Research on Mathematics Teaching and Learning,* edited by Frank K. Lester, pp. 225–256. Charlotte, N.C.: Information Age Publishing, 2007.

Gallimore, Ronald, Bradley Alan Ermeling, and Swen Nater. "Timeless Lessons." *Athletic Management* vol. 24, February–March 2012.

Gravemeijer, Koeno, Anton Roodhardt, Monica Wijers, Martin Kindt, Beth R. Cole, and Gail Burrill. *Expressions and Formulas.* Mathematics in Context. Chicago: Holt, Rinehart, and Winston, 2006.

Hiebert, James, and Douglas A. Grouws. "The Effects of Classroom Mathematics Teaching on Students' Learning." In *Second Handbook of*

Research on Mathematics Teaching and Learning, edited by Frank K. Lester. Charlotte, N.C.: Information Age Publishing, 2007.

Lampert, Magdalene. "How Do Teachers Manage to Teach? Perspectives on Problems in Practice." *Harvard Educational Review* 55 (May 1985): 178–94.

———. *Teaching Problems and the Problems of Teaching.* New Haven, Conn.: Yale University Press, 2001.

Lappan, Glenda, James T. Fey, William M. Fitzgerald, Susan N. Friel, and Elizabeth Difanis Phillips. "Prime Time: Factors and Multiples" (Connected Mathematics Project). Palo Alto, Calif.: Dale Seymour, 1996.

Lemov, Doug. *Teach Like a Champion: 49 Techniques That Put Students on the Path to College.* San Francisco: Jossey-Bass, 2010.

Mueller, Claudia M., and Carol S. Dweck. "Praise for Intelligence Can Undermine Children's Motivation and Performance." *Journal of Personality and Social Psychology* 75 (July 1998): 33–52. doi:10.1037/0022-3514.75.1.33.

Nater, Swen, and Ronald Gallimore. *You Haven't Taught until They've Learned: John Wooden's Teaching Principles and Practices.* Morgantown, W.Va.: Fitness International Technology, 2010.

National Council of Teachers of Mathematics (NCTM). Curriculum and Evaluation Standards for School Mathematics. Reston, Va.: NCTM, 1989.

———. "Enhancing the Learning Environment through Student-Led Mathematical Discussions," by Fran Arbaugh and Patricia Avery. In *Mathematics for Every Student: Responding to Diversity, Grades 9–12,* edited by Alfinio Flores and Carol Malloy, pp. 7–16. Reston, Va.: NCTM, 2009a.

———. *Professional Standards for Teaching Mathematics.* Reston, Va.: NCTM, 1991.

———. *Principles and Standards for School Mathematics.* Reston, Va.: NCTM, 2000.

———. *Curriculum Focal Points for Prekindergarten through Grade 8 Mathematics: A Quest for Coherence.* Reston, Va.: NCTM, 2006.

———. *Focus in High School Mathematics: Reasoning and Sense Making.* Reston, Va.: NCTM, 2009b.

National Governors Association Center for Best Practices (NGA Center) and Council of Chief State School Officers (CCSSO). Common Core State Standards for Mathematics. *Common Core State Standards (College- and Career-Readiness Standards and K–12 Standards in English Language Arts and Math).* Washington, D.C.: NGA Center and CCSSO, 2010. http://www.corestandards.org/.

Senk, Sharon L., and Denisse R. Thompson, eds. *Standards-Based School Mathematics Curricula: What Are They? What Do Students Learn?* Studies in Mathematical Thinking and Learning. Mahwah, N.J.: Lawrence Erlbaum, 2003.

Skemp, Richard R. "Relational Understanding and Instrumental Under-standing." *Mathematics Teaching* 77 (December 1976): 20–26. Re-printed in *Arithmetic Teacher* 26 (November 1978): 9–15, and in *Mathematics Teaching in the Middle School* 12 (September 2006): 88–95.

Smith, Margaret Schwan, Victoria Bill, and Elizabeth K. Hughes. "Thinking through a Lesson: Successfully Implementing High-Level Tasks." *Mathematics Teaching in the Middle School* 14 (October 2008): 132–38.

Stein, Mary Kay, and Margaret Schwan Smith. "Mathematical Tasks as a Framework for Reflection: From Research to Practice." *Mathematics Teaching in the Middle School* 3 (January 1998a): 268–75.

———. "Selecting and Creating Mathematical Tasks: From Research to Practice." *Mathematics Teaching in the Middle School* 3 (February 1998b): 344–50.

Stein, Mary Kay, and Suzanne Lane. "Instructional Tasks and the Devel-opment of Student Capacity to Think and Reason: An Analysis of the Relationship between Teaching and Learning in a Reform Mathematics Project." *Educational Research and Evaluation* 2, no. 1 (1996): 50–80.

Stein, Mary Kay, Barbara W. Grover, and Marjorie Henningsen. "Build-ing Student Capacity for Mathematical Thinking and Reasoning: An Analysis of Mathematical Tasks Used in Reform Classrooms." *American Educational Research Journal* 33 (Summer 1996): 455–88.

Stein, Mary Kay, Margaret Schwan Smith, Marjorie A. Henningsen, and Edward A. Silver. *Implementing Standards-Based Mathematics In-struction: A Casebook for Professional Development*. 2nd ed. Reston, Va.: National Council of Teachers of Mathematics, 2009.

Takahashi, Akihiko. "Characteristics of Japanese Mathematics Lessons." 2006. http://www.criced.tsukuba.ac.jp/math/sympo_2006/takahashi.pdf.

Wood, Terry. "Alternative Patterns of Communication in Mathematics Classes: Focusing or Funneling?" In *Language and Communication in the Mathematics Classroom*, edited by Heinz Steinbring, Maria G. Bartolini Bussi, and Anna Sierpinska, pp. 167–78. Reston, Va.: National Council of Teachers of Mathematics, 1998.

Yackel, Erna, and Paul Cobb. "Sociomathematical Norms, Argumentation, and Autonomy in Mathematics." *Journal for Research in Mathemat-ics Education* 27 (July 1996): 458–77.

Appendixes

SUCCESS
from the START
Your first years
teaching SECONDARY
MATHEMATICS

appendix **one**

Games for Basic Skills, Number Sense, and Reasoning

These resources
are also available
electronically on
More4U.

The games in this section offer opportunities to increase your
students' skills, number sense, and reasoning in mathematics.

"FIVE STEPS TO ZERO"

"Five Steps to Zero" gives students experience with basic operations and some important ideas about factors and multiples. In discussing strategies, students should have to reason about using factors to compose and decompose numbers and should gain experience with divisibility rules. Through extensions it also allows students to gain facility manipulating fractions, decimals, and signed numbers. Finally, it introduces a powerful way to represent functions.

Directions:
Start with a given number. Your job is to reduce this number to zero in five steps by using the four operations multiplication, division, addition, and subtraction, and whole numbers from 1 to 9. Look at the steps in the following example.

Example: 673

  1. Add 2. $673 + 2 = 675$

  2. Divide by 5. $675 \div 5 = 135$

  3. Divide by 5. $135 \div 5 = 27$

  4. Divide by 9. $27 \div 9 = 3$

  5. Subtract 3. $3 - 3 = 0$

Circle notation:
Circle notation is a great way to track this game. (The idea of circle notation is widespread. Arthur Powell, of Rutgers, Newark, and the writers of Mathematics in Context [Gravemeijer et al. 2006], among others, have used it extensively.) Use circle notation by following the steps below:

  1. Start with the initial number in a circle.

  2. Each "step" is an arrow to a new circle, with the operation and the number written above it.

  3. The new number goes in the new circle.

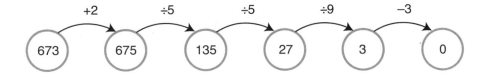

Notes on circle notation:

- You can use this notation later to introduce the concept of functions, unknowns, variables, and inverse operations. (See Expressions and Formulas from the curriculum Mathematics in Context for an example of using this notation in other contexts.)

- You can put in partially filled-in circle expressions and have students fill in numbers, operations, or both.

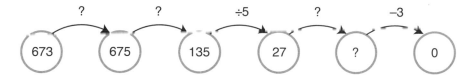

- You can have students go backward and fill in the numbers if you give them the operations.

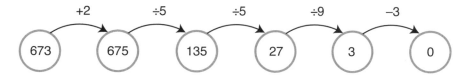

Common questions/mistakes:

- Can I use the same number twice?

  - Yes, you can use the same number up to five times.

- Can I use the same operation twice?

  - Yes, you can use the same operation up to five times.

- Students often use numbers over 9 (not allowed) or zero (not allowed) or negative numbers (not allowed).

Introduction and discussion:

1. Start with something simple, and maybe make it one or two steps to zero to begin with (two steps to zero with 11, then with 20, then three steps to zero with 29, etc.).

2. Have students play in pairs and have them discuss their moves.

3. After playing for a while, have students discuss their strategies. While discussing strategies, press for why a particular strategy works. Generally, the strategies are concerned with the relationship between factors and multiples. So if I can divide by 3, and then divide by 2, I know that 3 and 2 are factors, so therefore 6 must be a factor. Instead of using two steps to divide by 3 and then by 2, I can use one step to divide

by 6. This game is a great way to get students to think about and make sense of how factors fit together to form numbers, a basic idea behind number theory and number sense. Possible discussion points include the following:

- Getting to a number that ends in 5 or 0 right away, so I can divide by 5.

- Dividing as soon as I can, preferably by a large number.

- Divisibility rules—

    - 5 (ends in 5 or 0)

    - 2 (even number, ends in 0, 2, 4, 6, 8)

    - 3 (digits add up to a multiple of 3)

    - 6 (divisible by 3 and an even number)

    - 9 (digits add up to a multiple of 9)

- The idea that I can combine division steps (for example, if I divide by 4 and then divide by 2, I could just divide by 8, which is 4 × 2).

- Getting to a multiple of 10 and looking at the first two digits; if the first two digits by themselves are divisible by a number, then so is the larger three-digit number. (For example, 720 is divisible by 9 because 72 is 8 × 9. If I have 727, I will choose to subtract 7 to get to 720, rather than add 3 to get to 730, because nothing goes into 73.)

Extensions:
You can modify this game to target specific skills:

- Change the initial number. Make it a decimal, fraction, negative number, or a combination of all three.

- Change the operations allowed. Make it only addition or only subtraction, but allow any number between −9 and 9. Or allow square roots.

- Ask students to come up with a starting number that you cannot turn into zero in five steps.

"TWENTY-FOUR"

"Twenty-Four" is a great game for basic number sense, the idea that numbers can be broken down and manipulated. I can think of 24 as 12×2, 3×8, 4×6, $25 - 1$, and an infinite number of other ways. These different ways of thinking about 24 help me play this game.

- Give four numbers from 1 to 9 (you can give the same number twice).

- You have to use these numbers, along with any operations you want, to make the number 24.

- You can use a number only once, unless it shows up more than once in the initial four numbers.

Example: 2, 3, 4, 6
You can make 24 by doing $(2 \times 6) + (3 \times 4)$ or $6 \times 4 \times (3 - 2)$ or $\dfrac{6 \times 4}{3 - 2}$.

Logistical considerations for a full-class game:
Make teams. Give out four numbers; wait a few minutes. For each team, allow multiple solutions. Give five points for the first, three for the second, two for the third, and one for each one after that.
Raise the level:

- Make students state their answer in one number sentence with as few parentheses as needed. You could give extra style points or bonus points for doing it this way.

- Use negative numbers.

Strategies you might look for and discuss:

- Start by simply adding.

- Look for ways to make 12 two different ways.

- Look for ways to make 6 and 4, or 8 and 3, or 12 and 2, and then multiply these two.

- Look for other pairs that subtract to 24, such as 25 and 1.

- Look for ways to make 24 with two of the numbers and then find a way to make one with the other two.

- Use square roots, exponents—

  - for example, 2, 3, 5, 2 could be done $2^3 \times (5 - 2)$;

  - 2, 2, 3, 4 could be done $\sqrt{4} \times 2 \times 2 \times 3$.

"HIT THE TARGET"

"Hit the Target" stresses estimation, guessing and checking, and the huge idea that multiplying can make a number larger (by multiplying by a number greater than 1) or smaller (by multiplying by a number between 0 and 1).

1. You play this game with calculators.

2. You start the game with a range of two numbers (say, 650–670). This is the "target." The object of the game is to get inside this target.

3. You also start with a single number (such as 26). This is the "ball."

4. You try to "hit the target" with the ball by multiplying the ball by a number that you choose.

5. If the result is in the target, you win.

6. If not, the result is the new ball, and the other team tries to hit the target with that ball.

7. And so it continues until there is a winner.

Example: Target, 650–670; ball, 26
Team 1 guess: 26×22; $26 \times 22 = 572$. This is not in the target, so it becomes the new ball.
Team 2 guess: 572×1.5; $572 \times 1.5 = 858$. This is not in the target, so it becomes the new ball.
Team 1 guess: 858×1.1; $858 \times 1.1 = 943.8$. This is not in the target, so it becomes the new ball.
Team 2 guess: 943.8×0.7; $943.8 \times 0.7 = 660.66$. We have a winner!

Details:

- Teams must guess; they are not allowed to check their guess before they try it. This game is about estimation and using previous guesses to make better ones. You might want to limit moves to a few seconds so that teams will not check their answers. In the end, they need to use number sense, not calculation.

- This game has several big ideas:

  - You can make a number smaller by multiplying by a number less than 1.

  - You can make a number a little smaller by multiplying it by a number close to 1 (say, 0.95).

- You can make a number a little larger by multiplying it by a number a little bit more than 1 (such as 1.05).

Until students know these ideas, the game is incredibly frustrating. You want as many students as possible to discover these ideas on their own, but you may need to scaffold it for them. Stop the game and ask, "How can you make a number smaller?" Have them experiment and then have a discussion. Through lots of experience they should begin to get a sense of these big ideas.

- At some point you might want to discuss estimation strategies:

  - Looking at first digits, and disregarding others.

  - Rules for multiplying by 10, 100, 0.1, 0.01—this game has a big place-value element.

- Decimals can get cumbersome; you might want to have students round to the nearest whole number, or even set the calculators to show only whole numbers. You might want to discuss this. Of course, you can just have students press the multiplication button followed by their guess, and the calculator will automatically multiply the former answer by the new guess. No need to round at all.

- Students track their guesses on a chart that looks like this:

Target: 650-670

Move	Ball	Guess	Result	Hit (Yes or No)
Team 1	26	22	572	No
Team 2	572	1.5	858	No
Team 1	858	1.1	943.8	No
Team 2	943.8	.7	660.66	YES

- Watch for graphing calculator habits:

  - Students should not press Clear after each guess.

  - They can just press the multiplication button followed by their guess; they do not need to enter the new ball.

Extensions:

- Make the target much smaller (for example, 450–455 or 450–450.27).

- Make the operation division; to hit the target, you need to divide the ball.

  - You could start by making the target smaller than the ball (35–40 with a ball of 785) and then go to a small ball and a higher target.

- For students struggling with more basic number sense, make the operation addition. You can then turn the tables by making the ball higher than the target; you have to add a negative number to make the original number smaller.

- You can make the operation subtraction; you need to subtract by a negative to make the number larger.

- You can make the operation addition or subtraction, but use decimals.

Remember, the point is not for them to get the answer right away; it is to give them many experiences seeing what they get when they perform operations with certain numbers. Ideally, they should make predictions about their guesses and look at the results. After playing this game for a while, they should have seen many times that multiplying by a number less than 1 yields a smaller result (as long as all the numbers are positive).

"WALLY'S NEPHEW'S GAME"

"Wally's Nephew's Game" is a great way to practice operations with signed numbers. It also forces students to strategize, thinking several moves ahead to determine what their best move may be. Playing in teams encourages discourse.

- The game has two teams, the number team and the letter team.

- The game uses a 5 × 5 grid containing numbers from −5 to 5 scattered randomly.

- Rows of the grid are labeled A–E; columns are labeled 1–5.

- The referee chooses a letter (row). The number team then chooses a column (number). The referee erases the number in that box in the grid, puts some sort of playing piece in the square, and adds that number to the number team's score.

- The letter team now chooses a row. The referee takes the playing piece and moves it along the same column to the new row, erases the number in that box, adds the number to the letter team's score, and places the playing piece in the box.

- You are not allowed to move to an empty square.

- The game continues until a team has no possible moves.

- The team with the highest score at the end of the game wins.

Extensions:

- Add three multiplication turns. A team can decide to take the number in the box and multiply their total by that number, rather than add. For instance, if the letter team's total is 13, and they move to a box that has a 4 in it, they can say, "multiply," and instead of the referee adding 13 and 4 to get their new score, the referee would multiply 13×4, for a new score of 52.

  - This extension allows a team to get a negative number and turn it into a positive number by multiplying by a negative. Students figure out that the absolute value of the number is the most important thing until the end.

- Use decimals or fractions instead of whole numbers.

- Give teams an extra point for doing the calculation correctly.

Think about the logistics of running the game. You might want to have the grid on the overhead. You might want teams listed, and at each turn the team spokesperson is someone new. You might want to give a time limit for each turn. Some teachers introduce the game and then say nothing once students know the game; teachers just check off each name as each team goes and time the moves.

Example grid:

	1	2	3	4	5
A	2	−1	−2	−5	5
B	4	3	4	4	0
C	−3	1	0	−4	−1
D	−2	5	2	1	−3
E	−4	−3	0	3	−5

TIC-TAC-TOE

This game is like traditional tic-tac-toe, with some adjustments. It gives students practice using coordinate grids and naming points on the grid. It forces them to use precise language. It also forces them to strategize.

- The game is played on a coordinate grid from −4 to 4 on the *x*-axis and −4 to 4 on the *y*-axis.

- The game has three teams: *O*s, *X*s, and Δs.

- A team makes a move by telling the referee the coordinates of the point where they want to place their mark (for example, if the *X* team wants an *X* at 3 over and 2 up, the spokesperson tells the referee "3, 2" during their turn).

- You need to get four (or five) in a row to get a tic-tac-toe.

- The game does not end with one tic-tac-toe; it keeps going until the board is full. Each team can get multiple tic-tac-toes.

- Each team gets a point for each tic-tac-toe they get.

- You may not add on to a tic-tac-toe in the same direction, but you may build on to tic-tac-toes in a different direction.

  - Using a horizontal and a diagonal is allowed.

  - Building a second horizontal onto an existing one is not allowed.

Extensions:

- Give an extra point for saying the direction of the tic-tac-toe (horizontal, vertical, diagonal).

- Give a point for the slope (0, −1, 1, undefined).

- Give two points for the equation of the line that the tic-tac-toe lies on.

- If a team says, "tic-tac-toe," but gets the slope or direction or equation wrong, the next team gets a chance to steal their slope point. If the next team gets it wrong, the third team gets a chance, and then it goes back to the original team for a last chance.

- Give tic-tac-toe to four points that lie on a line, such as (−2, −1), (0, 0), (2, 1), (4, 2).

- Allow tic-tac-toes that are not lines, such as four or three points on an absolute value function or a parabola. Students must say, "tic-tac-toe," and give the equation. Once one equation is taken, it cannot be used again.

Again logistics are a concern. You might want to have each team listed, and team members take turns being the spokesperson, and the referee listens only to the spokesperson. Give a time limit for each turn. If they do not make a move in the time allowed, they forfeit their turn.

MENTAL MATH, STRINGS, CLUSTER PROBLEMS

Mental math, strings, and cluster problems all describe short activities designed to help students develop computation strategies. The point of these activities is not simply to find an answer, but to use bigger ideas about how numbers and operations work in order to develop shortcuts for computation and lay the foundation for algebra. It is, in the end, all about number sense.

Example:
The goal of the following problems is to get students to understand the idea of compensation—that when adding, they can take from one of the addends and give it to the other addend without changing the total.
Ask students to add, in their heads, 100 + 23. Write "100 + 23," horizontally, on the board. (Do not write the addition vertically because this will elicit a strategy of adding in columns.)
Ask students how they did the problem. You want to highlight the following strategy: "I just know that 100 plus a two-digit number is 100 and that two-digit number. I don't need to do any adding in columns."
Depending on how many students can do the above problem easily, give one or two more. Once a critical mass of students have the strategy above, give 99 + 23.
Again, ask how they did the problem. You are trying to highlight the following strategies:

- I took 1 from the 23, and gave it to the 99, so now I have 100 + 22.

- I added 1 to the 99 to make 100. I then did 100 + 23 = 123. Then I took 1 away, because I had added 1 at the beginning.

Try with more problems. Begin with 99 + some two-digit number.
Then move on to 98 + _____.
Then try 1000 + _____, and then 999 + _____ and 998 + _____.
Depending on your students' sophistication, you can move to 990 + _____, compensating or borrowing larger numbers. The big idea is to get to a friendly number that you can add in your head.
Highlight a particular numerical strategy and pick problems that will elicit that strategy. Below are some strategies you can think about.

Addition:
Skip-counting by tens first and then adding ones (you can use a number line model)

$63 + 46 \rightarrow 63 + 10 + 10 + 10 + 10 = 103 \rightarrow$ Now I have 6 more, $103 + 6 = 109$

Splitting, that is, adding tens and then adding ones
$60 + 40 = 100 \rightarrow 3 + 6 = 9 \rightarrow 100 + 9 = 109$

Subtraction:
   Counting on
   Counting back
   Number line models work well for subtraction problems.

Multiplication:
   Distributive property
   $13 \times 7 \rightarrow$ I did 10×7 and 3×7, and then I added them.

Area model

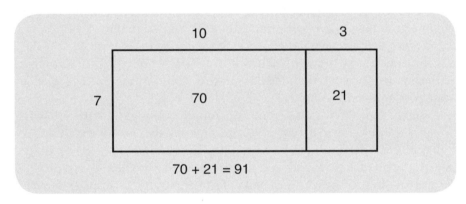

The following are excellent books about strings and how to use them:

Fosnot, Catherine Twomey, and Willem Uittenbogaard. *Minilessons for Extending Addition and Subtraction: A Yearlong Resource.* Portsmouth, N.H.: Heinemann, 2007.

———. *Minilessons for Extending Multiplication and Division: A Yearlong Resource.* Portsmouth, N.H.: Heinemann, 2007.

Imm, Kara Louise, Catherine Twomey Fosnot, and Willem Uittenbogaard. *Minilessons for Operations with Fractions, Decimals, and Percents: A Yearlong Resource.* Portsmouth, N.H.: Heinemann, 2008.

"THE FACTOR GAME"

"The Factor Game" (adapted from Lappan et al. 1996) gives students experience with numbers as multiples and factors, as well as strategy. This game is played with a sheet that looks something like this (after students learn how to play the game, they can make the sheets on their own):

1	2	3	4	5	6	Player 1	Player 2
7	8	9	10	11	12		
13	14	15	16	17	18		
19	20	21	22	23	24		
25	26	27	28	29	30		

Here is how the game works: Player 1 crosses out a number (let's say 21). She then puts 21 in her column. Player 2 then crosses out the factors of 21 (1, 3, 7) and puts those numbers in his column. After the first round, player 1 has 21 points, player 2 has 11 points, and the board should look like this:

~~1~~	2	~~3~~	4	5	6	Player 1	Player 2
~~7~~	8	9	10	11	12	21	1, 3, 7
13	14	15	16	17	18		
19	20	~~21~~	22	23	24		
25	26	27	28	29	30		

For the second round, player 2 crosses out a number (let's say 27) and puts that number in his column. Player 1 then crosses out all the factors of 27 that have not already been crossed out in her column. Here, the factors of 27 are 1, 3 and 9, but 1 and 3 have already been crossed out from round 1, so player 2 can add only 9 to the column. After the second round, the board looks like this:

~~1~~	2	~~3~~	4	5	6	Player 1	Player 2
~~7~~	8	~~9~~	10	11	12	21	1, 3, 7
13	14	15	16	17	18	9	27
19	20	~~21~~	22	23	24		
25	26	~~27~~	28	29	30		

If a player, when he or she is the first to go in a round, chooses a number whose factors have all been crossed out already, this is an illegal move. The player gets no points; the number is "uncrossed out" and is back in play, and the next round begins. So if 1 and 5 were already crossed out, and a player chose 25, this would be an illegal move, forfeiting that player's turn. The game ends when no possible legal moves remain. At that point, the player with the most points wins.

Discussion points for extension:

- What is a "good" first move? Why?

- What is a "bad" first move? Why?

- What is the "best" first move? How do you know?

- Do any first moves result in a tie?

- Which first moves result in the second player's circling only 1? What is special about these first moves?

- Which first moves result in the second player's circling only two numbers? What is special about these first moves?

- If, at every turn, the player made the "best move," who wins the game?

Vocabulary/ideas:

The ideas are more important than the vocabulary, except that students should know what prime and square numbers are.

- Proper factors: Factors that are positive whole numbers, not including the number itself.

- Prime numbers: Numbers whose only proper factor is 1; the only factors are the number itself and 1.

- Composite numbers: Numbers that are not prime, that have factors other than 1 and itself.

- Perfect numbers: Numbers whose proper factors add up to the number itself.

- Abundant numbers: Numbers whose factors add up to more than the number itself (such as $1 + 2 + 3 + 4 + 6 > 12$).

- Deficient numbers: Numbers whose factors add up to less than the number itself (such as $1 + 3 + 7 < 21$).

- Square numbers: Numbers that are the result of a whole number multiplied by itself (25 is a square number because it is 5×5. So is 36, because it is 6×6).

"THE PRODUCT GAME"

"The Product Game" (adapted from Lappan et al. 1996) gives students experience with numbers as multiples and factors, as well as strategy. This game is played on a board that looks like this:

1	2	3	4	5	6
7	8	9	10	12	14
15	16	18	21	22	24
25	27	28	30	32	35
36	40	42	45	48	49
54	56	63	64	72	81

Factors:
1   2   3   4   5   6   7   8   9

Rules:

This is basically tic-tac-toe; the object is to get four in a row. Player 1 is *X*s and player 2 is *O*s. Each player has a marker (such as a penny, chip, or paper clip).

- Player 1 puts his marker on one of the factors.

- Player 2 puts her marker on one of the factors, multiplies the two factors that have markers, and marks that number on the factor board with an *O*.

- Player 1 then moves his marker to a different factor, multiplies the two marked factors, and puts an *X* on that number.

- This process continues until somebody has four in a row.

- If a player moves such that the factors multiply to a number already marked with an *X* or an *O*, that player does not get to mark a number.

Search the Internet for "product game" to find computer-based interactive product games.

SUCCESS
from
the START
Your first years
teaching SECONDARY
MATHEMATICS

appendix **two**

Beginning Lesson for
The Geometer's Sketchpad

These resources
are also available
electronically on
More4U.

Too his lesson shows how you can introduce The Geometer's Sketchpad to your students. It embodies some basic teacher moves effective for introducing new technology. Using this technology offers several benefits:

• Students work at their own pace, rather than move together through a set of oral instructions all at once. Students do not spend much time waiting for others to catch up.

• It encourages students to help each other and to communicate and make sense of their interactions with technology—especially if you have students work in pairs and you alternate which member can touch the technology. By allowing only one "operator," and alternating who that operator is, you ensure that one student does not take over the process.

• It encourages experimentation and discovery, as well as directing students to think about the relationships between objects that they make. For instance, by asking students, "What do you need to highlight to construct a segment parallel to an existing segment?" you emphasize a basic element of the program: objects are defined by a minimum set of givens. Here, a parallel line is defined by a given line and a point, and so to construct a line parallel to a segment you must highlight the segment and a point.

- The questions force students to think about how the software works, asking them to attend to software features that will come up repeatedly.

- It poses constructions and tasks as puzzles to figure out, not as directions to memorize.

You will create half a picture and then reflect it over a line to make a whole picture. Your picture will have a title and your names on it.

Sketchpad Basics

1. Open Sketchpad by double-clicking on the sketchpad icon on the desktop.

2. Click on the white part of the document. Make the document fill the screen. If you do not know how, ask a friend.

3. Make sure that the people around you have a blank document on their screen before you move on. Help them if they need it.

4. The upper-left part of the screen has a series of boxes. Click on the box with a dot on it. Then click on the screen several times. What does this dot tool do?

5. Click on the box with a picture of a circle on it. What do you think it does? Try it.

6. Click on the box with a line on it. What do you think it does? Try it.

7. Click on the box with an A on it. What do you think it does? Try it.

8. Click on the box with an arrow on it. What do you think it does? Try it.

   Try moving around various things on the screen. See how they behave.

   What happens if you move just one point?

   What happens if you move a line segment?

Now you should be able to make points, line segments, and circles and write words in your document. You should also be able to select any of these things and move them around. If you cannot do these things, make sure you ask someone how until you can.

Some Tricks

1. To undo something, click on Edit on the top of the screen and click on Undo. You can keep doing this and undo everything you did.

2. If you want to select something and move it around, click in an empty part of the sketch first. Otherwise you might end up moving other things that are already selected. This is called "clicking on the white."

Now for the Picture

1. First you have to make a line that will be the mirror. Just make a line down the center of the sketch.

2. On one side of this line, draw a picture that, when reflected, will make a complete picture.

3. Once the half of the picture is done, select the mirror line and click on Transform at the top of the screen. Click on Mark Mirror.

4. Select your whole picture.

5. Click on Transform again. What should you do to reflect your half-picture over the line?

6. Once you have reflected your picture, select some points and move them. What happens?

7. Give your picture a title, including your names. Save it with your names in the title, and show your teacher.

Extensions:

1. What happens when you move a point on one side of your picture?

2. What happens if you move a point over the line?

3. What happens when you move the line of reflection? Be specific.

4. Look at one point and its reflection. When you move the line of reflection, what happens to these points? How are those points related to the line of reflection? Can you make a rule about a point, its reflection, and the mirror line? Write your rule as clearly as possible.

Complete each of the following tasks, and check them off as you do so.

1. Using the Display menu

_____ Construct a line segment.

_____ Make the line segment dashed.

_____ Make the line segment thick.

_____ Make the line segment a different color.

_____ Label the line segment.

_____ Hide the line segment.

_____ Use Animate to make the line segment move on its own.

2. Using the Construct menu

Construct a line segment and then:

_____ Construct its midpoint.

_____ Construct a line parallel to the segment. (What do you need to highlight?)

_____ Construct a line perpendicular to the segment. (What do you need to highlight?)

_____ Construct two segments that intersect. Construct their intersection.

_____ Create three points. Select them and then construct a triangle interior. Make the triangle green.

_____ Create a solid circle.

Construct one other thing by using the Construct menu and write down what it is:

3. Using the Measure menu

Open a new sketch. Construct a line segment.

_____ Measure the length of the line segment.

_____ Move one of the endpoints of the segment; notice what happens to the measurement.

_____ What do you have to highlight to use the distance measurement from the Measure menu?

_____ Create a shape with straight sides. Measure its perimeter.

_____ Measure its area.

Make a circle. What can you measure if you highlight the circle?

How do you measure an angle?

_____ Construct two segments. Measure their lengths. Use the Calculate command from the Measure menu to add their lengths.

4. Using the Graph menu

_____ Open a new sketch. Use the Graph menu to create a grid.

_____ Construct some points. Then on the Graph menu select Snap Points. Now construct some new points. Figure out what Snap Points does.

_____ Construct a line. Using the Measure menu, what can you find out about this line?

5. Exploring on your own

Look through the other commands and menus and try to figure out what some of the commands do. What did you teach yourself how to do?

6. What questions do you still have? What would you like to be able to do with this program?

INDEX